/104

Date Due

MAY 3 1	MAR 1 4 '03		
JUL 3 1 '97	MAR 3 0 2005		
SEP 20 '97			
NOV 2 9 '97			
DEC 1 9 '97			
FEB 2 8 '98			
NOV 5 '98			
MAR 2 4 '00			
DEC 7 00			
OCT 2 3 2002			
FEB 1 8 2003			

4/97

The Writer's Journal

40 Contemporary Authors and Their Journals

EDITED BY *Sheila Bender*

Delta
Trade Paperbacks

A DELTA BOOK
Published by
Dell Publishing
a division of
Bantam Doubleday Dell Publishing Group, Inc.
1540 Broadway
New York, New York 10036

Permissions follow on pages v–vii and constitute an extension
of the copyright page.

Library of Congress Cataloging in Publication Data
The writer's journal : 40 contemporary American writers and their
   journal / edited by Sheila Bender.
        p.   cm.
     Includes bibliographical references.
     ISBN 0-385-31510-4
     1. College readers.   2. Authors, American—20th century—Diaries.
   3. Authors, American—Diaries—Authorship.   4. American
   literature—20th century.   5. English language—Rhetoric.
   6. Creative writing.   7. Authorship.   I. Bender, Sheila.
   PE1417.W664   1997
   818'.540308—dc20   96-21346
                                                              CIP

Manufactured in the United States of America
Published simultaneously in Canada

January 1997

10 9 8 7 6 5 4 3 2 1

BVG

Acknowledgments

I wish to thank my agent, Elizabeth Wales of the Levant and Wales Literary Agency, for finding out about interest in a book like the one I have assembled. I want to thank Trish Todd, formerly of Dell, for giving me the chance to run with her interest in a book about writers' journals and put this book together. And I want to thank Cherise Davis Grant of Dell for her expert editorial help.

I also want to thank the people who staff the King County Answer Line and the Seattle Public Library's Quick Information Service for their help in getting me books I wanted to see before I left home, and my friend Jeanne Yeasting for her help with the on-line *Books in Print*. We perused it on more than one occasion from her laptop computer. I want to thank her also for the trips she made to the U.W. Library to procure books for me to look at that were not as quickly available through the other libraries.

Many thanks to Kay Morgan and Paula Jones Gardiner for reviewing my bibliography of books on writing journals and on published journals and making helpful suggestions. Thanks to Seattle University professor Sharon Cumberland for graciously introducing me to East Coast poets. Thanks also to Adrienne Reed for her early reading of these pages, her diligence in finding word-processing errors, and her enthusiasm for the manuscript.

Many, many thanks to my husband, Kurt VanderSluis, for his technical assistance once again—this time in setting up a scanner and teaching me the process so I could assemble forty different manuscripts into one. And thanks once again to Christi Killien for reading my chapters in this book and encouraging clarity.

Contents

There is a pleasure in the thought that
the particular tone of my mind at this
moment may be new in the universe;
that the emotions of this hour may be
peculiar and unexampled in the whole
eternity of moral being.

Ralph Waldo Emerson,
April 17, 1827
Charleston, South Carolina

Introduction

IN THE SUMMER OF 1994, I attended Ron Carlson's fiction writing class at the Centrum Foundation's summer writing conference in Port Townsend, Washington. For ten days, Ron proved a wildly witty and generous teacher. A day that especially stands out for me, though, is the one where he went around the room asking us all to describe our writer's journal, how we kept it and how we used it. On my turn, I confessed I had a box—those cardboard flats you can buy at the variety store and fold into a box with a cover with two openings to grab it for lifting and moving.

"What goes into this box?" Ron asked.

"Scraps of paper on which I have written things—bank deposit slips, napkins, other people's business cards, other stuff."

"How do you use the box?" he continued.

"I just go through it from time to time when I'm between projects or I am stuck on something I'm doing."

He nodded, then called on the next person. I had a sinking feeling that I had made a fool of myself among the more experienced fiction writers. What was I doing as the only poet in the room? I moaned to myself. Oh, well, I had been honest.

Months later when I began to explore the topic of writers' working journals, I invited Ron Carlson to participate. Can you imagine my smile (and relief) when I read about his method of keeping scraps of paper? I had interpreted his silence in that workshop as a sign that I had been using an inferior process. Actually, Ron wasn't judging, advocating, or suggesting a particular type of journal. He was giving his students a forum to begin to understand how different the process of keeping a journal may be for each writer. We saw the enthusiasm many writers have for their journal-keeping, and we saw that even what does not look like a journaling process actually can be one.

I hope you, the readers of *The Writer's Journal,* will enjoy the results of my continuing exploration of how writers keep journals. This book has forty sections, one for each author. In each section, journal excerpts are followed by the author's commentary on how journal-keeping influences his or her work. At the head of each author's section is a brief excerpt from that author's commentary.

I hope you will feel free to co-opt journal-keeping ideas from this book's contributors to invent or sustain a journal-writing process for yourself. I hope you will feel affirmed rather than silly in whatever process you choose.

Many of the writers in the book told me how enjoyable it was for them to look into their own process and articulate it. But some felt vulnerable and uncertain talking about and showing what they wrote in journals.

"Why did I have to write it down?" one of them said to me about one of her entries. "Isn't it obvious? Won't other writers think I am really incapable?"

Another writer said that when a friend read her commentary for this book, the friend didn't think the writer sounded at all like herself. The friend was surprised by the writer's voice on writing and this made the writer feel uncertain.

I think each writer did an accurate and admirable job for this book. I want to thank them all for their willingness, courage, and caring in revealing their methods and in risking being seen uncovered and unedited. I have left authors' idiosyncratic abbreviations, spelling, spacing, and use of punctuation in the journal entries in order to preserve the sanctity of the written journal. I want to thank the authors for doing the self-conscious and sometimes nearly impossible work of explaining how they do what they usually do at an intuitive level. I also want to thank them for sharing with me which published journals most influenced them. I have included citations for the books and/or authors mentioned in the biographical notes on each contributor at the end of the book.

I hope you will take the time to look through each of the book's appendixes. In addition to the biographical notes there are three bibliographies: books about keeping journals; writer's anthologies; and published journals of literary and historical figures.

The desire to share as much information as I could on writers' journals began early in my work on this book, as I listened to poet Henri Cole speak to students at Seattle University. He used the term "commonplace book" for his journal. I had not heard the term before, so I asked about it. Many writers, it turns out, cite W. H. Auden as the source of the term "commonplace book" because he entitled a collection of his most personal prose writings *A Certain World: A Commonplace Book*.

According to the Oxford English Dictionary, however, the term is actually mentioned as early as 1598; keeping a commonplace book was advocated by the English philosopher John Locke in the second half of the 1600s and employed by Emerson in his early diaries in the 1800s. The dictionary says a commonplace book is a "place to record passages or matters to be especially remembered or referred to, with or without arrangement."

In his book *Emerson and the Art of the Diary*, Lawrence Rosenwald includes a chapter entitled "From Commonplace Book to Journal." In the chapter, Rosenwald describes Locke's recommended method of keeping a commonplace book: One was to sit down and make an index composed of empty boxes. One would later fill in the boxes with subject headings that categorized transcriptions one kept in the book. These transcriptions were to be made as quotes without added context or notes from the journal-keeper's life.

Beginning with Locke's method, Emerson grew to take a more relaxed approach, and in sharing his journals with his Transcendentalist circle, he helped make the commonplace book into what Rosenwald dubs "a writer's workplace" organized according to time and intertwined with the occurrences of a life.

Some of the writers in this book keep journals of quotes as in a commonplace book; some transcribe their own musings. Some of the writers alternate between the two forms, and some have invented another kind of record by including descriptions of their writing process. Others are fond of the journal's first cousin, the letter. Some are used to sharing their journals as Emerson did; most are apt to have kept them private. Some habitually read their journals over; some never go back to see what they have written there. Each, however, teaches us about writing and the commitment one must make to turning out his or her very best work.

I hope *The Writer's Journal* will prove accessible, interesting, inspiring, and useful for all who want to absorb and use for themselves the many ways of journal-keeping that enrich writing and help sustain one's ability to keep at it.

Diana Abu-Jaber

Reading old journal and outline notes helps me to see what richly layered beings we are. I recognize odd currents in my work, repeating words and images, patterns, as if we were each embedded with private themes, symbols that could help unlock the mysteries of our existence. . . . Working with journals helps me to remember how vulnerable I make myself within the creative act and how vigilant I must be to stay honest.

1

10/13

The birds of New Jersey are going full force, all sorts of whistles and grackles and cawing this morning. We're at Gram's place, brick apartment complex with the drying "trees" for hanging laundry.

Being here reminds me of our first day back from Jordan (or was it the first day before school in America?), my school uniform, plaid jumper-dress, the nuns.

Now it rains, open windows, humid. Grey blinds in the windows, ragged lawn. Visiting Gram at the hospital, thinking: the powerlessness, being so sick and dependent that all you can do is show thanks, thanks, thanks, because it's terrifying, ghastly to feel so weak.

After years of Gram's sidling, sidelong prejudice, she is cared for mainly by black and Asian attendants. There is a terrifying young nurse who fixed the choking woman in the bed beside Gram's with a cold, concrete stare.

Elizabeth NJ is running endlessly down, never quite a slum, always, it seems, just arriving, though maybe I continually lower my expectations of it. The downcast at the bus stop, blue-collar and the unemployed, St. Elizabeth's Hospital with its huge saint's (Jesus? Mary?) statue in the lobby beside the woman selling raffle tickets, old men sulking around outside the front door.

10/14

Bird sounds echoing back over the trees, an amazing, eternal sound that takes me back and forward all at once. Light full in the sky and trees. Gram must have liked waking up in this room on her soft, narrow bed with the lavender bedspread all ruffles. Everything arranged just so: stacks of books and magazines, tissue-flowers propped from the stem of a lamp. The little statue of Jesus, rosary, painting of Mary, the prayer cards.

Trach tube. Learning how to read her lips—it comes. I must first learn to focus, not let my eyes blur over. The sense of disproportion diminishes. Depression lifts with the sunrise. It is good to have a bright sunrise.

Remember—Easter mornings, walking in Waranaco Park to see the new flowers, tearing into the Easter baskets after church. The deep plush and fur of Mrs. A.'s coat on the Sundays I rode with them to church. Her son Ed driving us, waiting outside through mass. I wonder at the silent light in his apartment downstairs now, as he must wonder at ours.

The floorboards creak. Gram was forever telling us to walk softly, not to disturb Mrs. A. I live in a different country now. I don't even bother looking at the Jersey landscape—I've already got it memorized.

10/21

Gram always hated the way I took care of my clothes, dropping them on the floor. She used to say she'd buy me something if only I'd try to hang it up.

She darned my socks for me, and had an ancient black sewing machine that I didn't see out too much. She knitted sweaters for several boyfriends: R., K., even C., I think.

But most of all for Michael, whom I think she truly had great feeling for. Tell Michael I love him, she said, the last time I saw her, just a week ago.

I remember the little steel cart she would wheel groceries back from Elmora Ave. in. I thought, as a child, it was the longest walk in the world.

She bought me clothes on Elmora, a favorite shirt, salt sticks from the bagel store, movies: 10,000 Leagues Under the Sea; in Linden, Jaws, books—one magic summer from the little library, "Chinese food," a mod watch on a green plastic strap that I gazed at adoringly throughout the bus ride back from Elizabeth.

Daffy Dan's, the 5 & Dime, the store counters with plastic place mats stamped with pictures of the food, tiny baby dolls in pink blankets, a baby bottle that seemed to empty its milk when you inverted it. Real stuffed

baby chicks from that funny little corner store where she got the paper.
Always at Easter. They had to stop selling them . . . because of disease,
did he say?

The trip to the Hershey factory, huge, cranking gears full of chocolate.
And the smell, better, blacker than dirt.

I had her for 30 precious years. So short, but we were very close in the
past, distant at other times, but always I loved her. And even in dying she
has surprised me with death, bringing it closer. Now it is more familiar, it
seems a bit less formidable. Gram has done it.

Where is she now? Is she reading this? Stay near me, Gram, stay near
if you can.

The Tenor of Memories

THIS IS A SLIGHTLY SHORTENED though not straightened-up version of the
entries. (Still not hanging my clothes, I guess.)

I kept a detailed journal around the time of my grandmother's
death, trying hard to record, honor, or just to get at our very complicated
and powerful relationship. There's a lot of nostalgia in this entry—she
was a potent force in my childhood. While my parents struggled over our
family's national and emotional identities, her home was a steady point
of reference. She seemed always, wonderfully, maddeningly, to know
who she was.

Interspersed with entries on my grandmother's illness are notes for
my second novel *(Memories of Birth)*. At that time, I hadn't quite finished
my first novel *(Arabian Jazz)*, but I did—wonder of wonders—have an
honest-to-goodness literary agent who was "interested" in the work
(and who eventually did represent the manuscript).

Now that my second novel is complete, it seems that I can see in its
pages strings of details and memories lifted directly from this journal. Or
close approximations. But then it turns out that for me it's not the

specific details that are so important, but the general tone, the tenor of the memories.

In *Memories of Birth,* I was trying to evoke the particular taste and smell and touch of my childhood. And through one of the central characters, a woman called "Mam," I worked hard on trying to express the character and music of my grandmother's Jersey voice.

Reading old journal and outline notes helps me to see what richly layered beings we are. I recognize odd currents in my work, repeating words and images, patterns, as if we were each embedded with private themes, symbols that could help unlock the mysteries of our existence.

I like keeping a journal because it helps make plain to me what intimacy and daring—or as one family member put it—what shamelessness is part of being a writer. It brings me face to face with issues of privacy and respect. I hesitated over submitting this entry—such a personal event, but then I also know how grateful I feel when I've read novels or stories that are deeply felt and personally honest. The voices of Philip Roth in *Portnoy's Complaint,* Maxine Hong Kingston in *Woman Warrior,* Etel Adnan in *Sitt Marie Rose,* and Louise Erdrich in *Love Medicine* all speak nakedly and at times defiantly. They do not try to protect themselves as authors or gloss over political, social, or privately emotional events. There is a quality of trust and revelation in such work that is immediately recognizable, impossible to fake, a generosity of spirit and fearlessness that I wish to emulate. Working with journals helps me to remember how vulnerable I make myself within the creative act and how vigilant I must be to stay honest. How hard it is to work against silence, shame, how hard to be brave.

Kathleen Alcalá

I needed to see my own handwriting telling me that "This is what Mexico is really like. I did not just imagine it." Of course, that's impossible, since we re-imagine everything our senses tell us just as soon as it enters our brains. But still, I thought I would try.

24 de Mayo, 1990
Chih, Chih, Mex.

Chih. Is much the same to me, though big and dirty and noisy. Priscilla says they have built machinaderas (industrial towns) so people have come from all over, from the south, to work in them. Impoverished-looking settlements, raw cement bricks with no trees, are springing up everywhere. There is not enough water for them. The land is stricken. I don't remember it ever so dry.

My aunt and uncle have moved. It's only a block from Calle de la Llave, a street name I loved. They live on Paso Leal, and Priscilla next door.

It looks beautiful walking in—a spacious tiled passageway full of plants one story high (the plants). It leads past a living room and dining on the right, a patio, a stairway on the left.

At the back, the kitchen on the right, a room with my uncle, now bedridden, on the left. He lies in a hospital bed, blind, unable to talk, but he responded to my talk and touch, and loved touching Ben's soft skin. He is 84. The rest of the room holds a big bed with a colorful spread, cozy furniture. This is clearly where my aunt spends her time. The upstairs is unused, the patio full of weeds. The back of the house peters out to a vacant lot.

26 de Mayo

Francisco was born on a hacienda near Saltillo of working people. 84 means he was born in 1906. Mexico had changed little from the 1500s to 1910, so he was born into the old class system, poor. He had to work since he was a boy, so it was important to him to have a big house. Wayne and I walked around upstairs—1 huge room after another, many with their own baths. There is no water connected upstairs. There is a big studio/ library which I will visit tomorrow. On a drawing board is a pastel study of an owl. He had been painting owls before he lost his eyesight. Ruth and

Prissy each have one. Julieta says I can take any painting I want, but I don't want to take any off the wall, although I love them. Some of the still-lifes of fruits and vegetables are so vivid and so much a part of my permanent childhood memory that when I see them, I almost don't see them.

The land is dry. El llano en llanas. People yearn for rain.

Jan Feb Mar Apr May Jun Jul Aug Sept Oct Nov Dec
    Dry   Wet
    Easter   Christmas

27 de Mayo
Francisco's Library

Books all dusty and mixed up. Books on Mex history, esp. Northern Mexico; famous artists' biographies, bios of famous musicians and composers (classical); books on homeopathic and natural medicine; books on Christianity; world encyclopedias; many Spanish dictionaries; profiles of historic Mexican figures; popular novels by Mex. Writers, books from Spain; translations of books by Am. Authors—Pearl S. Buck, Hemingway, Dostoyevsky, Steinbeck. "Yo, Robot," por Isaac Asimov; a Spanish/English dictionary printed in the late 1700's. Books by relatives, including Manuel Acuña and José Garcia Rodriguez. Books about Sor Juana; Gabriela Mistral; important women in world history.

Many of the books in F's library had titles like "Hidden Pages," or "Stolen Pages," or the "Hidden Mexico." The tables upstairs have bookends—a small, ornate globe—a colorful painting of birds on cuero, popular for the last 20 years or so—beautiful pottery on the bookcases. Priceless. Candy and wrappers left by Priscilla's children. Photos and portraits of F all over. Many of the books are inscribed by the authors to Prof. Cepeda.

Julieta played some really old gospel records for Wayne while I was upstairs. It sounded like Perry Como sings hymns or something. Scratched and well used. She also knows all about Julio Iglesias. Ruth went to Las Cruces to hear him.

BOOKS

Medicamentes Indigenes por Geronimo Pompa, 1972

Relatos misterio y realismo por José Garcia Rodriguez, 1947

Los Mexicanos Pintados por Si Mismos, orig. 1855, reprinted 1946.

Cuentos del Mexico Antiguo, por Artemio de Valle Arizpe, 1953.

Anthologia de Poetas y Escrituras Coahuilenses. 1926.

Los judios bajo la inquisicion en hispanoamerica. Boleslao Lewin, 1960.

Libro de Chilam Balam de Chumayel.

Manuel Acuña, por Francisco Castillo Najera, 1950.

Obras, por Manuel Acuña (poesias, teatro, articulos y cartas), 1965.

Poesias de Manuel Acuña, segunda edicion, 1968.

Obras completas de Concha Espina, 1944.

Francisco's Library

IN 1990 WHEN MY SON was three months old, I completed my first book, *Mrs. Vargas and the Dead Naturalist,* and entered the manuscript in the King County Publications Project in hopes of receiving funding for its publication. I was ready to turn what little attention I had left over to a new novel which I would call *Casas Grandes.* My uncle, who was eighty-four, was sick and dying. My cousin had three children I'd never seen. *Casas Grandes* would take place in Saltillo, which is 500 miles east of Chihuahua, the city where I had spent part of every year growing up and where my relatives still lived. The cities were similar enough in ambience that

I could research as I visited my family whom I had a terrible urge to see.

At an early age, I learned that nothing I wrote down was private, and so I learned to keep my private thoughts in my head. This probably gave me a very good memory, for even now, I can recall exact scenes from my childhood going back to age two. It was my birthday, and we were in Chapultapec Park in Mexico City. We were by the giraffes, and I was self-conscious over the fact that my twin cousin, Ruth, was already toilet trained, wearing pretty, frilly panties, and I was not. I'm sure that she was making this clear to me at the time, in her own, "more-princess-like-than-thou" way.

I am not a journal-keeper. Nevertheless, I realized that this was a special trip, different from the rest, because I was coming to Mexico of my own volition, a grown woman, and needed to gather material for my novel. I needed something to hold in my hands in the far north, in the rainy winter of Seattle and be able to say, "No, I didn't imagine it. It really is like that in Mexico. People really *do* sing in the streets and advertise cooked food for sale and the sky is bluer and the mangos sweeter. People *do* live in the moment instead of waiting for something better to come along." I needed to see my own handwriting telling me "This is what Mexico is really like. I did not just imagine it." Of course, that's impossible, since we re-imagine everything our senses tell us just as soon as it enters our brains. But still, I thought I would try.

The novel I was working on, *Casas Grandes,* takes place in the late 1800s in a city another 500 miles east of Chihuahua. It is where my aunt's and mother's ancestors were from, and is not much known or written about. It is also difficult to get to from Seattle, Washington, and it would have been impossible to visit both Chihuahua and Saltillo in one trip. I opted for my living relatives, especially since my uncle was not expected to live much longer. Even though my son was less than a year old, I felt it was important for them to meet Ben, and I suppose there was sort of a "baptism of dust" involved in bringing Ben to Mexico, the home of his ancestors.

On the other hand, life in northern Mexico has not changed all that much. Chihuahua is known for its Federalist (mid-1800s) architecture and its revolutionary history, and while the city is not the same, I felt that a lot of the ambience would be duplicated in both Saltillo and Chihuahua. Both cities are commercial centers, rather than tourist destinations. Both cities have been in existence for several hundred years, and both have been heavily influenced by their proximity to the United States. Most interesting to me is the mixing of cultures—Indigenous, Spanish, and European—that has been going on all this time, and the particularly fierce and independent outlook it has fostered.

My uncle Francisco Cepeda Cruz was both unusual and typical of the citizens of Northern Mexico. Born to peasants on a hacienda, he became, at the age of twenty-one, director of a prestigious private school in Chihuahua, a post he held for fifty years. Upon his retirement, he received a medal from the president of Mexico for his outstanding service to education. A self-made and largely self-educated Renaissance man, he painted in oils, sang, composed poetry, and read prodigiously. A devout Protestant, he was generous with his friends and silent about his enemies. I had found him both formidable and wonderful as a child.

Francisco's library had been a source of wonder since my childhood. It probably helped to shape my bookish nature as an adult, and I was eager to spend time in it, since I knew that it had invaluable source materials for my own writing. At the same time, I was interested in the space of the library, the idea of the library. I had come to realize, walking around Chihuahua, that architectural space in Mexico reflects the public and private lives of people. Plazas, fountains, and grand buildings are set aside for communal use. Houses present a forbidding facade to the street and are turned inward, built around an open courtyard where the family can move freely, and the division between interior and exterior is loosely defined. Catholic homes often have private shrines inside, and the idea of a personal library seemed even more private and interior to me. Perhaps, in our Protestant subculture, a love of learning had replaced faith in the institution of the Catholic Church.

It had not exactly been off-limits to us as children, but we were not supposed to bother Francisco if he was working in his combination library/studio. With five children plus their friends and cousins, this was probably a matter of survival. Still, it retained an air of the tantalizingly forbidden, which I was to use for a library in my novel:

> Within the enclosure was a miniature garden almost gemlike in its perfection. Low boxwood hedges hugged the wall on two sides, filling the air with their pungent odor. A veranda, or portico, flanked the other two sides along the house. Next to the portico grew blood red roses, almost funereal in their intensity of color.
>
> Huge pots of fuschias hung from the protruding vigas of the portico, catching the sun and contrasting sharply with the deep shade against the house.
>
> At the center of the garden, a fountain as squat as the house itself gurgled softly; the cold spring water spilled over its thick, green-stained lips and ran obediently along channels in the flag-stone paving to form a shining ribbon that laced the garden in severe Moorish symmetry before disappearing under the hedges. The fountain had run steadily since the house was built, the springs within the earth seemingly inexhaustible.
>
> Esaías walked along the wooden portico to a small door and knocked. This was his father's study, and only the old man had a key to this door. After a moment, the door swung slowly inward, leaving Esaías straining to see into the gloom of the interior before stooping to enter the doorway. His father was already reseated behind his massive desk, as though he had willed the door to open of its own volition.
>
> The small, sallow-skinned man sat regarding his second son with large unblinking eyes like some nocturnal creature.
>
> Esaías always felt awkward in this study, large and clumsy among the fragile books and stacks of tissue-thin papers that would crumble to dust in a good gust of wind.
>
> Here lay his father's treasure. Here were his books, the books accumulated one at a time, sometimes a few pages at a time, smuggled in saddle bags surrounding preserved foods, or wrapping a trinket from overseas. It had taken thirteen generations to com-

pile this library, thirteen generations since all things Jewish, all signs of learning and Hebraic study had been burned by the towns-people of Saltillo, since Esaías' forebears had gained the lives of their wives and children by changing their names and agreeing to be rebaptized into the Holy Roman Catholic Church.

Esaías stood in this dark, crowded room, hemmed in by pre-cariously balanced stacks of books, half-empty inkwells, broken quills and glass vials of mysterious chemicals. He stood too tall, his shoulders hunched under the weight of thirteen generations, under the name he bore, pinned against the six-inch-thick door at his back by his father's unblinking gaze. Esaías had no love of books, of tradition, or of enclosed places. He had come to tell his father goodbye.

One thing I discovered was that it was difficult to find informa-tion on women in Mexico in the late 1800s. I could find where all the trains ran, all the battle lines, all the crops and the names of all the mines, but information on domestic life was scarce. I was interested in more than just the facts, of course. I wanted to know about attitudes and, most of all, what a woman in that time and place might have thought about herself, dreamed and aspired to, if anything. One clue came from a book in Francisco's library, and I copied out the table of contents:

Breves Biografias Intimas de Mujeres Celebres
Spain, 1949

Cleopatra
Teodora
Juana de Arco 1412–1431
Santa Teresa de Jesús
María Estuardo
Catalina de Erauso (la Monja Alférez)
Cristina de Suecia
Madame de Maintenon
Madame de Stael

Carlota Corday
La Malibrán
Carlota Brontë
Concepción Avenal
Sara Bernhardt
Condesa de Pardo Bazán
Jane Addams
Isadora Duncan

The main female character in *Casas Grandes* is Estelá, a merchant's daughter who marries for love, then discovers that her husband is a wastrel, intent on spending their resources on prospecting for gold in the desert. Often alone with her children, the subject of gossip, in this excerpt from the novel, she turns to books for solace:

A sudden flight of birds, or movement of wind, made Estelá stop and gaze out the window. She could not say why, but she felt a lightness she had not felt in many years.

She should feel terrible, thought Estelá. Left alone to cope with the household by herself; her surly father, the prying neighbors; an abandoned woman. Estelá tried to feel sorry for herself, something she had done often enough before, but today she could not.

The last flowers of the season were still blooming. Her daughters played in the courtyard, their embroidery in a careless heap on a table. Gabriel read in a corner of the patio, his feet up, sweet tea at hand. My little man, she thought.

Esaías was gone again, but this time she had done something about it. Perhaps that was the difference.

Leaving the kitchen, Estelá wiped her hands on her apron and pulled it off over her head. She walked into the parlor and opened its wide windows onto the sunny yard. Normally reserved for guests, it stood unused most of the time. Estelá picked a book of verse out of a shelf, sat down in the most comfortable chair near the window, and decided to read until it got too dark.

Somewhere, a cock crowed, a horse whinnied, a cry of elote,

elote, roasted corn, floated on the evening breeze. She smelled sew-
age for a moment, followed by orange blossoms.

"Oh wretched moment of my birth," said the first verse she
read:

> When I opened eyes that one day would gaze upon
>   you,
> That one day would see the hand that never would be
>   mine
> Eyes that would see you speak the name of another,
> See your lips tremble on that name . . .

Normally, Estelá would find her heart beating rapidly when
she read such things, but today the words were full of air. A pleasant light came in from the west-facing window, bathing her in its
golden glow. Soon it would be too cool to enjoy the evenings like
this. A light wind lifted the leaves of the trees, the wind from the
mountains that blew everything clean, that cleansed the air of the
town from the eternal dust of the desert.

My grandfather, Miguel Narro, unlike me, kept journals from his
mid-teens until his death in 1955. A minister who traveled and lived all
over the Southwest, his journals also functioned as his sermon notes and
business records, but on occasion, he included long descriptions of people
and places otherwise lost. They include some of his dreams and his notes
from teaching himself how to read Hebrew. I now have these journals,
and they seem to radiate a magic of their own when I open the brittle
covers and see his careful handwriting. They are his legacy to me, the
only living writer in the family.

There is an air about life in Mexico that keeps it from ever seeming
quite of this world. Perhaps it is true in all of Latin America, where the
past and present run together, where reality is determined as much by
faith as by scientific evidence. No amount of journal-keeping can pin
down this quicksilver quality, which is just as well. In any case, I came

across a paragraph that seemed to sum this up, and I hope that it applies not only to the books in Francisco's library, but to my writing as well:

Foreword to "La Mandrágora," a story in the *Antologia de la Literatura Fantastica Espanola,* 1969, ed. Jose Luis Guarner:

La presente historia, aunque verídica, no puede leerse a la claridad del sol. Te lo advierto, lector, no vayas allamarte a engaño: enciende una luz, pero no eléctrica, ni de gas corriente, ni siquiera de petróleo, sino uno de esos simpáticos velones típicos, de tan graciosa traza, que apenas alumbran, dejando en sombra la mayor parte del aposento. O, mejor aún, no enciendas nada; salta al jardin, y cerca del estanque, donde las magnolias derranam efluvios embriagadores y la luna rieles argentinos, oye el cuento de la mandrágora y del barón de Helynagy.

In English:

This story, although truthful, cannot be read in the clear light of the sun. I advise you, reader, don't try to deceive yourself: turn on a light, but not electric, not of gas, nor of petrol; perhaps one of those quaint lanterns, so graceful-looking, that barely cast any light, leaving in shadow a major part of the room (lodging). Or better yet, don't light anything; go outside to the garden, and near the pond, where the magnolias pour out their intoxicating fumes and the moon makes silver tracks, hear the story of the mandrake and the Baron of Helynagy.

Robert Alexander

In fact, most of my play ideas first started off as entries in my dream journal. And just like my mother, I, too, would sometimes turn my dreams into songs, healing songs . . . the background music to my life.

Dream Journal Entry #29

Woke up this morning. A year older, if not a year wiser. Think I'll shave
my head bald. That'll keep the gray out. Why am I turning grey already?
I'm just 36. Today—I turned 36. 36 in nigger years, I guess is kinda old.
Seen a lot. Dreamed a lot. Here's what I remember from last night's dream.

THE LINE-UP

Last night I was having a dream
Not a wet dream/Nothing obscene
I was in a police station, a crazy situation
Something 'bout an extension cord and strangulation

I had been in a line-up at this station before
Under suspicion for being a nigger
In my time I've done some crime
Working as a freelance grave-digger

In my dream they keep holding me without charging me
Then I see Geronimo Pratt with a baseball bat
Fifty brothers had his back, each with a gat
They stepped to me and gave me a gat, 'cause it be like that

The whole scene was groovie, like something out of a movie
Then Pratt said, this ain't about no breakout
'Cause this scene calls for a turnabout
Turnabout is fair play come Judgment Day

I followed Pratt into another room
Where I saw Huey Newton pushing a broom
Huey said, there's a heap of shit that needs cleaning up
After two centuries of taxation without representation

Then Malcolm X entered with an extension cord, looking bored
He told me, "You know what to do."
Then I went myself into another room inside of yet another
room,
Rooms inside of rooms, sort of like chinese boxes
And then I saw J. Edgar Hoover holding a sign
It read, "Will fuck for food!"
And there were more rooms inside of rooms
before I came to the last room
Before I came to the line-up
This line-up was more like an assembly line
Marking time, blowing my mind
with a strange cast of historical characters
They entered one at a time and I strangled each and every
one of them, slowly, with my extension cord
Christopher Columbus, fuck you. Chris, you're falling off the
cross like Jesus. George Bush, Ronald Reagan, trickle down
death in effect
Adolph Hitler, Alexander the Great, Napoleon,
Thomas Jefferson

No further explanation required

Healing Songs

I FIRST STARTED KEEPING a dream journal in the summer of '72 when I was a young college student traveling through Ghana and Nigeria. My journal entries were sporadic, coming in random, measured outbursts of impulsive writing. Like my mother, a published poet, I was guided by my impulses and guided by my dreams.

My mother kept a journal of her dreams. She used to turn her dreams into songs, into lullabies, and she would sing them to me. She would rock me to sleep, singing me her dreams.

My head was filled with more nightmares than dreams. The Sandman always threatened the dreamer. Violence was always lurking in the shadows of my imagination. Growing up in Washington, D.C., and later in Arlington, Virginia, one had to learn how to fight to survive. One didn't go out of his way looking for trouble, trouble just seemed to be a fact of life. And violence always went hand in hand with trouble.

I remember 1989 as being a year of big events. Spike Lee's *Do the Right Thing* opened around the same time as the first Batman movie. Later that summer, Huey P. Newton was gunned down on the mean streets of Oakland by a crack dealer. That fall the World Series had two representatives from the Bay Area and was interrupted by an earthquake. A big earthquake.

I had lived in the Bay Area since '77 and in Oakland since 1980. I was living in S.F. when Newton returned from exile in '77 to stand trial for murder. I had run into Huey Newton on more than one occasion at social events. I never really got to know the man, but I had been thinking about him a lot before his murder. Even had a premonition about his violent death. Then after he was blown away, I started thinking about him all the time, as more visions of Huey began showing up in my dreams. My dreams were telling me to write a play about the man. *Servant of the People; The Rise and Fall of Huey P. Newton* was the end result of all those dreams. I was attempting to redefine Huey Newton on my own terms and to demystify the iconoclast Huey P. Newton became when distorted by the media.

My dreams had been a guide to my art for a long time. In fact, most of my play ideas first started off as entries in my dream journal. And just like my mother, I too, would sometimes turn my dreams into songs, healing songs . . . the background music to my life.

James Bertolino

While keeping a journal is one of the pleasures of being a writer, it also provides a place to find solace when the inexorable loneliness of poetry, of the poet's life, haunts you with feelings of frustration and powerlessness.

FOOD CHAIN GENUS

*It is in the world of essences that the genius finds her community, and the
ultimate love and generosity of her acts, her creations, are best estimated
there. On the level of daily events and creatures, the genius may seem
unfeeling, self-centered, even ruthless—but isn't that the way the
magnificent forms at the top of the food chain always appear to those
below?*

**17 May 1992 / written after reading about Martha Graham's autobiography,
Blood Memory, and Agnes de Mille's biography Martha, in the New York
Times Book Review**

TRUE SCIENTISTS

*Perhaps in thirty years, when our understanding of the
physical world is profoundly more sophisticated than now,
and we've truly moved into an era when information is
more real than things, we may discover what was once
known as supernatural—the range of powers and events
we had associated with the world of spirits—is actually a
complete system whose dynamics we can comprehend.
Such people as poets and mystics, whose value to post-
industrial society had been uncertain at best, may then
be recognized as true scientists of the numinous universe.*
4 April 1993

A Journal Where the Mind Can Live

THE POETS WHO most interested me back in the late 1960s and early '70s were known for keeping journals. Robert Creeley, Edward Dorn, Gary Snyder, and others often included dated journal passages and fragments in their books, and a few literary magazines were committed to documenting the process behind their poetry. I felt privileged to have access to the raw thinking and moments of inspiration that preceded their polished work. When I took the serious step of going to graduate school in creative writing in the fall of 1970, I began to make dated scribblings in a *spiral* notebook. By February of 1971 my notebook was disintegrating, and after I complained in class of my problem, one of my poetry writing students brought me a black, hardcover journal from an art supply store in Spokane. Since then I have never been without one, and the gaps in dated entries are rarely longer than a few weeks. My stack of journals is now eleven books high, and they continue to be an active source for my writing.

There are primarily two types of passages I write in my journals: one is the brief phrase or sentence that captures an unusual image, word combination, or thought; the other is a relatively complete statement that, with some tinkering, usually becomes a poem. No matter what the approach or style, the important thing is when I'm alone with my journal I feel free to write absolutely anything that comes to mind, no matter how bizarre or tasteless. Some passages try out concepts: "Terror and Capital: the gravity and light of the New Age." Others may play with a sound progression like "first brain / membrane / remembers." On occasion there'll be a phrase or sentence that begs to open or close a poem: "Sleeping below the full moon he remembered his womb."

There are times when I recognize the feeling, the poem-writing feeling, and if I don't have a particular thought or theme to play out, I will flip through my journals—looking for passages to leap out at me. And they always do. When I'm in this mode, my style of writing is the collage approach, and the poem that results is typically one where the reader does a lot of leaping. For several months back in 1991, I was meditating on this sentence: "Who do you become when you stop to look at a blossom?" (dated February 19). On May 12 I wrote: "the poises of being." On July 26 "time is an opinion." When on July 30 I wrote "I sing the body holographic," I knew I was on my way to a poem that might be a contemporary response to Walt Whitman's "I Sing the Body Electric." The sentence "God is watching you in the mirror," entered on August 10, clearly affirmed a metaphysical direction.

One of my favorite strategies for making a poem out of an assortment of loosely related lines is the Pantoum form. In the Pantoum the lines are repeated twice, each time in a new context, which provides an excellent opportunity for the "gestures" of the poem to become more familiar to the reader. Because the Pantoum is a mathematically described structure, there's a kind of rational elegance to the form; on the other hand, each time a line reappears in new surroundings, chance relationships may play an important role. In this sense the Pantoum is a complete and immensely satisfying form—it has the two great systems that together weave the fabric of the universe: predictability and chance. Here is the Pantoum that used versions of the lines noted above. (The poem was published first in the British magazine *Qrbis,* then in my book *Snail River, 1995,* Quarterly Review of Literature Poetry Series, volume 34.)

The Body Holographic

We sing the poise of being
in a room where time is an opinion
and the universe gazes from the mirror.
Here loss is lucid shadow

in a room where time is an opinion—
the empty throne of spirit.

Where loss is lucid shadow,
no gesture too small to move the mind.

Before the empty throne of spirit,
worship is a leaf turning to light.
No gesture too small to move the mind
through the implicate history of love,

where worship is a leaf turning to light.
Time learns the syntax of eternity
through the implicate history of love.
So we hum the body holographic.

Time learns the syntax of eternity
as the universe gazes from the mirror.
So we sing the body holographic,
we hum the poise of being.

A typical case where a complete poem was written into one of my
journals occurred the 21st of August, 1992, in Honduras. I was sitting
alone high in the stone "bleachers" of the ball court in the Mayan ruins
outside the village of Copan. Just a few minutes earlier our small group
had met and touched a monkey who lived there among the overgrown
structures, and I was still feeling moved by the encounter. Looking down
to the stone-surfaced playing field, I imagined the wild sounds of the
athletic contests, and they were blending with birdcalls in the present. A
sadness rose in me as I recognized the permanence of the grand architecture, in stark contrast with the impermanence of the thousands of human lives that seemed to echo there.

Here is the complete journal entry:

> *As the years go by, and as one finds their view of*
> *the world to be more clearly identified with*
> *history, it must be a comfort to have a field of*

> *study, a steady involvement, to return to*
> *regularly—something large and enclosing which*
> *does not change dramatically with the years. In*
> *this way a love, or an abiding friendship, might*
> *be of greater value as time passes more and more*
> *rapidly.*

The poem, published in the summer 1995 issue of *River City: A Journal of Contemporary Culture,* English Department, University of Memphis, required only careful line breaks and minor revisions:

What Abides

As the years go, and you find
your view of the world

to be ever more identified
with history, it is a comfort

to have a field of study, a steady
involvement to return to each day—

something large and enclosing
which time does not transform.

In this way a love, or an abiding
friendship, might grow in value,

might become more true, as all
that promised you permanence

begins to twist and diminish
with the years.

A third type of journal entry, which is a subset of the single passage/ sound progression approach, is the pun and a variant on puns I call "lyrical abstractions." I think of them as poetic aerobics—they help keep the intellect toned up and sometimes split open new fields of comprehension. Here are a few examples: "Bible boning," "whale curtains," "accupummeling," "psychic pheromones," "libido bugs," "platyporpoise," "RepubliKlan" and anagrams like "Newt went" and "spider pride." These all come from a period of entries from May of 1993, when I also wrote "Judas in Waco," "liquids of bliss," "The AIDS of Aquarius," and "pampered by hooligans of love." Sometimes a single pun can sum up an entire period of history, as this character's name gathers the monstrous aspects of the Atomic Age: Frank Einstein.

In fact, it was a punlike thought that changed the entry "True Scientists" at the start of this section into a piece for the summer 1995 Artist Trust Tri-Annual Journal for Individual Artists and Arts Supporters:

Virtual Scientists

Perhaps in thirty years, when our understanding of the physical world is profoundly more sophisticated than now, and we've learned how to recognize the relationships that are the basis for all that exists, then we may truly move into an era when information is more *real* than things. We may discover that what was once considered supernatural—the range of powers and events we often associated with the world of spirits—is actually a complex system of relationships whose dynamics we can comprehend. Such highly skilled people as poets and mystics, whose value to industrial and post-industrial society had become uncertain, may then be recognized as virtual scientists of the numinous universe. We may come to see that a poem is as grand as the United Nations, or a bacterium. We may once again grasp how a poem is a dazzling technology for drawing on the past, present and future, from the inner and outer, the known and unknown, to create something new that enjoys actual existence not limited by time and space. Perhaps a technique may be developed for projecting—holographically, virtually, or even physically—the multi-dimensional, implicate model of the poem. When this happens, I would expect that all who witness such a project would find it instantly familiar—the kind of being they've always found in their dreams.

While keeping a journal is one of the pleasures of being a writer, it also provides a place to find solace when the inexorable loneliness of poetry, of the poet's life, haunts you with feelings of frustration and powerlessness. The following passage became, without revision, the opening paragraph of an essay I wrote called "What's the Big Idea?" published in the Spring '91 issue of *Mississippi Review*. It's a good way to end this piece about journal-writing:

Sometimes, feeling isolated, I think writing poetry is like going alone into the mountains each day to make an artful arrangement of pebbles—under overhangs, in dry stream beds, on ledges— knowing none but the whistling marmots and mute deer will ever see the beauty, yet trusting that somehow these small orderings make their contribution to the world.

Linda Bierds

Typically, my poems are triggered by images recorded in my journal, images often received long before a poem begins.

1/6/89

—It snowed most of the night and morning, confined primarily to the north end. Two huge limbs broke off the fir tree in the front yard. One cracked the fence, the other dented the gutter. This strange sensation: every five minutes or so there is the sound of an ax—sharp and short—and it isn't an ax at all but the breaking limbs of the dozens of large fir trees around the house. Another just fell near my study. Its gray/green needles are covered with a plump snow so that the branch against the ground is almost invisible, a feathering, but the jagged scar where the break occurred is flesh-colored and stark, threatening and pathetic and exhilarating, too, where the moist sap slows.

The Journal and the Poem

I'VE KEPT A JOURNAL for as long as I have written poetry. Through the years the two have become so interdependent that I can't imagine one without the other.

I write in longhand, my sheet of paper with its ink scratches of poetry in front of me, my journal just to my right, open to its next blank page. Its functions are threefold: to store images that might lead to future poems; to document my research; and, with increasing importance, it seems, to record my correspondence with myself when I'm deeply involved in a poem.

Typically, my poems are triggered by images recorded in my journal, images often received long before a poem begins.

Here, taken from dozens of entries following the one above, are brief journal entries I made before starting the poem "White Bears."

—*Lascaux caves—paintings suggest movement*

—*Canary in mine shaft to predict loss of oxygen*

—White Bears and Other Unwanted Thoughts: Suppression, Obsession
. . . *Daniel M. Wegner. "Go stand in the corner," his brother told young
Leo Tolstoy, "until you can stop thinking of a white bear."*

—. . . *still warm from the polish cloth*

—*In Wyoming, cattle and farmers or ranchers have been killed by sudden
hail storms—hail falling in great round stones on them.*

Then, on July 15, I began the first of seven drafts that led to "White
Bears." The first draft was a short lyric set in the young Tolstoy's parlor.
The poem changed and grew as the metaphoric significance of the white
bear unfolded for me.

—*Tolstoy—what first attracted me to the idea of using him in a poem?
White Bears. Obsessive thoughts.*

From July 17 to July 31 the journal is thick with research notes.
Here are a few:

—*"flying accident, 9 years old—throwing himself out the window of a
Moscow apartment house"*

—*"precocious speculation on the nature of reality"*

—*"Countryside in spring—absinthe sprouted; coltsfoot swelled with buds;
the walnut tree, the willow tree, rye paled, wild wood, sorrel"*

—*"in summer—undulant rye, sea of oats with its yellow flowers, sweet
smell of field mustard with clover"*

(All of these quotes are taken from Edward Crankshaw's *Tolstoy: The
Making of a Novelist.*)

8/3/89

—This is the happiest time for me in my writing: to have the research over, to feel the diverse details begin to align, to feel the whole poem shift and settle and begin to be visible. Yet always at the back of my mind the knowledge of the teeth-grinding frustration ahead! And also, that the finished poem will never be as magnificent as this half-formed vision of it.

8/5/89

—Not much to show for today's work.

—I am thinking how the white bear is consciousness turned inward, excessive self-awareness, obsessive concentration "on the heartbeat," "on thinking . . . . I am thinking about the fact that I am thinking." The self so wrapped up in the self that the world drops away. And finally the snow image, just beneath the lavender coltsfoot, the magenta rye.

8/7/89

—The white bear: on an ice floe, surrounded by whiteness, it is black eyes only, a smatter of claws, a little purple at the eyelids, a little violet at the palate. Like the ultima thule line, of course, as if it were fading away, crossing into oblivion with just those parts remaining.

How does Tolstoy fit here? A supreme egoist, always creating rules for this life which then he would then break.

What are rules but borders? Perhaps he feels that without rules he will fade into nothing?

8/10/89

—Nothing of worth today.

—Form. If the poem is in the first person, then the last revelation—the comparison of snow, with its lavender grin of clover, to the white bear/ annihilation—will be known by Tolstoy. He will be looking back on his life with a certain wisdom, a final understanding, and a certain scorn. This is too tidy, I think.

8/11/89

—Have him on the train to Astapovo, near death, remembering: great sweeps given naturally. And the rhythm of memory, a unifying chant.

August 14

—So my writing marathon weekend is over. 14 hours later I have the approach, 20 lines, and the direction . . .

White Bears:
Tolstoy at Astapovo

The wheels of the train were a runner's heartbeat—
systole, diastole, the hiss-tic of stasis—
as they flipped through the scrub trees and autumn grasses,
slowing at last at the station lamps.
And perhaps the fever had carried this memory,
or the journey, or, just ahead in the darkness,
the white, plump columns of lamplight:

He is five, six, locked at the center
of the evening's first parlor game:
Go stand in a corner, Lyova, until you stop thinking
of a white bear. To his left
there is pipesmoke. Behind him
a little laughter from the handkerchiefs.
And in his mind, white fur
like the blizzards of Tula! He studies the wall cloth
of vernal grass and asters, a buff stocking, trouser cuff,
but just at the rescue of a spinet bench
two claws scratch back. A tooth. Then
the lavender palate of polar bears.

I cannot forget it, he whispers. And would not,
through the decades that followed—
the white, cumbersome shape
swelling back, settling, at the rustling close
of an orchard gate, or the close
of a thousand pen-stroked pages,

white bear, in the swirls of warm mare's milk,
at the side of the eye. White bear,
when his listless, blustery, aristocratic life
disentangled itself, landlord to
shoemaker, on his back a tunic, in his lap
a boot, white bear, just then,
when his last, awl-steered, hammer-tapped peg
bit the last quarter sole.

In the gaps between curtains. And now,
in the lamp-brightened gaps between fence slats,
there and there, as if the bear
were lurching at the train's slow pace,
and behind it—he was certain—the stifling life he fled
rushing to meet him: family, servants, copyrights,
just over the hill in the birch trees.

Simplicity, he sighed. Dispossession.
A monastery, perhaps. Kasha in oil. At eighty-two
his body erased to the leaf-scrape of sandals.
And even the room near the station, the small bed
with its white haunch of pillow,

even the mattress, where he shivered
with fever or a train's slow crossing, and whispered,
and, just before morning, died,
was better. Deep autumn. Already the snows
had begun in the foothills, erasing
the furrows and scrub trunks, erasing at last
the trees themselves, and the brooks,
and the V-shaped canyons the brooks whittled.
There and there, the landscape no more
than an outreach of sky, a swelling, perhaps,
where an orchard waited, then boundary posts, fence wire,
then, below, the lavender grin of the clover.

Ron Carlson

I am still inking odd inklings:
. . . names and coined words, what
ifs and descriptions, titles and dreams,
images and connections . . .

24. How it's impossible to point someone's hand at a star, the star you're talking about.
38. Getting off the phone, she always put a fire in the excuse.
55. Names: Nan Moist, Margaret Ability.

The Shopping Bag

WHO HASN'T TAKEN WORLD NOTES? Who hasn't written down some comment or observation that had absolutely no use or application to the current projects, some phrase that insists on being sketched in the margins of a history notebook or the back of an envelope? What are these things? I remember as an undergraduate worrying that I wasn't fit for college because I couldn't resist all the marginalia potshots that suggested themselves during lectures. What do you do when you're acting sophomoric and you're a senior? What about later—and later and later unto now—as I am still inking odd inklings: names and coined words, what ifs and descriptions, titles and dreams, images and connections? What I once thought was an entertaining quirk has become my clear custom and I've learned a few things about getting some good out of it.

60. All the songs were taking their lyrics from tattoos.
61. Titles: Asides.
88. Make love the way a construction worker has an accident with a wheelbarrow of cement.

In some ways these scraps are the physical manifestation of the way my mind works, sparks flying off the wheel. They're pretty, but you couldn't cook with them. The challenge is always to find a way to utilize each of these minute inventions, line them up and make them work. Well, that's not exactly going to happen, but I continue to write and gather these strange and distracting odd bits.

99. I discover myself on the verge of the usual mistake.
110. Painting: Landscape with fortified building.
30. They discovered that the elevator in their dilapidated building acted as
a bellows for the air conditioning, so they sent the child out an hour every
afternoon to ride up and down.

The day I finished the first draft of my first novel, *Betrayed by F. Scott Fitzgerald,* in the summer of 1976, I cleared my table and dumped my journal onto it. My journal those years had been a large Z.C.M.I. shopping bag which by that August was full of half a bushel of little papers on which I had scribbled: envelopes, folded memos, torn slips, wedding announcements, rodeo programs and such. It made quite a pile. What I did was sit there and type them up, one item at a time, dropping them back into the bag. I'd already rescued this treasure chest from the curb where my wife had put it as garbage, which it resembled more than a little—though I hadn't inscribed any remarks on banana peels or tin cans. This transcription took me all afternoon and was just the kind of exercise that's almost refreshing after finishing a manuscript. There was little thinking involved. What remained of my journal now were about nine sheets of single-spaced items, some only a word or two, some several paragraphs, and one (transcribed from the theater program for *The Mousetrap,* a school production my wife had been in) was more than a page. Immediately, I went through this freshly typed miscellany and penciled where I thought each entry might fit into the novel. It was fun, having all these smart remarks. Like working with a committee of the alert, the off balance, the witty. I'm only smart from time to time and here were many of the times. I was able to find a home for three quarters of my observations and I wove them into the book when I did the second draft, thickening the broth nicely.

I find that if I'm in a project, writing a story, my current observations are likely to find an immediate home. If I'm between things then my random notes go into the random file which is literally a file folder in the filing cabinet in my study. It's a first cousin of the shopping bag.

Once or twice a year when I am in need of an activity that requires no thinking, I pull this folder and type it into a computer file titled "Notes," which is simply a second cousin of the shopping bag. Right now there are several hundred items in "Notes," more fabulous gems, I fear, than I will ever find proper settings for. This hasn't stopped me. I continue this irregular activity regularly adding to my eclectic inventory. I appreciate what Dawn Powell said about journals and notebooks, their being a writer's "promissory notes." That's got it. All these things are little debts, most of which I will never pay.

204. Stark as in stark naked.
271. You can tell by the way people drive in a city how many lies have been told there.

Omar S. Castañeda

It is important to practice reliving places concretely and to write these "envisionings" down. Special project notebooks are ways to focus on the needs of the work and to do "exercises" of visualization or of dialogue or of characterization, etc.

27 June 1989
Santiago Atitlán, Guatemala

There were the twelve Nahuales of Santiago. They lived here before. The ancient ones talk about them, some know them. In the old days, then, people travel to Mazatenango to sell. They went there along the roads and came to the city. But there was this powerful dog. It was a magic dog. They say that it was a man. It smoked cigars and everything. It was the government's dog. The people went and stayed in a salon to sleep, but the Government Dog was powerful, magical. Who knows what kind of magic it had, but nothing would kill it. The people slept in the room and then the dog entered. It put its cigars on the feet of the people and killed them. The magic did it. The dead people never came back. The dog told the horses to carry the corpses back. And the horses carried the bodies back to the government. The government sold the bodies to the United States.

Well, the Nahuales met and divined. They divined because people were dying. They met and divined to find out. They found out it was the Government Dog. And what force, what magic this animal had! Nothing killed it. People fought with machetes, with everything, but nothing killed it. So the Nahuales went and they fought. They battled against the dog, and one turned into an eagle. See the dog was very powerful, very strong. Very, very magical. But the Nahuales were great eagles. They knew everything. Just like you and I speak and understand each other, they understood everything. The Nahuales met and found out it was the dog. They said, "You, turn into an eagle, I will fight the dog. You, fly up as an eagle; I will have this stone." So they went and pretended to sleep. They lay down and closed their eyes. The dog came in. It was heavily armed. It had a metal armor suit. It was ferocious. Nothing could kill it. The Nahuales fought and one became an eagle. The one fought hard against the dog. Suddenly, the eagle came down and snatched the dog, lifted it to the top of heaven. The other threw the stone. A little stone, but it grew very big. The stone was very large and the eagle let the dog drop and it smashed into the stone. It had armor and it was smashed. And that ended the terrible dog, the Government Dog.

The Nahuales were powerful. There are many stories about the Nahuales. The old ones, the ancient ones, know many. I only know a few stories. The old men don't trust. If you go to them, they won't speak. To ladinos, in Castellano, they won't share the stories. If you learn Tzutujil, they will tell all the stories. They say that the Nahuales will come some time. They are traveling in a car. They will come.

They say that they have passed recently. Five years ago they came. I don't think they'll come. The old ones say they will be gringos that speak Tzutujil and have "experience." Some have come and speak, but they don't have experience. They will come. Gringos who speak.

They met in the mountains up there past, in the back, up there. Who knows what they say or do?

Specific Project Notebooks

I DO NOT KEEP a writer's journal. I keep scraps of napkins, clippings, full-page notes, unordered quotes, character sketches, interesting lines, paper-clipped photographs, ripped-out-of-magazine things, miscellany, some of it placed together within a folder or box, most of it scattered and making a mess throughout my home. I do not have one of those "books" with empty pages on which to write my general musings, or a loose-leaf binder with pages joined for something approximating more a diary than the inchoate-in-form-and-content thing that gathers inside pockets and drawers, by my telephone, in loose vertical files, and is taken like stacks of overdue bills to every new place I move.

But I do keep a specific project notebook.

I used to feel guilty for not having a writer's journal. It seems such a sign of a writer that it is the most efficient way for those nonwriters in coffee shops to keep alive their highly visible pretense of ambition while avoiding most of the hard work and solitude that real writing demands. You know the type: They are full of romantic ideas of being a writer yet have a strong distaste for the nuts and bolts of the job—like endless revision! But then I have seen hardworking writers with journals, too. I have also seen "serious" writers who talk a lot about "journaling" as a way to get ideas, a kind of trove from which to draw. It took me a while to see that there may be a spectrum of writers, those who use journals "religiously" at one end and those who only use specific project note-books at the other end. I am of the second kind. While working on a specific book, I keep a binder full of photos, drawings, outlines, quotes, overheard comments, etc. I do not include material that is interesting but too far disconnected, and *this* may be the principal difference be-tween a specific project notebook and a writer's journal: The notebook has a proscriptive nature.

So, for instance, while writing my novel, *Imagining Isabel* (set in Guatemala), I developed a specific project notebook that gathered photos, interviews, details of environment, etc. One day, I sat in a small Chinese restaurant and looked for the time. The peculiar clock had a properly functioning hour hand and second hand, but the minute hand lifted toward :37 or :38, wobbled with effort, and tumbled back to :30. You see, the minute hand was decorated with a large, perhaps ivory, butterfly with bright and beautiful colors. Throughout our meal, the clock shuddered and fell. This trinket of observation did not make it into my *Isabel* notebook. It did, however, make it onto a torn napkin that later moved from a refrigerator magnet to a plastic cup filled with paper-clips. I thought the clock would make a good metaphor for the over-writing that some beginning writers do: where the writing is nice, very nice, but counterproductive; or when the author feels too precious about material that really should be cut in revision. There are other uses for the detail, as well. Then when I began working on a fiction writing textbook, this scrap sprang from the cup to my specific project notebook called *Textbook.*

I began special project notebooks as early as 1980, while finishing my first novel, *Cunuman,* though it wasn't published until 1987. I have stopped feeling guilty for not having a journal and have had the good fortune to use my notebooks in unexpected ways. My most developed notebook was one I used for my novel, *Among the Volcanoes.* I received a Fulbright Grant to do research in Guatemala for a novel I have yet to publish, though many sections have been published. I split the research over two summers of three months each. While doing the Fulbright project, I also gathered information that went into my *Volcanoes* notebook, though at the time it was called *Lake-Sea.* It is a thick red book marked Daily Reminder 1989. A quick skim of the notebook reveals that a high percentage of the material has been used, and most of it for the *Volcanoes* project. I see, too, that the notebook served as a resource for at least two published stories and two novels. The directedness of the note-taking surely accounts for some of this luck.

I used the entry I shared above in my novel, *Among the Volcanoes,* and in a collaborative work with Sergio Duarte called "The Government Dog" (Left Bank Books, Blue Heron Press, 1995). At the time I wrote the entry, I was focusing on ways of speaking in Santiago Atitlán, trying to capture the rhythms of dialogues for my novel. I entered three dialogues and one monologue that particular day: one I had with two boys about school; one with a man taking votes for the town's "Queen of the Lake"; one with a man about bus schedules; and the most useful, a story told to me by a young man in a bar. I was paying attention not only to content but to the way people spoke and to their mannerisms in different types of speaking situations. In the young man's case, I tried to capture all his particularities of speech. I did well on that day, I think.

My two teachers, Philip Appleman and Scott R. Sanders, were the ones who most influenced me in keeping some kind of notebook/journal. Philip Appleman always encouraged my doing serious research for my fiction, and recommended careful notekeeping. He also suggested I take photographs of the places I'm writing about, to make drawings and to spend as much time as possible "soaking up" the details, rhythms, patterns of the place. I feel I can only pass this wisdom on. I notice in my teaching of young writers that the most common problem is a lack of "visualization" of place, characters, interactions, etc. It is important to practice reliving places concretely and to write these "envisionings" down. Special project notebooks are ways to focus on the needs of the work and to do "exercises" of visualization or of dialogue or of characterization, etc. They, by their proscriptive nature, focus the mind on all the subtleties of the novel's milieu and increase the likelihood of creating a believable world, an "undisturbed dream," as John Gardner would say.

Henri Cole

I keep a daily journal whenever I travel. At home I am much more irresponsible, but keep a commonplace book like a bank for depositing passages from whatever I am reading. When I am writing a poem, I sometimes make withdrawals from both.

Hiking along the talus of Cap Canaille, its terra cotta ledge 1,365 feet above, one often meets naked fishermen of all different shapes. One afternoon as I was reading out on a pinnacle of stone and feeling as if it could as much have been the 1st or 2nd century B.C. before the Romans conquered Gaul, or modern day Provence, with neither man or boat in sight, I noticed a surge of bubbles nearby breaking the surface of the sea. Suddenly two orange Day-Glo flippers appeared and then a head with a shiny black rubber hood and mask. It moved sluggishly toward me like a beast and seated Itself on a giant oyster-white rock next to mine. Its body was so tightly molded Its wetsuit, it seemed It could as much have been squeezed from a toothpaste tube. From S-hooks on Its belt, two octopuses dangled, their muscular, sac-like bodies limp, their pink suckers in perfect rows. I looked at their inky necks to see where It had bitten them, for I knew that was how a diver kept from being paralyzed by their poisonous secretion. Crossing Its legs, It took a sharp sea urchin from a crocheted pouch, sliced the spiny husk in half with a Tarzan knife, and sucked out the delicate roe. When It sliced another, It looked at me sympathetically and offered the briny hemisphere like a curate might a Host.

The Mind in Repose

THIS EXCERPT from my travel journal was written during 1989 when I was living in Cassis, a small port village near Marseilles (where my mother's family lives) in the South of France. Several years after making this entry, during summer, when I do most of my work, I was searching for ways to write nonnarrative poems. At least nonnarrative in the orthodox sense of telling a story through a linear progression of sentences. I chose, instead, to compose a long list of fragments, many of which document sensoria I'd already noted in my journal. As the Pointillist makes little lozenge brush strokes cohere into something recognizable and true, I hoped my fragmented sentences would arc mysteriously toward the poem's last line, when the self declares what it is that's in the self's heart. Here is the poem:

THE PINK AND THE BLACK

The sea a goblet of black currant liqueur.
The pink sky regarding me sadly.
The hand that was mine, motionless,
    between passages in a story.
The sucking sound of underwater breathing, spitting.
The limy bubbles sequining the sea.
The mutable shape we call man, rising out of it,
    all nostrils and lips behind glass.
The Day-Glo flippers striking against limestone
    like a Spanish fan on pearls.
The limp, sac-like bodies, pink suckers in perfect rows,
    hooked at the belt.
The oyster-white rock on which we sat.
The sleepy face that looked at me.
The crossed ankles.
The inky cloud, like an octopus's secretion,
    moving overhead.
The sun a watery white mess.
The dainty, crocheted net where the sea urchins slept.
    The long spines of the one shucked for me.
The Bowie knife, sharp as a curate's words, cutting, cutting.
The intractable sea flattening and flattening.
The metallic back of something escaping,
    reveling beneath the shadows.
I had been so lonely, hungry as a snake.

Contrasting modes of composition between these two texts are self-evident. All the extra calories are gone from the latter. Language is not only leaner but more focused and dramatic. Rhythm and juxtaposition factor into the lyric equation, where they were not consequential before.

And the last line, though dangerous for its exposition of emotion (something I do not like in art), underscores the narrator's private experience (absent from my journal)—the *raison d'être* for my poem. In my commonplace book, I find, perhaps, the seed for this bald declaration in something preserved from Colette's *The Vagabond:* "Oh, to throw my arms round the neck of a creature, dog or man, a creature who loves me!" The poem originally appeared in *The New Republic,* which was the fifth magazine I submitted it to for publication. And it is the opening poem in my most recent collection, *The Look of Things.*

The commonplace book is a genre I know little about; I expect most remain unpublished and unread except by their makers. Not so long ago I read Bruce Chatwin's *The Songlines,* which has as a centerpiece his commonplace book with a theme. The first journal I remember reading addictively is that by the youthful Wallace Stevens, preserved in *Souvenirs and Prophecies.* It radiates with what only a journal can reveal: the mind in repose, the heart excavating itself.

Chitra Banerjee Divakaruni

There's something about those cryptic gnarled notations on the journal page. Something cathartic, something that unlocks. Or maybe what it really does is lock up the intimate insidious voice which whispers in my ear, *not this, oh no, not this at all.*

August 1989

Have been trying to write about the trip, make sense of it, a series of poems, call them Via Romana? *Line breaks don't feel right. Rhythm too short, cut off. Prose poems? How to convey the feel of Rome in July, the heat—like a fist? And also what I've been thinking a lot lately, god, why do people go through all the trouble of travel, putting themselves at the mercy of strangers, their quick indecipherable lips their eyes their everywhere pointing hands. The helplessness of being lost and sweaty and constantly thirsty. Give it distance. How? Third person? Anonymous? Everyman and woman. At the end, I need a glimpse, an epiphany. What could be epiphanic and relevant and yet fit in naturally here? Image: bougainvilleas on a crumbling brick wall. How? How?*

(Written after a month of traveling through Italy with my husband)

The Journal and I

I AM A JOURNAL WRITER by default, brought to it kicking and screaming. I would rather be writing poetry or fiction. I would rather be composing directly (fluidly?!) onto my computer. I have had my current journal since 1985. It is a fat notebook; nevertheless, those are a lot of years, and its size betrays my resistance to the act of journal-writing. Perhaps this is because I turn to my journal only when in trouble.

For me the journal is a threshing ground, a place to wrestle with writing ideas that refuse to take satisfactory shape. It is a place where I discuss with myself what my hopes for a certain story or poem are—the emotions I want to convey but cannot, the characters who will not let me coax them out of their stubborn woodenness, the feel of a place, a day, a certain quality of light that keeps falling flat.

My journal entries are brief, tortured, punctuated with many question marks. They take me a long time to write. The spaces between the few words weigh heavily on me, stretch into the greyness of uncertainty, the fear of mediocrity. I go back to them many times when writing the problem piece. Sometimes the piece is too difficult. I am not in the right place in my life yet to give it form and voice, and so I have to abandon it. In those cases I circle the journal entry with my yellow highlighter, an illuminated failure to draw my eye whenever I visit the page. Or perhaps the seed of the idea is gestating within its golden skin. That is what I like to think at more optimistic moments.

But most times I do go on to write. There's something about those cryptic gnarled notations on the journal page. Something cathartic, something that unlocks. Or maybe what it really does is lock up the intimate insidious voice which whispers in my ear, *not this, oh no, not this at all.* Perhaps it is just acknowledging fears and frailties, giving myself permission to falter, to fail.

Whatever. The words begin to come, the images. Some fast, some slow. Tumbling, trickling, pooling onto the page until I have enough to take back with me to the computer screen, to begin a successful first draft.

Here is the poem the journal entry above became, the first in a series called "The Tourists," in my collection of poems, *The Reason for Nasturtiums* (Berkeley Poets Press, 1990).

The Tourists

The heat is like a fist between the eyes. The man and woman
wander down a narrow street of flies and stray cats looking for
the Caracalla Baths. The woman wears a cotton dress embroidered Mexican style with bright flowers. The man wears Ray-Ban
glasses and knee-length shorts. They wipe at the sweat with
white handkerchiefs because they have used up all the Kleenex
they brought.

The woman is afraid they are lost. She holds on tightly to the man's

elbow and presses her purse into her body. The purse is
red leather, very new, bought by him outside the Coliseum
after a half-hour of earnest bargaining. She wonders what they
are doing in this airless alley with the odor of stale urine rising
all around them, what they are doing in Rome, what they are doing
in Europe. The man tries to walk tall and confident,
shoulders lifted, but she can tell he is nervous about the youths
in tight levis lounging against the fountain eyeing, he thinks,
their Leica. In his halting guidebook Italian he asks the
passers-by—there aren't many because of the heat—*Dove
terme di Caracalla? and then Dove la stazione? but they stare
at him and do not seem to understand.*

*The woman is tired. It distresses her to not know where she
is, to have to trust herself to the truths of strangers, their
indecipherable mouths, their quick eyes, their fingers each
pointing in a different direction, eccolo il treno per Milano, la
torre pendente, la cattedrale, il palazzo ducale.* She wants to
go to the bathroom, to get a drink, to find a taxi. She asks if it is
O.K. to wash her face in the fountain but he shakes his head.
It's not hygienic and besides a man with a pock-marked face
and black teeth has been watching them from a doorway, and he
wants to get out of the alley as soon as he can.
The woman sighs, gets out a crumpled tour brochure from
her purse and fans herself and then him with it. They are
walking faster now, she stumbling a bit in her sandals. She
wishes they were back in the hotel or better still in her own cool
garden. She is sure that in her absence the Niles lilies are dying,
in spite of the automatic sprinkler system, and the gophers have
taken over the lawn. Is it worth it, even for the colors in the
Sistine Chapel, the curve of Venus' throat as she rises from the
sea? The green statue of the boy with the goose among the
rosemary in a Pompeii courtyard? She makes a mental note to
pick up some gopher poison on the way back from the airport.

They turn a corner onto a broader street. Surely this is the one
that will lead them back to the Circo Massimo and the subway.
The man lets out a deep breath starts to smile. Then suddenly,

footsteps, a quick clattering on the cobbles behind. They both stiffen, remembering. Yesterday one of the tourists in their hotel was mugged outside the Villa Borghesi. Maybe they should have taken the bus tour after all. He tightens his hands into fists, his face into a scowl. Turns. But it is only a dog, its pink tongue hanging, its ribs sticking out of its scabby coat. It stops and observes them, wary, ready for flight. Then the woman touches his hand. *Look, look.* From where they are standing they can see into someone's backyard. Sheets and pillowcases drying white-ly in the sun, a palm scattering shade over blocks of marble from a broken column, a big bougainvillea that covers the crumbling wall. A breeze comes up, lifting their hair. Sudden smell of rain. They stand there, man and woman and dog, watching the bright purple flowers tumble over the broken bricks.

And so I thank my journal, my book that I hate and love. I kiss its cover as I put it away. I hope not to open it again for a long time.

Postscript: Several years after I began keeping this journal, I felt it needed an epigraph, something that encapsulates the writing life. I was tempted to inscribe, on the inner cover, "Abandon hope all who enter here." But after some deliberation I decided to go with what Robert Hass once told us at a writer's conference at Squaw Valley: "It's hell writing and it's hell not writing. The only tolerable state is just having written."

Janice Eidus

*f*or most of us who keep journals in whatever form, there's no need to revise, no need to search for the perfect metaphor, the perfect title, the "hooky" opening paragraph, the climax with the "inevitable surprise."

November 14, 1994

Dear EL.,

What a nightmare my birthday yesterday ended up being. My father was rushed to the emergency room of the hospital due to kidney failure at three a.m., so I spent my entire day in the emergency room with my mother, brother, and John. My father is in bad shape. I think—hope—he'll pull through, though. (He was just there, same emergency room, in September, when he fell, so this is becoming a pattern.)

Finally, this morning, he was given a room. I have no idea what will be involved, how long he'll be in the hospital. I'm really exhausted. I'm giving a reading tomorrow, which I'll do, somehow. I'll rally— but I'm going to cancel a radio interview I'm supposed to do on Thursday; it's too much—I have more root canal on Wed., the reading on Tues., my IRS audit on Friday, and I'll be running to the hospital. It's all too much.

Love, Janice

November 15, 1994

Dear EL.,

Well, the latest news on my father is that the kidney failure/infection is being treated, but the doctors think he may have also had a massive stroke. So they're going to do tests today to determine whether that's what happened. He's in a bad way—has no idea who he is, where he is, who anyone else is, can hardly talk. . . . It's really frightening. To imagine him remaining like this. My mother is pretty hysterical.

*I've got to do a reading tonight. It's at The Knitting Factory. Can't
even decide what to read; I guess I'll have to decide at the last
minute and just walk through.*

Also have teaching, and business to take care of.
Love, Janice

*P.S. Tomorrow is the second root canal visit—in the midst of all this
with my father. Just what I need.*

November 21, 1994

Dear EL.,

*The latest on my father . . . the kidney failure/infection has been
treated—there's no more infection. He still is in an extremely bad
way, though. He still has no idea who he is, where he is, who
anyone else is, still can hardly talk. . . . It's unbelievable.*

*The doctors are speculating that a "contaminant" got into his
bloodstream when his kidneys failed and oxygen wasn't delivered to
his brain and that he had some kind of brain damage at that time.*

*That's all they can come up with, but they don't really know. They
have some idea how to treat the kidneys. But the doctors have no
idea how to treat his mental state. That's a mystery; unfathomable.*

*So sad. I can't bear it. He can't sit up by himself and he behaves in
a really disturbed, and disturbing, way until he falls asleep. He's
also in terrible pain, and he hasn't eaten in about eight days, and he
ripped the IV out the other day. . . .*

I had nightmares all last night and could hardly sleep. So frightening. To see him alive like this—in such pain and such a bad way—and there's no way to reach him at all.

At moments, he _is_ lucid; but they're very isolated moments, few and far between.

So, the doctors have advised us just to wait. They continue to do tests. He seems to be getting relatively decent care. My mother sits with him every day for hours and hours.

My second root canal visit was much much more painful than the first; horrible. I have one more next week. I know that you're in the midst of much dental madness yourself (with caps and implants, etc.), so we can truly _empathize_ with each other.

Oh, I ended up doing the reading _and_ the radio interview. And, somehow, even in the midst of all this craziness, they both went very well.

Also our IRS audit began this week—we had one meeting on Friday and now they want all sorts of documents; we spent all Sunday doing that, putting it all together, and now John will mail it off, and we'll see whether this will be the end of it or not, but I doubt we'll know for a while.

Love, Janice

November 23, 1994

Dear EL.,

My father still can't sit up, etc.—and, worst of all, he remains totally out of it mentally. His doctor told my mother that he won't *be able to come home when the hospital is ready to release him—which will be quite a while, it seems—that he'll have to go into a nursing home. This is a terrible blow to us all. We will have to begin to deal with this.*

He continues to have brief moments of lucidity but they're very rare.

What are you and R. doing for Thanksgiving?

Friday night T. [a mutual friend, also a writer] is going to be the subject of a cable TV show—"the wild East Village performance poet," I guess, will be how he'll be presented. Maybe seeing him on TV will take my mind off some of this. Also am going to order the Rolling Stones live concert on Pay Per View and watch that. I need distractions: poetry; friends; rock n' roll (all three are among my favorite things on earth!).

On Saturday, we have to take Antigone to the vet in the morning for her annual shots, and then in the afternoon we'll go to the hospital to see my father.

I have to go. Have to rush to therapy.

Love, Janice

P.S. Am so distracted and disoriented and stressed, am having difficulty writing at all.

November 27, 1994

Dear EL.,

So so sad. My father is in a coma, on life support—and should he recover, the doctors have told us that the brain damage is quite severe. So so so so sad.

Putting him on life support was not a decision I would have made, given the circumstances, I think. I'm not certain that my mother understood what she was doing at the time; in fact, I'm sure she didn't. But it's an irreversible decision. I, a firm believer in one's right to die with dignity, know that this is an excruciating choice to have to make. My father does not have a Living Will.

So I just go to the hospital now and watch him in this very sad state, lingering on. It's heartbreaking. There's no telling how long he'll remain like this, but I can only hope—for his sake—not too long.

Love, Janice

November 28, 1994

Dear EL,

Things have taken a major turn for the worse with my father. He began to die today, truly, and the doctors asked my mother whether they should use "extraordinary means" to try to revive him, and she said yes.

I am not sure why she said yes—I think it might have been the wiser decision to do otherwise, and she agreed with me when I spoke with her later but she said that she didn't have it in her heart to say no, although should she ever take a turn like this, she said, should she ever get ill like this, she wants me not to try to revive her. I told her that if she has such strong feelings, she ought to make a Living Will. She balked at first, and then in fact she agreed and felt an intense urgency to do so, right away. These are not easy things to discuss with a parent—and certainly not at a time like this. But in my family it seems that it is only in times of crisis that one can discuss such crucial issues. I'm glad that John and I are very different, very willing to communicate openly, and to anticipate issues, before they arise.

Meanwhile, I'm sort of numb. I'm waiting for John to come home, and for her to call me again—she's at the hospital, waiting for the doctors to come out and tell her whether or not they've been able to revive him or not. I want to go to the hospital tonight. I hate her being there all alone.

My brother is out—not at home, not at work—unreachable, and he doesn't have an answering machine.

When she calls again, after she hears from the doctor, and when John comes, we'll decide whether to go or not. She said she doesn't want me to see my father, that he's in such a bad way, near death, and she's frightened for me to see him like that.

But I just want to say goodbye to him, in my own way. This has all been so sudden.

And should they succeed at reviving him, this could go on a long time, I guess. I don't really understand it all. I mean, he'll never get his mind back, that's clear.

I'll let you know. I so appreciate your concern.

Love, Janice

December 1, 1994

Dear EL,

I'm just so emotionally and physically spent and exhausted.

I was talking to John's cousin, who's a psychotherapist, and she said first I need to absorb and integrate what happened the last weeks

while he was so ill (it was so shocking and sudden) and then only
after that will I begin to absorb the fact of his death.

Love, Janice

———————————

December 6, 1994

Dear EL.,

Am so weary; I feel that only now is the fact of my father's death
sinking in. And I feel so much worse, day by day, instead of better. I
seem to have somewhat delayed reactions to these things—with my
sister's death, as well—the reality is too awful for me to comprehend
at first.

I know what you mean about once feeling that if your mother died,
on some level you wouldn't be able to survive, either; I always felt
that way—in some deep part of me—about my father. I remember
saying to friends when I was twenty that I felt so connected to him I
didn't know how I would go on living if he died. As your mother
was for you, he was a "larger-than-life" figure for me, much, much
larger than life. And now—lifeless. It's incomprehensible to me, still.

Love, Janice

———————————

December 9, 1994

Dear EL,

Just time for a quick note. Have come back from therapy, done some
writing on the new story I'm working on, and now have to make
some calls and then meet John at the gym.

Am particularly nervous today; I suppose I'm not emotionally ready to go through my father's things tomorrow.

Love, Janice

P.S. My mother just called—she wants to know whether or not John and I will trust her to make us a good cup of coffee tomorrow. She used to make only instant coffee, which I simply can't drink. So John and I used to stop at a coffee shop and get our own before we visited. This insulted her terribly, we later learned, although we hadn't meant it to. Anyway, she said she's been practicing how to make "good" coffee. So she wanted to find out if we'd be "willing to try" her "new" coffee!

December 29, 1994

Dear EL.,

You said you and R. are having <u>three</u> couples stay with you for a week or so, over New Year's? That's a lot! How will you cope? Will you be able to get any writing done?

Haven't spoken to my mother in a few days; maybe things are a tad back to normal. John and I are going to her apartment this weekend for a couple of hours, to continue to go through some of my father's things.

I owe so many people calls; I don't see how I'll ever get to call them all back.

I'm working on a new story, and for some reason it just isn't working. I keep trying different beginnings, different endings, but something just isn't clicking. It's very frustrating. I don't know whether I should just put it aside with other stories of mine that ultimately didn't make it, or whether I should keep trying for a while longer. It bothers me so much these days when a story isn't working.

I did finish a new story—a very strong one—a week or so after my father died, and that was cathartic. But what I really want to do is get back to my new novel. That's been difficult to return to, since my father first fell ill.

Love, Janice

March 25, 1995

Dear EL.,

My mother's birthday is very soon, in April. She'll be 77. My father would have been 77 next November (two days before my birthday). I'm sure it will be a difficult day for her; it will be difficult for me, too.

I got her a music box. She loves music boxes, and I've bought many for her over the years. He used to love them, too. It was something they shared.

It's so interesting for me to see the distinct personalities of Antigone and Poe. They both are loving and affectionate to me and John. But Antigone loves people, in general; she'll cuddle up to strangers within seconds. Poe, however, is skittish and frightened of strangers. He's more like Margot [EL's cat] in that way.

Love, Janice

April 18, 1995

Dear EL.,

Just have a minute—am spending the morning trying to catch up on business and correspondence, but I found your letters and realized I didn't answer all your questions.

So, first of all, yes, seeing my mother on her birthday was fine. I didn't give her the music box, after all; I decided it wasn't quite as "classy" as most of the music boxes she has (it was sort of "campy," which isn't really her style, I realized). And I decided, as soon as I'd wrapped it up for her, that she wouldn't like it. Instead, I gave her a book of paintings of cats—she adores Antigone and Poe. It's one of our "bonds," actually. I also gave her a box of delicate, embroidered linen handkerchiefs; she seemed pleased.

She's devastated, of course, but she's trying to fight it, trying to figure out "new meaning to her life," she said. But she also said to me the other day that she's "mostly just trying to get by day by day."

Love, Janice

June 29, 1995

Dear EL.,

You asked how my mother's doing—she's okay, but emotionally, naturally, she goes up and down. She's taking an aerobics class for the first time in her life—well, it's sort of aerobics for elderly people—and she goes three times a week and it makes her feel very "exhilarated." She also walks a few miles every day and does calisthenics every morning at home. For a woman of 77, she's in great shape. She says that her best days are the days she takes the aerobics. (I'd never before realized that she and I share such a passionate love of physical exercise; it's really startling to me.)

My brother's planning on moving to the Dominican Republic. He and his wife are in the process of building a house down there. It makes me sad; and it also makes me see that I'm going to be the child who'll have to take on the most responsibility for the parent. With my sister gone, and him living down there. . . . I gather there usually is one child who does become the primary "caretaker." You certainly were with your mother.

Have to go—spent the day writing letters and shopping for John. (I love shopping for him—probably more than I like to shop for myself; I like to own and wear lovely clothes but I don't enjoy shopping for them.)

Love, Janice

July 10, 1995

Dear EL.,

John and I went out last night to try to relax and unwind a bit; we ended up sitting at the bar at the Marriott Marquis Hotel, the revolving bar on the 48th floor with the most amazing view of the city. It was a gorgeous, clear night and I had a strong martini. I so rarely drink anything at all that I felt quite tipsy, and had a good time.

I needed to relax because my mother had fallen in the street two days ago (this from a woman who, as you know, since my father's death, has been taking aerobics classes three times a week; but she lost her balance very suddenly at the curb, she said.)

Being elderly, even if one is in good shape, can be very difficult. And we live in a society that so devalues the old, the infirm. (I know that you don't need me to tell you this, after what you've been through with your own mother; but it makes me so angry.) Luckily, no cars were coming, but she was bloodied and bruised and when some kids finally came to help her, she refused to let them call an ambulance, although they wanted to.

She thought she had broken her wrists (both of them), but she also refused to let me and John take her for an X-Ray. She's very feisty, very stubborn and cantankerous.

However, she called me this morning to say she's feeling almost one hundred percent better and is spending the day with a girlfriend. I'm so grateful that she's okay. She's such a survivor.

It all began to feel reminiscent of my father, who used to fall down frequently, in his last few years; but he was very frail, whereas she's really in terrific shape. John keeps reminding me it isn't the same thing at all.

I hope/trust your reading at the bookstore last night went well. You're such a wonderful reader, I'm sure it was a big success.

Now I want to go out and find a cafe or a hotel bar to sit in and sip something cold, while working on a new story in longhand (the old-fashioned way of writing, which I still love to do). I'd like to get away from the phone, which is ringing constantly, and also from Antigone and Poe, who still don't get along. I guess they never will. But they're both so darling and sweet despite the daily cat fights.

And then, when I've finished writing for the day, I'll go to my health club for a swim.

I guess I'm a survivor, too!

Love, Janice

Bearing Witness

THE LETTERS THAT I WRITE to my close friend, whom I'll call EL., are my current journal. I save all my letters to her on my computer. I stopped keeping a bona-fide, "official" journal—or diary, as I'd always thought of it—about ten years ago, although until then, I'd kept one regularly from age eleven on.

My letters to EL. (and to other friends, as well, although it is to EL. that I write the most frequently, and it is EL. who writes the most frequently to me) have evolved, naturally and fluidly, into both a personal journal and a way to sustain our friendship.

My letters to EL. "bear witness" to my life and thoughts. They are always accessible for me to reread. They help me to remember events, thoughts, people, and feelings. They are useful, therefore, for my fiction writing—as well as for my own self-examination and self-awareness.

EL. is a well-known poet. She and I met sixteen years ago when we were both on the faculty of a writer's conference in upstate New York. We grew very close during the weeklong conference. We've never lived in the same city, however (although we've each moved since we met). Every few years, we visit each other, and sometimes we speak on the phone. But it is really through our correspondence that we keep our close friendship alive.

The letter excerpts that I've chosen to include here span a period of eight months, and they revolve around the subject of my father's death in November 1994. Three years before I'd lost my sister to cancer. Naturally, I've grieved and mourned a great deal over the last few years.

Throughout this period, writing to EL. was helpful. When ELs'. mother—to whom she was very close—died a few years back, we also wrote regularly to each other. And EL. also found that writing back and forth in this way (sharing the daily sorrows and aggravations) was helpful.

I'm not yet ready to write fiction about either my father's death or my sister's death. I need more time, more distance. But losing them both (and watching my sister, who had a very rare cancer, suffer for nine years) will "inform" *all* of my writing for the rest of my life, in the sense that my own worldview has changed. My knowledge of the meanings of the words "family" and "loss" is far more personal now, and much deeper.

So in the meantime, before I can write about these subjects in my fiction, it is in my journallike letters to EL. that I've begun the process of writing about these difficult subjects.

My suggestion to other journal-keepers is simply this: Write freely, without self-censorship. Write as you need to, in whatever form you choose to at any given time (journals, letters, poems, stories, scrawled fragments on notebooks and napkins). Journal-keeping is different than making art (although some writers' journals are so magnificent they are deemed "art"). But for most of us who keep journals in whatever form, there's no need to revise, no need to search for the perfect metaphor, the perfect title, the "hooky" opening paragraph, the climax with the "inevitable surprise."

Writing letters to EL. tends to be a relaxing, calming experience for me—as opposed to writing fiction, which is wildly exciting and stimulating. I need both in order to survive as a person, and as a writer: the calm of the journal; the storm of the fiction.

Reginald Gibbons

So the keeping of a journal is a peculiar form of writing practice—whether deliberate or hasty, formal or casual, whether more or less honest (depending on one's mood and motives), it seems not quite fully meant to be private even at its most private. I feel the tension between the absence and presence of a possible audience.

A few journal entries selected to illustrate different impulses of the journal-keeper:

Nov. 8, 1990

In the still morning—sharply cool, and quiet—the sound of one leaf clattering down through others from the top of the beech tree—and then, free of them, it falls rocking in the air to the ground.

A wide flat yellow 20-pointed maple leaf.

Pet crow

The trees were writhing and thrashing overhead. Rain dripped from their faces, soaked and chilled their napes and shoulders.

January 4, 1991

The parallelism & steady accretion of the language of Genesis—at least as the seventeenth century cast it in English—is, as a gesture, a consoling—however authoritative. And its authority and consolation come from syntactic structure, which with its simple parallelism and repetitions is the language of adult to small child. Since it is my present belief that poetry recovers and restores to us some of the language-use or language-repertoire of childhood—after force of mature habit has accustomed us too much to discursive & communicative or rather informational use of written language—it's no surprise that this first language or first text (text about firstness) is more like a "primitive" (and of course oral-tradition) use of language.

January 9, 1991

> Blown to a tatter by the wind
> the cry of one gull or cat
> and a lost child's cry
> sound nearly the same.

May 19, 1991

On the plane, a vegetarian eating his special lunch, reading a potboiler about Nazis.

June 8, 1991

Miroslav Holub, "Poetry, Science and Survival after Communism," TLS 5/24/91, p. 10:

> The existence of some cultural phenomena here
> and the deep human understanding of the bulk of
> the population are proof that at least in the
> western part of Eastern Europe [a little
> chauvinism?] you couldn't really suppress normal
> human personalities [what is a "normal human
> personality"?]. Here nobody would ever accept
> the official line. Nobody accepted it deep inside.
> There were different levels of non-acceptance,
> from the dissidents to hidden non-accepting at
> home. It was enough culture, enough rationality,
> enough emotional self-cleansing just to state
> once a day, "That's a lie and we hate it." And we
> discovered in those days that we still know
> what's right from wrong. We are getting more

and more hypersensitive to empty words and lies.
In a way this is a very optimistic sign for
intellectual or cultural survival.

Why isn't it enough, in a western capitalist society like our own, to state
once a day, "That's a lie and we hate it?" It wasn't enough even in
Czechoslovakia, where if people did feel this way, it nonetheless required
an external aid from above—Gorbachev's giving up Soviet control—for this
feeling to issue in a change of government. And will any such "self-
cleansing" suffice against the invasion of capital and capitalists? Now
there is a panicked chaos of publishing and perhaps even of writing in all
the former Soviet bloc—no paper, no state subsidies, no money in the
hands of readers with which to buy books, a rash of translations of the
most socially clichéd American writing—Stephen King & hyper-male
"techno-thrillers," etc. What intellectual and cultural resources or resistance
will be erected against this sort of lie? I wish I had the resources to amass
packages of, say, 100 books, 100 packages for each country, & send them
to libraries or study groups, to try to make some alternative available. But
that is probably not only a hubristic scheme but also a futile one. I want
to write a book that encompasses the turmoil of feeling . . . and the
conundrum of thinking: freedom, free thinking, a human scale of response
to state lies, or the lies of money.

June 11, 1991

When someone reads my work, unknown to me . . . When C. reads my
work, in the very same room with me, then I sense very powerfully a giddy
disclosing of myself, an intoxicating addition to my being because this work
of my making is in the light of her mind, her knowing, her feeling. Ong, I
think it is, says that a desire to share consciousness characterizes our
species, or seems to. Neo-Platonists, I've read, although I don't myself know
the sources, believe evil is an absence of being. This seems slippery indeed,

but does it, might it, mean that full being, being in fullness of mind &
body, is the good? My being seems full as she reads—but perhaps this is
only because she likes what she is reading. If she disliked it or was
indifferent to it, would I rise on the same wave of . . . happiness? Of
course not. I write in the hope of adding to my being, or of being more
fully; to be read sympathetically, with fellow-feeling, is to share
consciousness at the height of being, & would be perhaps an
unendurable—but I would like to endure it—experience if the reader could
simultaneously with reading share her thoughts, her being and
consciousness, with the writer.

　　Some literary works reveal a writer's urge or impulse to dominate;
others, a desire to be loved; others a desire to merge consciousness with
another (the reader)—having already merged it with others (the created
consciousness and characters of the work)?

July 9, 1991

V told me that when someone at a Guild Complex meeting suggested a
poetry reading by cops who write poetry, someone else said, Yeah, and let's
have a night for poets who beat people up.

Writing a novel or poem may be, more than we want to admit, very like
writing in a diary when we are young those words that we do not want
anyone to read and that we nevertheless leave where mother or father may
find them.

July 16, 1991

I met a cultural journalist from Brazil, and heard of an anthology of new
poetry called As Artes e Of cios da Poesia (?)—the result of a symposium
in which poets gave readings and spoke about poetry. Thirty poets,

considered the best of the present day. The debate, he said, is (the old one) of formal values vs. content. Those who are playing with words are accused of having nothing to say; those saying something about life are accused of being poor writers. The old debate—rehashed often and again and everywhere—is there value in it, or only uninformed flailing?

My Own Particular Custom

I LOOKED THROUGH a journal of several years ago, to get a little distance on what I have written in this mode, and I selected a few entries that would illustrate how my journal-keeping feeds my writing of poetry and fiction and my thinking about them, as well. Amidst other jottings to which they were not related, the pet crow and the rainstorm in the entry of November 8, 1990, were the first germs of what became chapters of my novel *Sweetbitter,* which I had begun nearly two years earlier, on January 1, 1988. I see the crow and rainstorm in my journal as hints of what was already moving in my memory and unconscious; my writing down these few words is not really my first attempt to begin to create a scene, but rather a kind of marker buoy that I throw into the waters to remind me to go back and search the depths beneath it:

> The weather was gathering, threatening rain. A
> thunderstorm had been building, far off to the
> west, and now it was going to fill the quiet night
> with its threats. A sizzling bolt of lightning burst
> out sideways above them, searing its thick knotted
> length on the dark sky for a long instant like an
> engorged vein on the very arm of God. She was
> blinking up where the flash had been. The
> immense darkness of the woods around them had
> turned in the moment of the bolt into a frightening
> innumerableness of detail and in that lit instant

every leaf and twig, every thread of their clothes
and hair on their heads, was counted and recorded.
Then came the blasting thunder, pushing through
their bodies as if they were nothing, and beyond
them echoing away over half the world.

In memory and feeling, as yet unexplored by my conscious mind, either in pure thought or already in the wonderfully complex process of writing, lie these subjects that I sensed, on that day, were important to my novel. I didn't end up pouring rain down on my characters, only threatening to. The fallen leaf remains where it fell, not yet used for anything more in my writing.

The little quatrain I jotted down in January 1991 was the seed of something that took a long time to come fully into being, as my writing usually does, and finally became a poem called "White Beach" (published in the *Southern Review* [31:1, Winter 1995]). The finished poem preserves only a few words from this dull, original quatrain; but a mood that struck me, or into which I fell, that the quatrain marked, again like a buoy, was at the heart of the poem. Later came a process of drafting and revision, but without having written down these four lines, I would probably never have written the poem. I have the impression that this is the way many poets work.

The other entries are meant to example the mere noticing (the vegetarian) and the thinking-through of questions about writing and reading that also fill my journals.

When I was still an undergraduate student, I started keeping a journal that sometimes was a somewhat analytical diary of what happened and sometimes a trying out of ideas about what I was reading and writing. I have kept writing both sorts of entries, all these years, and added fragments that are those floating markers of my unconscious, which become more frequent as the years go by.

I use a notebook that I carry with me nearly everywhere, and there are several different sorts of entries in it—from the fragments and even single words to long passages of essayistic complete sentences—almost as if written for different audiences, although in theory at least for no audience at all. I write irregularly about my own life events; I sort out my observations about and relationships with others; about some of my dreams; I comment to myself on what I'm reading; I wonder about what I'm writing and what sort of a writer I am; I record anecdotes, observed moments among strangers, acquaintances and friends; I work out lines of thought about what I see happening around me in our common life as a society. I put down notes for poems and stories (I keep another note-book for notes toward the novel I am working on). I scrawl hasty scraps of language and writing that feel like beginnings, or endings, or possibili-ties, of poems or stories, and that have arrived, finally, from their origins in my unconscious. I write down things I hear others say. I sketch (and use these sketches as bases of larger drawings). I rant.

And from time to time—but not particularly often, because some-thing about the process disturbs me, embarrasses me, makes me feel an especially intrusive, cold voyeur of my own life—I go back through the pages and I read. More often, I scan quickly for, and recopy into a work-ing notebook, the first drafts, the isolated phrases, sometimes a few words out of the middle of something else—live words with feeling and thought still pulsing in them even though the mood of the moment of writing has long since passed. These are the tatters, bits and shards I want to make more of, and sometimes I do, although only of some of them.

———————

A number of years ago I was very taken by the published journal of George Seferis (and I included some especially striking excerpts from it in my 1979 anthology *The Poet's Work*). Seferis gave me permission to acknowledge feeling baffled or thwarted somehow, when the poem won't go forward—or anywhere—yet without losing hope of eventually finding a way to write what I could sense I wanted to write. He encourages patience and a deep sense of the body as the source of symbolic thinking. He records anecdotes of experience as if to confirm or even shape his sense of poetry. I have also been moved by the power of Gombrowicz's uncompromising and hard self-presentation and thinking, and also by the surviving fragments of the journals of Chekhov and Thoreau. Reading what was not exactly meant to be read by others is peculiar—for it always does seem to be meant to be read by others. It's somewhat like a black-and-white candid or news photo that seems to seize, out of what happens to happen, an inevitability of witness. So the keeping of a journal is a peculiar form of writing practice—whether deliberate or hasty, formal or casual, whether more or less honest (depending on one's mood and motives), it seems not quite fully meant to be private even at its most private. I feel the tension between the absence and presence of a possible audience.

And then there are at least two ways to use one's own journal writing. Keep the journal for the sake of reading back over it—simply to "refresh memory" (as lawyers say to witnesses)—and perhaps for the sake of using this record more fully in further writing or reflection. Another value of reading back over it is that, as well as in your own poems or fiction, over time, you can eventually see patterns of feeling, of perceiving the world and the people in it, of thinking, that help bring your own unconscious mental life into view. Your predispositions, assumptions, patterns of responsiveness, obsessions. For me, such inquiry into my own unconscious, however unavoidably incomplete, helps me to write with a greater self-understanding, and sometimes to move deliberately beyond past obsessions, or at least move into new ones. I have long believed Keats's assertion, and later restatements of it by other writers, that writing is self-making: at minimum, in our contemporary sense of its being a performative self-fashioning, but at maximum, a much deeper process than that, more like self-psychoanalysis.

A second way of journal-keeping is nicely described by Thomas Mann in the journal he kept in the 1930s, after the Nazis forced him from Germany and he lost all the routines and places that had been home to him. Having already won the Nobel Prize, having married money and made more of it, he was a materially cosseted public figure, enjoying even in uncertain exile and unstable health a sort of existence enjoyed by only a handful of other writers, then or now—admired by great minds, always attended by well-wishers, expected to make public statements on politics as well as art, spending all his working time on his books and correspondence, with few if any of the practical everyday duties and responsibilities of living, which were managed by his wife, Katia, and even by his daughter Erika. Nevertheless, his diary is very matter-of-fact, and I hear a voice kindred to our ordinary ones in this passage that he wrote on Sunday, February 11, 1934:

> These diary notes, resumed in Arosa during days of illness brought on by inner turmoil and the loss of our accustomed structured life, have been a comfort and support up to now, and I will surely continue with them. I love this process by which each passing day is captured, not only its impressions, but also, at least by sugges-tion, its intellectual direction and content as well, less for the purpose of rereading and remembering than for taking stock, re-viewing, maintaining awareness, achieving perspective . . .

I encourage students to keep a journal, and in it to try to find words not only for their intimate self-disclosures and record of experience but also for their reactions to the writing of others—for the sake or sharpen-ing their sense of what can be done, and of why it might be done, in fiction and poetry. I encourage them to use the journal to contain every-thing that has to do with beginning new writing: to try out styles, strategies, beginnings and endings, to assign themselves tasks of describ-ing or imitating. And of course to just spill, sometimes; to pour out words from one's being, from one's being-in-language. I suggest they choose a notebook sturdy enough to knock around with them, small enough to carry all the time, everywhere.

But I am only urging on them my own particular custom. Not only some writers but also some politicians, sycophants, torturers, doctors, bird-watchers, fly-fishermen, dreamers, blessed lovers, and all sorts of other persons keep journals. The keeping in itself refines no virtue, enforces no honesty. But then personal honesty and virtue are not required of a writer; only a way of looking at life and a way with words and symbols, with the pacing and shape of a story or the unfolding of a sequence of rhythms and images.

Patricia Hampl

It started for me, as it does for most girls, with one of those red leatherette five-year diaries, bolted shut by a diminutive brass lock whose ineffectual key I hid elaborately in my bedroom. A journal not only required secrecy—it *was* secrecy. Solitude implied scribbling. My soul poured forth. My brother, idly curious, didn't even bother to search for the little key; he coolly sprang the lock with a bent paper clip, and laughed himself silly. My first reader.

So Ian (who's okay most of the time, one of those guys who hums under his breath when other people are talking: he's chronically bored but tries to be polite about it), anyway he ambushes me! Asks sweetly, "So, Trish, are you much of a walker?" I think I have the right answer (that was my first mistake, right there: why do I always try to figure out what the other person wants to hear? Think about this).

So I say, "You bet I am, Ian, I love to walk, I walk a lot at home." This isn't even true, but I'm bursting with athletic good intentions and some misguided patriotic zeal to convince them all Americans aren't a nation of slugs.

"Oh," he says, and he's frowning. And he tells me about another hike he and Lollie took a couple of years ago when four Americans, Californians, came along and ruined everything, walking too fast. "They didn't even stop to look at the flowers," he says. Disapproval. I've given the wrong answer—the reply of a potential non-stopper for the flowers.

And then Cecil comes forward with that Porterhouse face of his and . . .

A Book with a Lock and a Key

IT STARTED FOR ME, as it does for most girls, with one of those red leatherette five-year diaries, bolted shut by a diminutive brass lock whose ineffectual key I hid elaborately in my bedroom. A journal not only required secrecy—it *was* secrecy. Solitude implied scribbling. My soul poured forth. My brother, idly curious, didn't even bother to search for the little key; he coolly sprang the lock with a bent paper clip, and laughed himself silly. My first reader.

Maybe it was there, at that early crossroads of betrayed confidentiality, that I gave up my faithfulness to the journal. I couldn't seem to "keep" a diary. Each year a few valiant entries (I have decades of early Januarys recorded in detail), and then the dwindling begins, until the frank silence of all those unmarked white pages resounds through the abandoned notebook. Why so many failed attempts? Did my life bore me—or shame me? Sometimes. But the reason I couldn't sustain a daily journal, I think, was that I hated to see all that writing go to waste. Into the journal, down the drain.

The problem with journal writing (aside from its notorious self-absorption, which is hardly a sensible thing to blame it for) is that journals have no retrieval system. You write and write, and it all swirls away into the unnumbered, unindexed pages of notebooks that stack up, year by year, in the dark of a closet shelf. You forget, but *they* remember. You say you're going to reread them—and sometimes you even begin to. But in the end, the inky lines blot into the non-acid-free paper, and you're too busy writing this year's journal to work your way through two decades' worth of old ones. Who was R? Why did I resolve never again to put up with such behavior? (What behavior?) Who is this breathless, overwrought person? It is me, me, me. Who cares? Nobody even bothers to pry anymore. Most of my journals lie on a shelf, passionately written but virginally unread, even by me.

Yet I rarely leave the house without a notebook tucked in pocket or purse. I sometimes substitute a microcassette recorder, but that's a stretch: I'm a notebook person. Hearing my voice, confiding *sotto voce* to the little tape recorder, startles me back to a wary surface self; I require the hermetic experience of subject, verb, object on silent paper to feel free. I am so journal dependent that I will even turn back home once I'm in the car if I realize I've forgotten my notebook. I never visit a new town without finding a stationery store and buying a notebook, the only souvenir I require of all places. I don't believe I have ever gone to a doctor's office or a dentist's without a notebook. I don't always write in it, but it is the one companion I seem to require in all public and therefore potentially alien, places—museums, cafés (of course cafés: there's a whole literature founded on café writing), auto-body shops, wherever waiting is done. And especially and most ardently—on airplanes, and in all forms of conveyance. For over the years it has become obvious that I am at my most devoted as a journal-keeper when I am on the road.

This is when such companionship is essential, I suppose, to assuage the solitude of solo travel. But it is also because a trip has the orderliness and reassuring form of art: you depart, you experience, you return. Beginning, middle, end. In the travel journal nothing, it seems, is wasted— unlike those chunky journals marked boldly with the year, 1972, 1973, 1974. They go on and on, with the blown-to-bits lostness of all lived time. Those are the journals I rarely open. But my travel journals, titled with the names of places, the years only a tag-along subtitle, reassure and welcome me: Prague 1977, London 1978, New York 1983, Iowa 1985, Vermont 1995. *Which* place is less important than the fact of *some* place.

Traveling sharpens the eye; it revs the engines of description. "I have to get that down," I'll think greedily. Travel gives the illusion of freshness; it offers the compelling pretense that no one else has ever observed this scene as you, now, are observing it. All of life should be this way, of course. But travel is the model for such avid attention. It is life understood as notetaking. Those Umbrian hills—get them. That burnt-gold wave of Iowa corn, cresting over the highway—get it. The gossip in the Duluth diner, the lovers hissing accusations at the next table in the London pizza parlor—get down the dialogue. For once, mortality becomes positive: you may never see this again—get it now. You pass here only once.

When I travel, the formlessness of the journal, which usually troubles me, becomes instead its essential charm and usefulness. It is the right tool for the job. And the job is what Thoreau, patron of all journal writers, said it is: *simply seeing.* It has helped that my two longest works, *A Romantic Education* and later *Virgin Time,* required much travel. Both are memoirs, and therefore inhabit that intermediate range between fiction and frankly nonfiction narrative. In the first, about my Czech family background in St. Paul and my travels to Prague, I consciously used the journal (or rather, several journals) as I researched and wrote the book. I had three notebooks, which corresponded to what I thought might be the three sections of the book. I used these notebooks pretty much the way most writers use notebooks—for daily, even hourly, notations. Later they were money in the bank. I cashed out the deposits of those casual notations—sometimes a whole paragraph, sometimes just a fleeting idea that needed pages of "real writing" to work in the text. *A Romantic Education* (Houghton Mifflin, 1992) was ghostwritten by those journals.

Virgin Time (Farrar Straus Giroux, 1992), a memoir of my Catholic upbringing and an inquiry into contemplative life and prayer, sent me on travels to Assisi (where I pursued the life of St. Francis first on a hiking tour of Umbria and then on a study tour with a group of nuns and priests) and later to a remote monastery in northern California on retreat. More journals, much note-taking. Once again, in these notebooks there is the typical writerly reliance on the fleeting impression, the quickly executed sketch of character, the shard of dialogue that is meant to trigger a whole encounter, a full scene. Because these memoirs engaged me in questions of history (of the Czech lands in *A Romantic Education* and of the early Italian Renaissance in *Virgin Time),* I also used my journals for research and note-taking from books I read.

None of this was unusual or perhaps even of interest except to me. But when I began writing *Virgin Time*—the book itself, not the "notes" from my various travels—I came upon a new usefulness for the journal. It was no longer simply a source; it became a character.

A memoirist must construct a protagonist just as certainly as a novelist must, though the character is traced more closely to autobiographical experience. Still, the task of finding that part of one's character which can sustain the particular questions of the book under construction is a similar job. Somewhere along the fumbling path of discovering/creating this protagonist-self for *Virgin Time,* I realized that the part of me who is an obsessive note-taker needed to be in the book, not simply of it. This notebook-toting scribbler—that *type*—was exactly the protagonist I needed to represent the religious search I meant to embody in this book.

It was a (briefly) startling moment, though I had long been convinced of the core value of these journal and notebook remarks and sketches, so hastily tacked down on paper. "The notes for the poem are the only poem," Adrienne Rich said (in a poem), and I believed her. I transcribed carefully (in my notebook) Henry James's dictum on "the rich principle of the Note": "If one was to undertake to tell tales and to report with truth on the human scene," he says in "The Art of Fiction," "it could but be because notes had been from the cradle the ineluctable consequence of one's greatest inward energy. . . . to take them was as natural as to look, to think, to feel, to recognize, to remember."

Still, it was a strange sensation to draw the journal forward from its backstage position where it usually directed so much of the action, and make it now a player, speaking lines directly to the audience. Yet the more I allowed myself to use the journal as a presence in the text, the more light it shed. In one Umbrian scene where I wanted to convey the peculiar frustration of being the lone American (and a Catholic) in a group of English hikers wary of popery, I found that the journal-as-character knit together this fabric of frustration as nothing else could. I frankly displayed the journal—the fact of my writing it and some of its contents—and it became the touchstone for emotional candor in the book. It became the *way* this protagonist—this me—was honest. It became the me I needed. And this "private" me was now, necessarily, "public." The journal inside-out.

How odd, after all these years, to pry open the secret book, after all, to do away with the lock and key, and display those hidden pages for anybody who wants to take a peek, as this section from *Virgin Time* shows:

We walked long hours every day, with a lazy two hours for lunch, moving in and out, back and forth across the Umbrian antiphon of light and shade. Sheets of poppies, Chinese red, papered the shallow dishes of meadows. In the early mornings, birds started up like ink flicked against the white sky.

Diana clumped through the hot days in khaki shorts and dingy T-shirts. Her hiking boots looked as if they weighed ten pounds each. She lacked only a machete strapped in a holster at her side to complete the image: intrepid girl explorer.

At night, she appeared, reincarnated in a brief slither of a black dress and spike heels, her washed hair swinging free to her shoulders like poured honey. She wore narrow chains of gold at her neck and wrists, and had a gold signet ring and gleaming hoop earrings. She was a dazzler, and easy with it.

Her great breasts swung free above the sheer fall of her leggy height. Cecil had the habit of addressing himself directly to her chest. "I say, Diana," he would begin, transfixed by the double oracle veiled by her T-shirt, "when are you thinking we might stop for a bite?"

She took it in stride, dipping her head to catch his glance. She drew him up like a fish hooked in the eye until he was looking her in the face. He didn't seem to register the casual, almost friendly, contempt that met him there.

We gathered after the day's march for elegant dinners at the small restaurants Diana ferreted out. We ate, in many courses and with much wine, the food she ordered. She always managed to get herself into the kitchen to do her choosing, then returned to our table with the appeased look of a shrewd interrogator who has her ways of getting information from the prisoner. "They *did* have truffles," she would say, vindicated by her kitchen reconnaissance after correctly mistrusting the false intelligence of a perfidious waiter, "and *we're* getting them."

Diana hiked with us; Will drove the Land Rover, hell-bent for election, billowing dust, to our lunch stop, where he laid out the picnic. After lunch he careened off to the night's hotel, and lugged the suitcases to our rooms, just as the tour brochure had promised someone would do. Then he took himself off to a corner where he read Petrarch (in Italian) from a ratty paperback, and bit his fingernails raw while the rest of us ordered Cinzano *bianco*.

Will was not Diana's lover, though Cecil did what he could to fan his own projected flames. "I say, Will, pretty close quarters for you and Diana on third. Sharing the bath up there?" Cecil encouraged Will to pursue romance with Diana based, it seemed, on their age difference. "Get yourself an older gal, my lad, that's what I did," he said, jerking his head toward Alma, who blushed. "Didn't I, darling?"

"*Ce-ci-il,*" cried Alma hopelessly.

Diana's Amazon to Will's boy Mr. Peepers: stranger things under the sun, of course, but they were clearly unsmitten. It was not entirely certain that Diana understood Will to be a person, even. He was a fluent-in-Italian kid, her gofer. She let it be known she was the girlfriend of the firm's owner. An older lover: his slightly disdainful face looked out from the firm's brochure, whose arch prose he had no doubt written. On the trail, though, Diana was the boss, wielding her invisible machete.

Will was afraid of her. Actually, Will was afraid of *everything,* of which Diana was only the most immediate manifestation. He jumped if you spoke his name, and his egg-beater-styled hair stood out from his head in permanent alarm. He scribbled covertly in a notebook. That we had in common. If truth be told, I thought maybe he was a little smitten with me—I qualified as an older woman (he was just past twenty), and I was an even more manic notetaker than he. We sat across from each other in the gilt salon of our hotel after the first day's hike, before the others gathered for dinner. We were both writing away in our notebooks, sweeping the day's bits and pieces into our ruled dustpans.

We happened to pause and look up, into each other's face, at the same moment. I had the uncanny, sure sensation that we had each been caught in mid-description of the other. I, for one, bent head to notebook and went right back to it shamelessly: *Skinny and lumpy. He looks thoughtful in repose—or no, I guess he looks hurt. But mostly, just young.*

He sought me out during the siesta the next day after lunch. The lunches were true to the brochure picture: the blue-and-white checked tablecloth, the cheese and leathery sausage, the liters of wine. Only the figs were missing—wrong season. The hike was offered twice a year. "In May you get the wildflowers," Diana said, "in September you get the figs." In the brochure we had gotten both as you do in fantasy, where travel most truly occurs.

The pages of my notebook were damp with pressed flowers, as if no written word could do justice to the trembling light and mist of the place. I tried and gave up, speechless with the fullness of the floating world. In my frustration, I imposed on the lines of my notebook pages, where all the words were supposed to be, the souvenirs I snatched from the landscape. Lollie named, and I reverently copied, a whole page of wildflowers, listed in ranks as she pronounced them for me: star-of-Bethlehem, wild gladiolus, love-in-a-mist, and convolvulus and forget-me-not, the grape hyacinth and buttercup and wild rose, which I could identify myself, cistus that looked like a rose but wasn't, and the oddly named Christmas rose, which bloomed in May. There were orchids and iris hidden in the sedgy parts of woods where truffles were supposed to be, and simple starry flowers identical in petal and leaf but washed in a range of blue and pink, depending on the soil they leached their color from. Even Lollie couldn't tell their name, and stood before them confounded, thumbing her flower book to no avail.

Will tended to eat his lunch furtively, removed from the rest of us, who were grabbing and reaching around the blue-and-white cloth. Some days he drank only *acqua minerale,* and frowned as our empty liters of wine fell on their sides off the cloth onto the grass, where he parsimoniously retrieved them. Other days he poured himself a tumblerful of Orvieto white wine and gulped it down like milk with cookies, and then sloshed himself another of red warmed in the sun.

Whatever he did—or in those things he refrained from doing (engaging in small talk, for instance)—there was a subtext written in invisible ink, an inchoate message he seemed to be guarding but also displaying for someone, anyone, to decode. Though he made much of carrying himself off to be alone with his Petrarch or his notebook, he stayed within view, and he rarely turned a page. He sat across a room as if across a desert, his pale eyes searching us as we sat in our oasis of Cinzano and chitchat, a mirage he could only rarely bring himself to join.

He had the look of a lost soul, waiting for someone to divine his thirst, to come forward with a cut lemon to rub across his lips so his invisible ink would reveal its message at last, liberated and open for all the world to read. Meanwhile, he held to Petrarch in the original. I asked him, pointing to the book, what it was.

"Love poems," he said in his startled way, as if I'd wormed an addiction to pornography out of him. He stood there twisting the soft cover and flimsy pages of the book as he spoke. "I—I was wondering if I could speak with you. I mean, if I'm not interrupting . . ."

I was writing in my notebook, trying to describe the hill color *. . . some kind of gray scrim over the green, but not muddy, not depressing . . .* The notebook was bulging with pressed flowers, and I wrote over a bumpy terrain like the one we had walked up that morning. Everyone else was napping. After the morning's walk, we threw ourselves on the picnic lunch in a frenzy of bread-ripping and wine-gulping. Then people curled up on the grass while the spring leaves shushed softly above, and they napped like good children on kindergarten rugs.

Ian slept nobly, like a statue, propped in a seated position against a rock, his burl walking stick straight as a rod next to him; Lollie lay nearby on her side, her hands clasped together, prayer-like, serving as a pillow for her small, high-boned cheek. Cecil hurled himself into the sun as if to defy it with his meat-red face; with an irritated gesture, he knocked off the straw hat Alma crept up and placed gently on his head to protect him before she took herself off to a shady spot, where she lay down, tugging at her culottes to be sure they covered the backs of her dimpled thighs.

Lloyd and Louise had found separate facing trees, like twin beds at an economy hotel. "I say, all of you," Lloyd had called to the rest of us while we were still sipping the last of our wine, "I've found the best tree. Too bad for you."

"And I've found the next best," sang out Louise.

Nigel and Jill lay in dappled light, their arms around each other, Jill's face tilted into Nigel's chest. They were smiling faintly. They looked so simply intimate they might have been at home, in the house attached to their clinic in Devon, rescuing a sweet moment in their own double bed, floating on the afterward of love. As for Diana, she had taken off in the Land Rover to settle arrangements at the next hotel and would be back to lead us there on foot after the siesta. Will had been reading until he braved the distance between us and stood there, wringing Petrarch by the neck.

I got up to follow him and closed my notebook where I'd intended to chart my journey over the hills and dales of St. Francis, spinning out my thoughts along the way about his quirky contemplative life, which refused to remain medieval, refused to disintegrate into mere oddity. His life that called me somehow. Had called me here, I thought.

But only my list of wildflowers and the squashed blossoms pressed between the pages showed I'd been to Umbria at all. My journal displayed the inner life of a score-settler and a hand-wringer. St. Francis was nowhere. And where was the contemplative mind he had staked his life on—and I this trip? I was filling the pages with a documentation of the English on holiday, licking my wounds, unable to detach from the social scene and float as the milky landscape did, into the life of the mind—or into the life beyond the mind which, I'd thought, was my goal, my desire. Instead, I was tracking my companions:

So Ian (who's okay most of the time, one of those guys who hums under his breath when other people are talking: he's chronically bored but tries to be polite about it), anyway he ambushes me! Asks sweetly, "So, Trish, are you much of a walker?" I think I have the right answer (that was my first mistake, right there: why do I always try to figure out what the other person wants to hear? Think about this).

So I say, "You bet I am, Ian, I love to walk, I walk a lot at home." This isn't even true, but I'm bursting with athletic good intentions and some misguided patriotic zeal to convince them all that Americans aren't a nation of slugs.

"Oh," he says, and he's frowning. And he tells me about another hike he and Lollie took a couple of years ago when four Americans, Californians, came along and ruined everything, walking too fast. "They didn't even stop to look at the flowers," he says. Disapproval. I've given the wrong answer—the reply of a potential non-stopper for the flowers.

And then Cecil comes forward with that Porterhouse face of his and . . .

So the pages were filling, not with Francis and Clare, but with Lollie's faded beauty and vague sweetness of mind, with Ian's lost-the-empire-but-not-our-honor manners. I took up my ballpoint to rage at Cecil for Alma's ineffectual sake, as if after all I'd accepted her initial invitation to stick together, two lost colonials. *He has the nerve to say, "Better watch those sweets, Trish. You don't want to lose your figure. Wouldn't want to thicken the way Alma has now, would she, darling?" Thicken—as if she's a gravy. And Alma just says, "Ce-ci-il." And I order the tiramisu, lapping up the cream to revenge us both.*

I wasted whole pages tracking the twin minds of Lloyd and Louise, marveling at the quantities of complacency they managed to cram into those tidy heads. Lloyd, I took a page to note, was troubled that I spoke a different English from his, one that must be wrong because his was so patently right—and my being an American was no excuse.

"I say, Trish," he had piped up at dinner, "why *do you* say 'driver's license' instead of 'driving license'?" He had noticed my use of the phrase the day before and had been brooding ever since. "I can't see the logic of it," he said. "One is not licensed to *be* a driver; one is licensed to go driving. Surely the Americans see that."

Nor could I let pass without notation the incident with Louise, who had been all in a false flutter because she had let loose with a casual anti-Catholic remark at lunch. Her point: The Franciscans were the worst of a bad lot, all the Catholic orders were positively *rolling* in money they extorted from these poor peasants and had done for generations upon generations.

Someone must have passed her the information that I was a Catholic. I had been seen lighting a candle in a chapel along the way. Great flapping at dinner. "I had no idea, Trish, I'm quite contrite. I must say I had no idea *what you* were. Lloyd and I thought perhaps Jewish, it's quite difficult to know with Americans." She was paralyzed with embarrassment, she said. "But I would be less than candid," she said, looking around the table with her pert face, "if I didn't maintain that I do find the Catholic orders to be . . ."

What do you do with such people? I gave myself over to them

heart and mind, driven as if by family bonds. I endured them, I reveled in them, I judged them in my little ledger, I forgave them and judged them all over again. I took umbrage, I took revenge. I wrote them up at night in the pitched-roof rooms of old hotels and the monasteries-turned-inns where we stayed.

I suppose I was lonely. They were, for now, my people.

Jim Harrison

I don't write in my journal daily or habitually. I limit it to notions and images I can't live without, which are mostly concerned with germinating work.

From the *Dalva Notebooks, 1985–1987*

The thirteen-year-old girl walks out into the damp moonlight. It's after midnight and I'm trying to imagine the freshness of her emotions.

Only when I'm fatigued do I worry about being vindicated.

I explained to Ms. _____ that life was a vastly mysterious process to which our culture inures us so we won't become useless citizens.

I'm inventing a country song, "Gettin' Too Old to Run Away." In the middle of these sloppy ironics I remembered the tremendous silence of the midday eclipse last summer. Nature was confused & the birds roosted early. I was full of uncontrollable anger because I had to leave for L.A. in a few days for a screenplay conference. No one liked my idea of the life of Edward Curtis except me.

In a dream a ranch foreman named Samuel Creekmouth appeared to me and told me how to behave. I became irritable but in the morning had a lush & jubilant vision of what the novel was to be.

On the walk there were two small beaver, a huge black snake, a great blue heron feathering into a southwest wind, sand dunes caving into a furious sea on a rare hot day in late April.

Hard to keep the usual interior balance when the dream life is kicking the shit out of you during, as usual, the waxing moon. In the same place I saw an actual wolf last year, I found a female wolf in a dream, her back broken. I went to her, knelt down and gathered her up, and she disappeared into me. This experience was frightening.

That peculiar but very beautiful girl I saw in a dress shop in Key West ten years ago reappeared. She told me you can't give up Eros. Then, as with most of my dream women, she turned into a bird (this time a mourning dove), and flew away.

I woke in the middle of the night and wrote down that it is important not to accept life as a brutal approximation. This was followed by a day of feeling quite hopelessly incapable of writing my "vision" of the novel which I haven't begun to compose.

In New York City staying with my agent Bob Dattila over by the river on East 72nd. We are trying to make business deals on the phone, and play gin rummy though we can't quite remember the rules of the game. Bob asked me what was even deeper than the bedrock in the huge excavation next door. I told him watery grottos full of blind, albino dolphins. Then in the night, in a dream, I climbed out of the excavation in the form of a monster: my eyes were lakes, my hair trees, my cheek was a meadow across which river ran like a rippling scar. In the morning it was a comfort to walk the dog up to Ray's for a breakfast slice of pizza. Since I have three at home it is a considerable solace to have a dog friend in NYC, and when I come to town Bob's dog knows she can count on me for a slice of pizza. In short, we make each other happy.

What I don't want for myself is called a "long ending" with the vital signs not altogether there. This thought occurred to me after reading a biography by John Dos Passos.

Upset that this novel is going to make me too "irrational" to earn a living. In my background it is inconceivable for a man not to offer the full support for his family. A half-dozen years ago I made a great deal of money but didn't have the character appropriate to holding on to any of it. This must take training. Now the accretion of beloved objects & images in my life and dreams has become more totemistic & shamanistic: grizzly-bear turd & tooth, coyote skull, crow and heron wings, a pine cone from the forest where Garcia Lorca was executed. Probably nothing to worry about as it began when I was half-blinded as a child, and for comfort wandered around the forest and lake and you don't find any trinkets there.

Always surprised on these days when the mind makes her shotgun, metaphoric leaps for reasons I've never been able to trace. Remembered that Wang Wei said a thousand years ago, "Who knows what causes the opening and closing of doors?"

Alliance: Nebraska reminds me of what America was supposed to look like before it became something else. Along Rte. 20 the almost unpardonable beauty of desolation. I could live along a creek in the Sandhills. I've established no strengths outside the field of the imagination, which is a fancy way of saying I'm hung over from an American Legion barn dance a waitress invited me to. She disappeared with a cowpoke who could wrestle a truck. Woke at first light laughing. Stepped on a steak bone.

Re: the banality of behavioral and emotional weather reports. My life is still killing me but I am offering less cooperation. I want to know what you do, rather than what you quit doing.

Up at my cabin more attacks of irrationality. Been here too long in solitude. Blurred peripheries so I "am" the bitch coyote that killed the rabbit in the yard. My longest & strongest literary relationship with McGuane—twenty years of letters and we don't even see each other once a year.

Rode an enormous crow, flying down to the Manistee River to drink from a sandbar. Used a martingale. Easier to stay on than a horse and better view! James Hillman says that dream animals are soul doctors. Bet I'm the only one around here who reads Cioran & Kierkegaard after working his bird dogs.

Disturbed that I am creating this heroine because I'm lonely and wish to have someone I can utterly love. Relieved of sanity fears by reading Angus Fletcher on the subject of the borders of consciousness.

There are many hidden, unnumbered floors in the apartment buildings in NYC, or so I have thought.

My coffin was made of glass and she ran out of the woods and shattered it! She is E. Hopper's girl at the window.

This must be a novel written from the cushion—silence, out of water, the first light, twilight, the night sky, the farthest point in the forest, from the bottom of a lake, the bottom of the river, northern lights, from the clouds and loam, also the city past midnight, Los Angeles at dawn when the ocean seems less tired having slept in private, from the undisturbed prairie, from attics and root cellars, the girl hiding in the thicket for no reason, the boy looking in the wrong direction for the rising moon.

At the cabin the fog is so dense you can hear it. A rabbit near woodpile, fly sound, crackle of fire in the hush. Can't drink much or my heroine escapes, evades me. The voice just beyond hearing

Hot tip from Taisen Deshimaru on the writing of this book. "You must concentrate upon and consecrate yourself wholly to each day, as though a fire were raging in your hair." Reminded me again of the injurious aspect of protestantism for an artist—one's life as inevitable, or predestined, causing a looseness in the joints, the vast difference between Calvin (and John Bunyan). You must transfer these banal energies toward self-improvement to your work.

The post-modern novel suffocates from ethical mandarinism. It is almost totally white middle class, a product of writer's schools, the National Endowment, foundations, academia. The fact that this doesn't matter one little bit is interesting. Who could possibly give a fuck during this diaspora. The literary world is one of those unintentionally comic movies they used to make about voodoo and zombies.

Who said, "You can't do something you don't know if you keep doing what you do know"? Drinking prevents vertigo and that's why I can't get her voice if I drink. A trip to NYC restored my vertigo. If you enter a bookstore or a publisher's office your life again becomes incomprehensible. Fear refreshes. Luckily you can head immediately for a good restaurant.

Back home the troubling dream image of myself emerging like the "Thing" from a block of ice full of sticks and leaves.

In another dream she ran backward nakedly into history which was an improbable maze. Another night an unpleasant visit with Herman Melville who didn't look well.

Went up to my winter retreat at a hotel in Escanaba to edit Paris Review interview. Can't get beyond first page by the second day because I'm not currently interested in anything I've ever said, what with a hot eyeball from being two thirds done. Zero degrees and a five-hour walk in the woods because I got lost, followed by rigatoni & Italian sausage, and two bottles of red wine. Next day I walked miles out onto the frozen harbor ice—a marvelous polar landscape of glittering sun & ice as far as you can see. Fishermen have driven their pickup trucks out on the ice and are pulling nets where the ice was divided by a fuel oil tanker. They are Chippewas and offer me a partially frozen beer that thunks in the bottle.

A strange March walk: broke, can't write, sick from new blood-pressure medicine, out in an area of juniper, dunes, pine culverts out of the wind. Thoughts about the degree to which I'm a slave or lowly employee of the system I've created: cigarettes smoke me, food eats me, alcohol drinks me, house swallows me, car drives me, etc.

"She" comes and goes. I had to talk to Hollywood today (to say why I was fired from the last project) and she fled top speed. An utterly enervating & fatal game of pursuit.

It seems that severe emotional problems, neuroses, are born, thrive, multiply in areas where language never enters. The writer thinks that if he can solve these problems his quality of language will vastly improve. This is the fallacy of writing as therapy. Dostoyevski maintained that to be acutely conscious is to be diseased. One could imagine a novel that murders the writer. You don't want to discover a secret your persona can't bear up under. But then you can't rid yourself of the hubris of wanting to create a hero or heroine of consciousness.

Completely flipped from nervous exhaustion on page 430. Take my wife and daughter to Key West, a place I had feared returning to after so much "disorder and early sorrow" from a dozen previous trips. Turned out pleasantly. Good chats with Brinnin, mostly on how to determine pathology when everything is pathological. Studied the giant ocean river, the Gulf Stream, where Duane committed suicide on his buckskin horse. We forget we have blood in us until it starts coming out.

All your aggression is directed toward discovering new perceptions, and consequently against yourself when you fail to come up with anything new. But then I "made her up" knowing very well we will abandon each other.

Bernard Fontana warned me about getting the "Indian disease." It takes a great deal of discipline not to shatter into fragments. The wonders of negative capability & allowing her to decide what she's going to do next. What Fontana meant is the intense anxiety I felt at the Umbanda session seventy miles outside of Rio de Janeiro when the ladies went into their whirling trance to heal the black drummer who was a drunk. If you've seen and lived the supposed best the white world has to offer it's "harmless" to

check out the rest of the world. We are all in the Blue Angel in that
respect. The actual world is Dietrich's thighs.

Startled to read in Jung that violently colorful dreams & physic events
occur to people in psychic flux who need more consciousness.

At the cabin just saw a chipmunk leap off the picnic table & tear the
throat out of a mouse, lapping vigorously at the blood. I am chock-full of
conclusions. Must write Quammen to find out what's going on here. Lopez
told me the only way to feed ravens is to gather road kills, a rather smelly
business. Peacock has studied bears so long he has become one, not entirely
a happy situation. Dalva is probably my twin sister who was taken away
at birth.

Nearly finished. It's like going outside to estimate the storm damage. Want
to avoid stepping into a thousand-story elevator shaft. As a ninth grader I
was very upset to discover that Ross Lockridge committed suicide when he
finished Raintree County.

My friend _____ thought that all of his concessions, like the Eucharist,
were rites of passage.
He forgot how easy it is to earn the contempt of your fellow writers.

Was amused to realize that the mess I am always trying to extricate myself
from is actually my life. The other night I played ranchero music & thought
how different the music is in areas of fruit, hot peppers, garlic, hot sun,
giant moths, & butterflies. An old woman in Brazil had a worn photo of a
group of men ice fishing in Minnesota which she thought was amusing. We
drank rum and I tried to explain away the lugubrious masochism of life in
the upper Midwest.

For almost ten minutes I looked forward to the second volume when
Northridge's voice will become mangled & intolerable, a prairie Lear.

Finishing any large piece of work makes one dense and irascible. I cooked the fucking brook trout too long! I demand more of myself and life than it is suited to offer. I look for the wrong form the reward is to come in—thus it is a full year before I realize how good a certain meal was: during bird season we stopped by a river, started our portable grill and watched four English setters and a Lab swim lazily in an eddy in the October sunlight. We grilled woodcock and grouse over split maple, had a clumsy salad, bread, and a magnum of wine, napped on the grass surrounded by wet dogs.

Nearly done at the cabin, a specific giddiness. Last night wild pale-green northern lights above scudding thunderheads. On the way home from the tavern I saw a very large bear on the two-track to the cabin, thus hesitated to take a midnight stroll, possibly disturbing both of us. He was not my friend, but a great bear, a Beowulf, trundling across the path & swiveling for a look at me, his head higher than mine was in the car.

Hard to develop the silence and humility necessary for creating good art if you are always yelling "look at me" like a three-year-old who has just shit in the sandbox.

Postscript. Finished the novel in July and have since driven 27,000 miles to get over it. Perhaps it is easier to write a novel than survive it. Driving is a modest solution as the ego dissipates in the immensity of the landscape, slips out into the road behind you. Watched an Indian, Jonathan Windyboy, dance seven hours in a row in New Mexico. That might work but as a poet I work within the skeleton of a myth for which there is no public celebration. Publication parties aren't quite the same thing. I can imagine the kiva late at night under a summery full moon; the announcer asks the drum group from the Standing Rock Sioux to play a round from the Grass Dance for Jim's beloved Dalva! But perhaps our rituals as singers are as old as theirs. Cadged my epigraph from Loren Eiseley's tombstone: "We loved the earth but could not stay."

Germinating Work

I STARTED KEEPING a journal when I was sixteen. At that time it was mostly piths and jists to keep myself alive. I was incompetent to write anything formal so this was my only emotional contact with the burgeoning notion that I should be a writer. I don't write in my journal daily or habitually. I limit it to notions and images I can't live without, which are mostly concerned with germinating work.

The notebooks to *Dalva* are probably a hundred pages or so but those included particularly germane or poignant thoughts to the actual book. So many journal entries are dead end but you don't know until you write them down and think about them.

My main influences in the whole idea in keeping a journal were, oddly, Henry David Thoreau and Tom McGuane. The latter used to keep his on tiny dime store notebooks, which he would toss in a box. The best and most influential journals for me were those of Dostoyevski, with Flaubert coming in as a close second, also Loren Eiseley.

It's important for a writer not to put too much in a journal for fear of losing the energy and attention that should be left for the work itself.

Robert Hellenga

. . . *A*m presently on notebook no. 71. That's a lot of notebooks to keep track of, so when I finish one, I make an index that will help me locate sketches, scenes, descriptions, accounts of what I've eaten, etc.

[Journal Entry #1: Thursday 28 May 1981. Florence. This is my first time in Italy. I'm living with an Italian family and struggling to survive in an intensive language class.]

What a difference a day makes. Yesterday (Tuesday) I was ready to pack it up. The pressure at the school is terrific, and not only from the 4 teachers but also from the other students. Felt really homesick—partly because I went home right after class—& home is a long way from downtown. House seemed empty. Lonely. Wed. Took laundry. Lavasecco first—near bus stop (dry cleaners). Left pants & shirts there. Got directions to a lavanderia. Left underwear in nylon bag. This was near the Piazza Cure—glad I discovered it—shops, restaurants, etc. Very near home.

Decided to find a groc. store to shop in regularly. Went back to Via Faentina—but everything was closed there. Had to go back to Piazza Cure. Bought some olives, artichoke hearts, salame toscano. (I already had some cheese at home). Bottle of wine. L1000.

The Raugeis not home. I studied for a while & then ate at kitchen table. The Raugeis came home just as I finished. Sat & talked for quite a while. Sig.a R. sewed up my new sweater.

———————

People. In morning—met a Swedish girl at bus stop. Very nice. Going to a different language school (Michelangelo).

Swiss girl whom I met first day. (This girl is staying with Sig.a R's sister). A bit snippy. Smart looking but not attractive. We spoke German. When I learned that she knew English, I said: "You prob. speak Eng. better than I speak German." She: "I hope so."

Rode home w. her on bus Tue. night.

Thurs.
    Grey day.
    no Swedish girl.

Swiss girl.

Much better day in school. More relaxed. I wonder if they have the psychology of the whole experience doped out. Are they delib. easing up, or are we just getting used to it???

I did better this morning. I think I'll be able to overcome the others soon, though the Swiss girl [Erika] is very strong willed.

Bernard, Erika, & I each missed 3 on a test. Sara went over each mistake. Anna Maria missed 8, and Elmer (from Austria) 14. He may be the first to crack.

Pranzo. Wed. Vitello con funghi.
Thur. Roast rabbit.—coniglio.
first rate. excellent sauce.

Ravioli for first course. OK. I gave Anna Marie a taste & she complained about too much salt.—made some snide remarks about Americans.

She tosses our salad. interesting. puts a little salt & pepper in a big spoon w. vinegar—Stirs it around & then puts it on the salad.

An idea for a story is emerging. X goes to Florence. Has a relationship with someone who doesn't speak English. THE IDEA OF THE STORY IS HIS ATTEMPT TO EXPLAIN SOMETHING VERY IMPORTANT (his daughter's death?) IN ITALIAN & CAN'T EXPRESS HIMSELF. Lots of possibilities here.

LANGUAGE is power.

1) Teacher-student. The teachers can intimidate the students because they know the language.—Even a young girl teacher can tyrannize over me.

2) Between equals, however, there are other factors. The Swiss girl who lives near me has the upper hand because she has forced me to speak English—to acknowledge that her English is better than my German.

But, I have gained the upper hand over Elmer by establishing German as the language we use when Italian fails. (I am sure that his English is better than my German.)

3) With the Raugeis I have (in a sense) the upper hand because I know (!) two languages & they only know one.

4) W. Swedish girl. She got upper hand a little by getting us to speak English. But I can get the advantage back by insisting that we speak Italian.

No doubt there are more possibilities.

————————

[Journal Entry #2: Friday 26 June 1981. Rome. This is the last day of my first trip to Italy. I did a little shopping, went on a bus tour, and mistook a Frenchman for an Italian.]

More shopping
Oil can. cannoli tubes—then bought more.
7 ties. For Ed, Brady, etc.
I did a lot of debating about this, but now I'm glad I bought them.
Olive oil—2 liters.
grappa.

Tour of Castelli di Roma. Rode around in the bus for quite a while [to pick up people at other hotels]. An old man complained: "How many more hotel we stop. Hotel hotel hotel. No see nothing."

I think there was a mix-up somewhere. We went to one place & then another—a long drive—to join [the actual tour] bus.

Drove around.

After first stop I decided to sit with an Italian who turned out to be French—no communication!

Wine at Frascatti. I cd. easily have drunk too much. Met an English couple—very nice—hell of an accent. from Manchester—daughter works for embassy in Rome.

———————

[Journal entry #3: Saturday 9 September 1989. Florence. Walking around the neighborhood where I lived with my family for a year in 1982–83 I encounter a Frenchwoman who doesn't know any English or Italian.]

Didn't get up till 12:30!

Pranzo. *Spaghetti w tomato & basil. Similar to "summer pasta."* (They said I cd. put cheese on it if I liked. Obviously you don't usually.)

Left-over arista *[pork roast]. Salame toscano. Veal scaloppini. Salad. wine & water.*

Studied most of the afternoon.

Went out about 6:00

Chilly!

Bus in station. I was going to go to Fiesole & walk to Settignano— senza carta. But no. 10 bus came first. Went to Settignano. Walked down to see Sig.a Marchetti. Fancy new gate—electric. TV viewer—speaker. It was after 7:00 & I was a little reluctant—But I pushed the buzzer. She was delighted to see me. We had a nice talk—some grapefruit juice. She told me about Paola—married & divorced. a baby. She helps a lot w. the baby. Alessandra studying in Colorado. Am. boyfriend who speaks Italian.

She was going to Paola's. Drove me down to bus stop (#14). Took bus into town—Got off by Post Office near our old apartment.

Walked around old neighborhood. Rush of emotion at the arch. had to do w. family associations. So much time there. Feeling of its being a special place. (a Chinese rest. on corner of Borgo Pinti.)

Street very narrow & dark. Walked past no. 31

Walked around past Trattoria Maremmana. Still pretty reasonable. Menu turistico for 15.000 to 23.000. Had a pizza at Pizzeria e Trattoria del Angolo. L5000, & L3000 for a large glass of beer! L1500 coperto. L9500 & tip. Not cheap.

Sat next to two Americans. young guy w. funny 2-layer haircut. Girl not esp. attractive.

He: this is where the Renaissance really reached its peak—Brunelleschi's dome.

She: Where?

He: the duomo.

He didn't want her to order a glass of beer. She was going to order milk but couldn't think of the word. Latta?

Two striking women. One w. streaks of blond hair in brown.

One w. huge tits that she stuck out when she put her leather coat on.

What do I want? not to have heads turn & to have people say, there goes the famous travel writer. To function inconspicuously in Italy. To chat w. the man at the bar—cash register. To discuss the menu w. waiter.

French woman in Pz. Ambrogio, asking for acqua. Acqua Arno. She wanted the river. Couldn't speak Eng. or It. Couldn't see map without glasses.

Walked home along Arno. No lights after Ponte _____. About an hour from Santa Croce. Not a specially pleasant walk. Finished <u>Falling in Place.</u> Didn't sleep well but not too bad.

———————

[Journal Entry #4: Monday 11 September 1989. Florence. I start to write about my first trip to Italy in 1981.]

I'd recovered from acute homesickness [back in 1981]—esp. as the end drew near & I knew I was going to make it. But I was glad to put Florence behind me. Went to Rome. Stayed in a hotel. Not especially nice, but I felt <u>free. libero.</u> To come & go as I pleased. Rome was big & breezy—like Chicago. Big wide streets—Big open spaces.

Confident—in restaurants—in the hotel. I was speaking Italian.

Bus trip on 3rd day. Via Appia from hotel. Wound up sitting next to some Americans. Wanted to speak Italian on my last day. Finally moved to seat next to a distinguished man who'd kept to himself. Looked a little funny to me—but . . .

He turned out to be French. couldn't speak a word of Italian.

I said: "Je parle un peu français."

He perked up a little.

It was true. I can read French & when I was in France I cd. sort of speak it. But Italian had driven it all out of my head. The only thing I cd. say in French was "Je parle un peux français"! That was it. Absolutely!

He must have thought I was very strange!!!

—————

[Journal entry #5: Thursday 21 September 1989. Florence. I spend too much money on a leather jacket.]

The jacket. After class went right to Raspini to pick it up—(to bank this morning.) Nervous. so much money—took off money belt. No one grimaced. On hanger—folded in a sack.

Didn't want anyone to see it! Didn't want to wear it!

Didn't want anyone to see me carrying the Raspini sack either!

went to bar—sandwich: Rustico: prosciutto crudo e salsa di carciofi. Not all that good.

Bus home. Snuck sack into my room before going in to say hi to Sig. e Sig.a

Tried coat on. Hung it in closet & hid other coat in suitcase; Raspini sack in suitcase too.

You cd. do quite a lot with this. Maybe write about "Traveler vs Tourist." Sometimes I want to be a tourist—

Buying the coat is a tourist thing to do—reveals a fundamental split.

Cf. reading Dick Francis instead of Nat. Ginzburg—can't even read her in English.

[Journal Entry #6: Tuesday 26 September 1989. Florence. A short story starts to come together.]

*Idea for a story:

Just a quick sketch: A man wants to be bilingual. After his wife's death he returns to Florence, where he spent a year w. his family.

Living w. a family

Not very comfortable.

Maybe in a room by himself—because language school can't find a family for a man his age. (much easier to place young girls)

Learns things about himself: he's really hoping for romance. Looking at the girls, etc. women on the bus. Thinks if he can master the language he'll have a better chance.

Finally the opportunity presents itself: wandering around old neighborhood Santa Croce. Eats a pizza. on way back to his room— beautiful blond woman—no longer young—not a kid—fashionably dressed, but not in a frightening hands-off way. Suitcase of sorts.

Wants to find the Arno. (what exactly does she say? Acqua. Seems to be calling for acqua.)

Doesn't speak English or Italian.

Protagonist has become pretty proficient in the language.

She's French.

He says: "Je peux parler un peu de français." (Title of story: "I Can Speak a Little French")

But then that's all he can say! She looks up expectantly. Tears of relief spring to her eyes—a warm welcoming smile. Starts to speak in French. Protagonist can't understand a word. And he can't come up with anything in French except the phrase: "Je peux parler un peu de français." He's trapped in that phrase. When he repeats it, she smiles and looks expectantly again.

He manages to point her in the direction of the Arno—Lets her go.

It all happened so fast. Took him by surprise. If he'd had a chance to think . . . He cd. have taken her to his room, and then . . .

You didn't need to know French or Italian or English . . .

But couldn't imagine . . .

NB: something more could happen. He cd. follow her. something cd. in fact develop.

or he cd. see her again.

They cd. have a little fling—going out to dinner—unable to speak to each other.

This might in fact be an interesting problem to set your protagonist.

Maybe: if she writes things out he can read them.—or maybe you should just work on them getting along without communicating.

—in contrast to his strong desire to communicate in Italian.

At end: "I can speak a little French. Not much, but enough to get by!"

One way to get started: He gets a letter from his daughter in France saying she's found a job and won't be coming [to Italy] after all. This cd. touch off a change from feeling on top of things to the bottom dropping out, i.e., the realization of how lonely he is—and how much he wants to hold someone in his arms.

All the defenses he's been building up fall apart.

Prospect of spending Thanksgiving alone (or at the Am. church, which wasn't quite the same thing—but almost)—

or maybe Christmas

spending Christmas with the French woman—His heart is so full of memories, stuff he wants to tell her—to show her—the apartment on Borgo Pinti—He'd been living right in the center then—the centro storico. *Now he had a room way out in the Novoli—upper left hand corner of the map—if you had the right map—otherwise it might not be there at all.*

Maybe taking a course in Enology—to fill up the time.

His writing project? discrepancy between the renaissance in the visual arts and the other developments political, economic, historical.

(You could do some interesting stuff with the daughter being in France—w. French—preparing for the French woman. Acqua Arno)

Also: sending American postcards to various friends acquaintances actually—saying that he was in Florence. But he doesn't hear anything— People who'd been glad to send their children to Chicago for a month at a time—friends of his daughter.

He'd written to them using the tu form—saying how much he'd like to see them again and perhaps their families too. But nothing.

He'd been careful w. money—saving up for a big splurge when his daughter came.

Gets involved w. the French woman.
Spends the money on a suede coat.
    that he's embarrassed to wear.
From Raspini.
Wears it in his room.
Afraid it's too big.
Goes back.
    asks for a brush (ostensible motif)

possibility of exchanging it.

No problem

But no smaller size.

Girl tells him that for a <u>morbida</u> jacket the line should be down over the shoulder—She touches him to show exactly where. it's just where the line falls. He feels better.

Christmas dinner w. French woman.

He thinks he'll burst—he has so much to say. *Imp. development. His Italian is at the point where he can sit down w. one or two people (Italians) and talk about anything—religion, philosophy, story of art, literature, family, love—his experiences in Italy. (This was where he'd left off before.)

But the prob. was getting one or two people to sit down and talk to you.

He's older than the students.

You can't just start talking about love & philosophy to the person sitting next to you on the bus. (What was more likely to happen wd. be that someone would turn to him & say something out of context. He'd be taken by surprise—wouldn't know what the person was saying—& then the person wd point to his or her wrist & say "time pleez" & he'd show him (or her) his watch—pulling up his sleeve.

VIP theme: TALK VS SILENCE (w. French woman)

Protagonist setting so much stock on talk—in speaking—Then the big surprise comes from a woman he can't talk to. A woman who offers herself to him (modestly)—& whose offer he <u>almost</u> turns down because she can't speak Italian—because they can't talk to each other.

(She really needs help w. her suitcase, which is very heavy.)

OK: what do they do? How does he communicate to her that he wants to see her again? At the hotel on the Lungarno? (when she sees the river she gets reoriented.)

All this time learning Italian, and now this! Je peux parler un peu de
français.

"Doman" "demain"

Maybe he remembers a few more French phrases:
    Dans le fond des forêts votre image me suit.
    On ne me suit merne pas sortir en hiver.
and one of the first phrases every student (male) figures out:
    Voulez-vous couchez avec moi.
(Of course one wouldn't use the 'vous' form!)

Maybe he remembers these at the hotel. Desperately wants to see her again.
Can't talk!

———————

When he entered her he had to bite his lip to keep from crying.
(Thinking earlier that he might never make love to a woman again! a real
possibility!)
    This is such a great gift.
    Sees her off at the station.
        That night: puts on his new suede jacket. Goes
downtown. To tell the truth, he'd been afraid that everyone wd. stare at
him. even follow him around.
    But nobody noticed. He was invisible. Takes a bus—rides to end of
line—cf. when he was a child riding the buses and street cars in Chicago.
    An invisible presence traversing the city—like Browning's _____ Il
padrone della città. Watching over the city—so far from home.
    If someone had asked him, he wd. have said, "I speak a little French.
Not much, but enough to get by."
    But there was no one to ask.
    Or: but no one asked.

Time for Amendment of Life

IN LOOKING OVER these notebooks I see that they are not one thing but legion:

   (a) a journal proper, i.e., an intermittent record of day-to-day life;
   (b) research notes;
   (c) free writing exercises;
   (d) first drafts;
   (e) notes on books I've been reading;
   (f) miscellaneous information (addresses, phone numbers, etc.)

The distinctions between these categories—especially between the "journal proper," the "free-writing exercises," and "first drafts"—are not always clear.

I began keeping a journal on Ash Wednesday 1979 with the following portentous announcement to myself: "Time for amendment of life." The *only* requirement I set myself was that I enter something every single day. Well, I have neither amended my life, nor have I entered something in my journal every single day. I have written a lot of stuff, however, and am presently on notebook no. 71. That's a lot of notebooks to keep track of, so when I finish one, I make an index that will help me locate sketches, scenes, descriptions, accounts of what I've eaten, etc.

In keeping a journal I've been very much influenced by Dorothea Brande's *Becoming a Writer,* and have tried to follow her advice, which I shall now pass on: write regularly (so you don't have to waste time and energy reinventing your schedule every day); write a lot (to develop writing muscles—cf. training for a race or practicing for a recital); write without stopping (so your inner critic doesn't have a chance to intervene).

Whether a writer's journal has value for someone other than the writer himself, or herself, is another question. The only journals I've ever read were written by Mrs. Tolstoy and Mrs. Dostoyevsky. From these journals I learned that Mr. Dostoyevsky was a nice guy and Mr. Tolstoy (my favorite author) a real bastard.

The journal excerpts I have selected for this collection are taken from two different trips to Italy (spring 1981 and fall 1989) and are linked by themes and experiences that have shaped a lot of my fiction: Italy itself, the challenge of living in another language, the meaning of "home," etc. They are also linked by the fact that in 1989 I began to write about things that had happened in 1981, and by the fact that on each trip I (a) had a brief encounter with a French person with whom I couldn't communicate and (b) spent too much money on a jacket. The last journal entry I've included incorporates these experiences into a sketch that eventually (several drafts later) became a short story: "I Speak a Little French" (*Crazyhorse* 43, Winter 1992). I include here a brief excerpt from this story—an encounter with a French woman that grew out of two seemingly insignificant encounters recorded in my journal:

> I was about to order another glass of wine when I noticed a young woman crossing the piazza dragging the largest suitcase I'd ever seen. The suitcase had wheels on it so that you could pull it down long airport corridors, but the wheels were too small for the rough paving bricks of the piazza and the suitcase kept tipping over, like a large dog that keeps flopping itself down. She wasn't able to go twenty feet without the suitcase falling, and it was so big and heavy she had trouble setting it upright again. I stepped out from under the arc to get a better look, and when she saw me, in the light of the piazza, she cried out: *"Acqua, acqua."*
>
> I shrugged my shoulders. After all, there were two bars in the piazza, in addition to the *bettola* [wine shop]. We were in the center of a modern city, not in the middle of the desert.
>
> *"Acqua, acqua."*
>
> I could hear the tears in her voice.
>
> *"Acqua Arno,"* she said, and it dawned on me that she was looking for the river.
>
> "Right down the via Verdi," I said, in Italian, pointing to the street.

The suitcase tipped over again and this time she left it.

"Acqua, acqua," she repeated.

"Parla italiano?" I asked, helping her right the suitcase.

"Acqua, acqua."

"English?"

"Je suis française."

"Ah," I said. *"Non parla italiano? o inglese?"*

"Je suis française," she repeated. *"Je suis française."*

I'd had two years of French in college and said the first thing that popped into my head: *"Je peux parler un peu de français."*

"Dieu merci." A look of relief rose to her face. *"Je cherche l'Arno, s'il vous plaît. . . ."* She kept going, but too fast for me to follow. Quite naturally she expected more, but unfortunately there was no more. To her rapid questions I could make only a single response: *"Je peux parler un peu de français,"* which I kept repeating, hoping that something would click. But nothing clicked. I was imprisoned in a single phrase. What had looked like an open door was a *trompe l'oeil.* *"Acqua Arno?"* This time it was a tentative question. She had given up. She was a damsel in distress, and I was her knight errant; but without the sword of language I couldn't come to her rescue, so I pointed her, once again, down the via Verdi towards the river—*acqua Arno*—and watched as she crossed the piazza. She reached the post office; the enormous suitcase teetered, tottered, and fell over again. She struggled to set it on its wheels, and then she disappeared around the corner and was gone.

Je peux parler un peu de français. It was ridiculous. It was maddening. *Je peux parler un peu de français.* It didn't occur to me at the time that if I'd gone on in French, in school, instead of switching to Italian, I'd probably be in Paris instead of Florence, or that if she had spoken Italian, she wouldn't be in the middle of the piazza asking for *acqua Arno.* No, all I could think of was that my whole life had been leading up to this point, and I'd studied the wrong language.

Robin Hemley

All writers are observers, fascinated with human goings-on, but journal writers are a special breed, I think, suspicious of their own memories, like tourists taking snapshots of everything they see. They're different from diarists, of course—diarists seem, as a whole, fascinated with their own lives— journal-keepers are snoops, fascinated with everyone else's life.

5:00 a.m. 8/25/92

Dreamed I wrote a story based on my relationship with AJ. Free spirit who drives trucks and sport cars from one location to another. Stops in town where I live. He's sort of my alter-ego, makes everything look simple. Always relaxed. People are attracted to him, his open personality. We wind up at a country bar listening to the music of a country star like Tanya Tucker, but her name is something like Swish Swander or Samantha Swan. At one point, he takes out some breath mints and she's singing her way through the audience. He says jokingly that he'll give her a mint if she sings one of her songs, and he names a famous one. She stops at the table and soon she and AJ are talking. She's someone AJ and I might make fun of, but I can't believe a famous star has sat down with us. She and AJ eventually go off together and I'm left to fend for myself. But then he reappears to give me a lift home. He's just given the woman a ride to her hotel and he's back. And we're friends again, and he tells me to relax.

- *Base everything on AJ from how he got his name to Sulfur Springs.*
- *The country bar is called "Gator's Bar and Boogie."*
- *Set story in Charlotte.*
- *Line dancing*
- *Then I realize I'm someone we might make fun of.*

A Special Breed

I KNOW THE EXACT MOMENT—time, date, and place—I started to keep a journal: Wednesday, November 13, 1974, at 7:15 P.M. I was sixteen years old, away that year at a boarding school in Sewanee, Tennessee, called

St. Andrews. The journal, thin and bright red, has the word "Record" imprinted on the cover. The price sticker is still on the inside:

STEELE'S $1.89

On the cover page there's a request in big block letters that anyone who finds this journal should please return it to my mother's address in South Bend, Indiana. Above that are the mysterious words "Scorpion, elephant," not some secret code I'm sure, but hurried jottings, notes to myself on some poem (that's what I was writing back then) I thought would be published in *The New Yorker,* no doubt.

The journal entry seems to me now none too remarkable, but it's my first, my virgin journal entry in more ways than one—and at least shows what preoccupied me—namely, being a virgin.

> *Walking from Mr. Feaster's house, overheard Beverly and Kurt talking.*
> *Bev: Everyone does it, you know.*
> *Kurt: Does what (while chewing gum)?*
> *Bev: Everyone tries to look sexually appealing.*

Details. It seems to me that that's what interests the journal writer, however one keeps a journal—the minutiae of life that one doesn't want to let go of. All writers are observers, fascinated with human goings-on, but journal writers are a special breed, I think, suspicious of their own memories, like tourists taking snapshots of everything they see. They're different from diarists, of course—diarists seem, as a whole, fascinated with their own lives—journal-keepers are snoops, fascinated with everyone else's life.

I don't know that I've looked at that first entry more than once or twice before today. I'd pretty much forgotten about it, but I think it's fitting that my first entry was an overheard snatch of dialogue. In the years since that time, I've filled my journal with such bits of dialogue, and anything else that struck me as unusual. But my journal is not simply a compendium of observations, collected for the sake of record keeping. I've also used my journal more self-consciously, as a kind of writer's sketch book, a place to try out ideas. So, besides overheard dialogue, I have included in my journals plot outlines, story ideas, character sketches, anecdotes that have been told to me, dreams, images, diarylike episodes—and the occasional grocery list.

I love the feel of a journal—the hard-shelled ledger variety especially (and they're getting more and more difficult to find. Who keeps ledgers anymore by hand?). I find that when I carry my journal around, things that are worthy of being recorded simply seem to pop up all around me, which leads me to suspect, of course, that these things are always happening around me. I'm just more observant when I have my journal with me. There are times when it's not practical for me to carry a large journal, and so I almost always carry a pocket-sized notebook and a pen for those times. I believe it's crucial to write down my observations or thoughts in my journal the moment these observations occur. As Thoreau wrote, "The writer who postpones the recording of his thoughts uses an iron which has cooled to burn a hole with." That's a quote I wrote down in one of my journals. Otherwise, I'm sure I wouldn't have remembered it.

My friend AJ grew up in Sulfur Springs, Indiana (I've always loved that name), but we knew each other at Indiana University in the late '70s. AJ is the original free spirit, or at least that's how I remember him from college. AJ was one of those people who seemed so open to knowledge and experience that people flocked to him, someone who always seemed on the verge of discoveries. The other characteristics that come to mind when thinking of AJ include an animated, almost manic intelligence, a generous spirit, and above all, a whimsical, unpredictable nature. He was also one of my most loyal friends, staying in touch with me over the years—not like clockwork, but unexpectedly calling or appearing when I didn't expect him. For a time, whenever I visited Chicago (once or twice a year), I'd run into AJ purely by chance on the street—this happened three or four times—and AJ didn't live in Chicago either. He visited the city almost as infrequently as I. In a way, I thought of AJ as an alter-ego.

AJ, by the way, is his real name. Not A period J period. "A" and "J" are his father's initials, but for some reason his mother wanted to give him his father's initials but not his full name.

And AJ had, for a time, the perfect job for a questing free spirit such as himself. For years, he delivered cars and trucks across country to various dealerships and individuals. Once he took me on a wild ride in a railroad truck across northern Indiana, and he'd always send me strange artifacts from his travels across country, or accounts of the odd tourist attractions and people he'd come across.

The night I dreamed about AJ, I wrote down the dream in my journal.

The dream, strange as it was, immediately suggested a story to me, partly because of the strong demarcation between my personality and AJ's. Obviously, the situation seemed a little skeletal and inscrutable (as dreams often are), but I figured I could work with it, and in any case, I'm often drawn to making incredible scenes seem credible. My wheels were turning as soon as I wrote down the dream, and I plotted the notes to myself below the dream.

I *did* base the story on AJ, though I transformed him somewhat, exaggerating him, making him even more of a prankster than I remember, and I exaggerated the personality traits of the character based on me, making him more harried and neurotic than I am (though that hardly seems possible). I also hinted that he was unhappy in his marriage, and that the narrator's wife disliked AJ. My real wife, when she read the story, told me that when AJ read this story I was to tell him that she didn't dislike him. I hasten to add that I'm quite happy in my marriage.

As much as I liked the name "Sulfur Springs," I had to leave it out finally. I didn't want this to be the real AJ, but someone modeled on him.

And my initial enthusiasm for the name "Gator Bar and Boogie" evaporated. I did, however, set the story in Charlotte, North Carolina, where I lived at the time, a place I had some antipathy towards, which came out quite strongly in the finished story. Line dancing also figured prominently in the story, as did that line that followed in my journal, the character realization that *"I'm* someone we might make fun of."

Wanting to stay in some ways true to the spirit of the dream, I decided to set the story in a country bar in Charlotte, with the main action occurring more or less as it did in the dream, with some crucial adjustments. Line dancing was in full swing around this time, and I'd never seen line dancing in person, so I enlisted two friends, and under the guise of research we went to a cavernous country bar on one of the main thoroughfares in Charlotte, a tawdry strip called Independence Boulevard. I took notes (of course), on the terrible band that was playing, on the race signs on the wall, the woman selling roses from table to table, the struggling, half-drunk line dancers. I even took notes on the conversations around me, and included some of what was said that night in the mouths of my characters.

Here's how the story, titled "Independence Boulevard," which was published originally in a magazine called, of all things, *Boulevard* (Fall 1994) opens:

> LD's in town, or maybe he's not. Maybe he's calling me from Nebraska and just pretending he's in some phone booth in a convenience store parking lot near the coliseum. His voice sounds like LD's: a hairtrigger laugh inside him, a little high, a little hyper. He says, "You want to play?"
>
> "I'll kick your butt," I say.
>
> "I'll whup your ass," he replies, our little ritual.
>
> "You near the old coliseum or the new one?"
>
> He laughs. "I don't know. It looks like something that Mc-Donald's used to package Big Macs in."
>
> "That's the old coliseum," I say. "Out on Independence. You want directions to the house?"

There's a pause. "Why don't you come meet me?"

He doesn't like to come over because he thinks Mary Elizabeth doesn't like him. It's not that. It's just that women are either insanely attracted to LD or repelled by him. There's no in-between. When Mary Elizabeth and I were living together before we got married, LD came over once and insisted on sweeping the kitchen floor. LD can be helpful like that, but Mary Elizabeth was suspicious. She called me at work and asked me if he was safe. Sure, LD's harmless, I said, but he's given her the creeps ever since.

I haven't heard from LD in three years, and I'd almost thought he'd forgotten about me, or given up on me, but being LD's friend is like belonging to the Mafia. One of these days, you're going to get a call, and you won't be able to pretend it's for somebody else. If you're LD's friend, you're stuck for life.

LD's real name is LD, with no periods in between the letters. He was born in Valparaiso, Indiana. His mother didn't want to name him after his father, Lester Dean Conroe, because she thought he was a jerk, but Lester was a big man in town and she wanted to give her son the advantage of being known as Lester's son. So she named him LD. Of course, in the outside world, people don't know who Lester Dean Conroe is, and they think LD stands for something. Like Learning Deficient. It's not that I don't like hanging out with LD. I've known him since college. I'm just not the same person I was fifteen years ago. But LD is. I've matured. I don't like scenes . . .

As I said, the story is an exaggeration of our personalities. I hope AJ and I aren't quite as childish in real life. We've never done that "whup your butt . . . kick your ass" exchange or anything like it, but it seemed to fit the mood of the story.

LD and the narrator, Kevin, meet at a shady convenience store near the coliseum, where LD pulls a prank on the narrator, centering on a pay phone and some drug-dealing kids. Then LD plays another prank on Kevin, and finally they wind up at a country bar along Independence Boulevard—a mixture of the one in my dream and the one I researched, with my imagination thrown in for good measure. By this time, Kevin, already in a questioning state over his life with Mary Elizabeth, and unbalanced by LD's sudden appearance and prank-playing, starts to question LD's choice of bars in an irritable and bitter way. The singer on stage, a Croatian country-and-western singer named Laurel Dove, has been belting out her tunes to a zombielike crowd who'd rather line dance to canned music, and she's been trying futilely to engage her audience in some friendly stage banter.

"Why did you bring me here?" I ask LD over the noise.

"What?" he yells back.

"Why did you bring me here?"

LD shrugs. I look at Laurel Dove prancing around, her hair flowing behind her. I wonder what's up with LD. This is the kind of place we would have made fun of ten years ago, but LD looks like he's really into the music, tapping his stubby little fingers on his Lone Star Beer coaster. What's with this Laurel Dove? She's the kind of person we would have made fun of ten years ago.

"You know, Kevin," LD yells suddenly. "You've changed."

"What do you mean?" I ask, warily.

"You've matured. I mean that in a good way. The well of your experience seems deeper."

I almost laugh at that one. LD can be corny sometimes when he's trying to sound wise.

"How can you tell? We've only been together for an hour."

"I can tell," he says wisely and goes back to his beer and the song Laurel Dove is singing.

When Laurel Dove finishes, she yells out, "How many of you . . . ?" and stops mid-sentence. "Hey, y'all out there? Any survivors?" She scans the audience with a hand in front of her eyes. "Oh, fuck this," she says, and walks offstage. For a moment, no one reacts, and then her band members slowly unburden themselves of their instruments and follow her. Then the place fills up again with canned country music, and almost everyone jumps up from their tables and rushes to the dance floor.

LD buys a rose from the rose woman.

"What's that for?" I ask.

"You never know when a rose is going to come in handy," he says, and laughs.

"Give me a break," I tell him.

Presently, Laurel Dove emerges from behind the stage and walks toward the bar. She sits down on one of the stools and the bartender brings her a longneck. She takes it and heads our way.

She stops right in front of our table as though she's on a string that LD's pulling. LD hands her the rose and she takes it and smiles. She sits on his lap, puts her arm around his neck, and gives him a kiss. Her hair surrounds them like a curtain.

I've got a buzz. Time has slowed and I'm in that frame of mind where almost anything is acceptable. My head's cocked and my mouth is slightly open and saliva's gathering in the corner for a drool. My voice is a croak, and I'm not sure whether I'm talking or thinking, but a voice in me says, "Yeah, I guess this is truly happening." A woman with hair down to her butt has stepped off the stage, ordered a beer, then made a beeline for our table. She's sat on LD's lap and the two of them are making out. Things like this happen to LD.

I wonder what Mary Elizabeth would think of this. I'd say, "You have to admit. He's got to have something."

While they're making out, I study the place. There's a cactus theme on the walls. My skin feels tingly, like I'm being pricked. I have a cactus in my yard, a big overgrown one that's taking over and choked out some daffodils that Mary Elizabeth planted. If you've ever been pricked by a cactus, you know it's hard to see the little quivers. You just bite them out and swallow, because they're so small. I guess maybe they're still stuck in me, but on the inside where I don't have nerves.

Then I think I'm the kind of person we would have made fun of ten years ago, and this depresses the hell out of me.

Laurel Dove scoots off of LD's lap and LD gives a little laugh. His face is smudged with stage makeup.

"Kevin," he says, "I'd like you to meet my wife, Mara Dovnic, a.k.a. Laurel Dove." Then he bursts out laughing and Laurel Dove nods her head at me. "We met in Nashville. I'm her manager, too."

She gives him an adoring look. "LD keeps me sane." She

glances out at the dance floor, gives the line dancers a death-ray look, and turns back. "I've never met anyone like him, have you?"

"No," I say, a bit dazed.

The story doesn't end there, of course. The narrator, angered by this final prank of LD's, asks to be driven home, and the story finishes back at the convenience store where it started. The narrator, in a somewhat altered state from the evening's events, commits, somewhat inadvertently, a convenience store robbery, turning the tables on the shocked LD, and putting *him* in a vulnerable position for once. Sounds crazy, I know, but so do a lot of stories and novels in synopsis. As a writer, my job is to make it all seem believable within the context of the story, just as in my dream all the crazy actions seemed credible as they were taking place.

You might notice that I've changed a lot from the original dream I recorded in my journal. In the dream, AJ drove the country singer home and then returned, and we were friends again. In the story, LD drives Kevin home, and the tension has only intensified by the end of the story. In my journal entry, Laurel Dove was Swish Swander or Samantha Swan, a famous country-and-western singer, but I knew that a real star wouldn't be appearing in such a place. Maybe a has-been or a pseudostar like Laurel Dove. I can't tell you exactly why I made her Croatian, except that I have a good friend who's Croatian, another writer, and maybe this was a subtle tribute to him. Or maybe it was just a quirky detail I liked. Of course, a breath mint didn't seem like much of an offering, maybe even an insult to someone like Laurel Dove who's just been ignored off stage—a rose seemed more appropriate—something that I'd set up earlier in the story and something that I'd seen being sold at the real country bar I visited.

You'll also notice that that original realization I noted in my journal, already somewhat in character—*I'm someone we would have made fun of ten years ago*—fit into the final story, and became one of the prime despairing epiphanies of my main character, Kevin. I feel the need to emphasize at this point that, although I wrote this thought down in my journal after the dream, it both was and wasn't how I was feeling personally at the time. As a writer, I was already thinking in terms of shaping this dream into a story (not something I do with every journal entry, mind you), and so I was thinking in terms of my character's thought processes. Of course, there was obviously some emotional resonance to me in my own life, and to say otherwise would be disingenuous.

This is fairly typical of the way I work from my journals. Whatever fascinates me or at least holds my attention—whether a dream, an incident, an idea, an anecdote, an overheard conversation, a quote—I write in my journal. These are the kernels for my stories, though I'm not saying that everything I write down needs to appear in a story—or should. I also use my journal, as in "Independence Boulevard," later in the process, for research on the story, if it's needed, or for blocking out scenes or character sketches.

I don't write in my journal every day. There are some months when I don't write in it at all. I tend to write in my journal in spurts, and this doesn't concern me. I certainly don't feel the same pressure to write in my journal that I feel to work on a story, novel, or essay every day—though I think I tend to write in my journal more often when my more formal writing isn't going well. It helps me stay in the game.

When my students tell me they're grateful for anything I've taught them, it's often the fact that I ask them to keep a journal in my writing classes. I rarely ask to see these journals, nor do I enforce my journal-keeping policy. To me, one either writes in a journal or one doesn't. They're not for every writer, and I don't think they should be shoved down anyone's throat. But for me, my only important rule in journal-keeping is that you should always keep your journal in one of those fine and rare hard-bound ledgers, not a three-ring binder nor one of those flimsy college notebooks with the wire rings. And certainly not on your computer! In this computer-addled age, it's nice to carry around something tangible that links one directly to the joy of writing in one's own lousy penmanship, rather than a collection of neurons to be autosaved on one's hard drive every fifteen minutes. It's nice to have a book to carry around, one that feels permanent but also unduplicatable, the nexus where world and writer meet.

Brenda Hillman

I feel writers should keep
... journals because when we
begin to lose a sense of private
pleasure, the assurance of a sacred
space exists in a journal. There is only
the purity of unstudied thought.

1/31/89

Woke this a.m. at 2. Large moth pattering, like wool slippers, in the room. Was disturbed, frightened, could not go back to sleep. Low, sick, couldn't wake up. V depressed about poetry . . . Whether to get to work on <u>Bright Existence</u> or on divorce series & if so how. The answer came that it didn't much matter but don't forget your insight. It was the first time I felt like proceeding without a plan.

. . . T called and said Linda had died last night. At first it seemed right, suitable that she had died. Then I felt an enormous bafflement, a sort of dazed and immense sorrow that I hadn't said goodbye . . . I remember hearing her outside the door and thinking, I miss her! And feeling for the first time that I was on my own, that she had given me a priceless gift and let me go.

Because she had died I found I could speak to her more quickly through the brocade covering my closed eyes.

2/1/89

. . . B came and we drove up to Russian River. First acacias along 101— first week of those. Past Healdsburg and followed river to coast to Jenner. Gorgeous rolling hills. New lambs including one tine caught lamb who shied when I got out of car to help it. "Near Jenner" I decided would make good title . . . one deer feeding. We kept driving and stopped at one place, then stopped here . . . One feeling I keep having is that living, being alive is so <u>clumsy</u> and bulky. As if only being dead is really the right amount of existence. I know this is a strange thing . . . I just can't believe she's dead and that I'm here without her.

2/2/89 Gualala rain and cold

Many complex dreams. One of being at some sort of conference thing
with big excited G. whose shirts were decorating the room like banners
hung upside down. Silk fabrics. . . . . Felt a clear sense of what she was
like, in heaven. Yesterday, at the sunset. The clouds must be so beautiful
from <u>behind</u>. Because the sunset was not very spectacular, but we could
see pink edges & knew it would be remarkable from behind. I thought
Linda would be seeing it. Continue to have the sense that living is clumsy,
bulky, compared to the finer, more private method of being, dead. But also
love life so much that I would never intentionally choose the other.

. . . A series of poems about the coast.

Many blackbirds on the top phone wire.

Like high G's
quarter notes

the doves actually more like quarter notes because their tails hang down

2/8/89

Can't decide whether to work on <u>Bright Existence</u> or divorce poems. Can't
decide. Step out of the way so <u>deciding</u> can decide . . . There is a small
mockingbird outside my window. It is making all kinds of sounds—it's
standing around just looking in. And I wish I could do something for it, it's
so cold outside. But has the black juicy berries it is sucking on, and its
own need to sing . . .

Grief tractates
—The tractates
—the codex

Over the ripped middle—
I try to arrive
at being born   ④

2/9/89

Yesterday was very crabby . . . We went up the Bucklin Trail. Walked up
a ways. Nothing in bloom but did see 2 or 3 violets, a few "footprints of
spring"—Bob loves that name, he keeps saying it over and over—and
much that was trying. One red maid, one milk maid and one wild iris.
Birds: hawks and the most amazing thing happened: we were walking
along and observed a small thrush on the path ahead. He was really fussy ④
and we watched a long time. Then he began hopping up the path ahead of
Bob as if he had a perfect notion of where he was going. John the Baptist
thrush. Hop hop hop! Bob bob bob! He went ahead. And he stayed on that
trail a good 15 minutes ahead of us, stopping only occasionally to eat a
little speck of something . . .

Feeling much less devastated about Linda. I "saw" this a.m. how her soul
was taken. She really was prepared & it filled with light & then she left it.
The it.

2/13/89

The question obsessing me at the moment is the one of voice. What is
mine.

Oh I get it. The watcher did not change. Phenomena streamed by in ⑤
speckles but she did not change.

—Everything is strange to me in this world

Just the taste of oranges, imagine!

Went to Linda's service . . . How wonderful her spirit was to people! Her courage, her clarity, her truth & how she loved people. She was so gifted, and deeply there. She didn't produce anything but change. It was odd that she is more important to me than G. whom I have also lost but whose life seems impoverished to me now . . . It made me cherish the notion of human togetherness . . . We need not feel that a very short life is a wasted one.

I think about

     poetry every
minute
like Spanish moss it's killing
the tree

(6)

     pink kleenex in the
street or is it
a camellia

(7)

Maybe I will and maybe I won't do
any such thing

(8)

That mockingbird outside has been trying one voice after another for hours like a
young poet   It's like she can't decide among the little trills and scallops

(9)

And you my beloved my earth bridge
where are you who is noticing.
Where is your thisness

waiting for Triple A I try to follow the three new voices
little trills and scallops then a wedge shaped

(10)

2/17/89

My tire was flat yesterday and it's flat again today. Am sick with a cold, called triple A twice. If I have to call tomorrow it will be triple triple A. I should be able to change a tire but I forgot a vital step: loosen the lugnuts before I jack it up. Couldn't figure it out so just kept trying. Two hours of work lost.

towhees on a conveyer belt

take the week off from writing. Trying to play with the idea of "tractates". Death tractates—for Linda. But mostly about spring, reincarnation, vividness.

—Remembering anything being like that documentary of chimps, when the mother chimp dies and the baby looks for her body for days—careening sometimes out of control into the unknown world of health

personal/impersonal
spiritual/physical
freedom of spirit/political
intimate/general
observations/statements
hieratic/demotic
health that includes one's former illness
ethereal/grounded

—when subject merges with object—Plath—where you stop being tied to yourself, you
are everything or you are dead
visiting creature mystery exegesis
as soon as you stop being compelled by the idea of life you can—

thus it is possible to hold two
thoughts in your mind
and forgive one of them

third heaven

2/20/89

Went to F's studio yesterday and saw her unbelievably beautiful art. As we
walked in the whole show kind of just hit us. I was so moved by the sight
of those little canvases with all the pretty colors and zaniness I burst into
tears. Great art I think . . . she really has no idea how talented she is

2/21/89

the idea of the scraps of the universe. Of the dying person not taking the dress but
*   taking the*
scraps

winged one

about her grandmother telling her there is hell
about her being afraid she will be caught on one of those planes

subtle bodies

she died, she gave you back completely
what you were

fully being open to what is there. The little vireos swinging upside down, in
*   another*

universe
I felt along the edges of the panel

then this idea came to me (use this like slang)

B liked new moon poem F adored it. I had thought it wasn't much I guess
my expectations are too high. This business of writing—will it ever finish?

Did a meditation—talked to L about J and she was wise noting that this
feeling will pass. Natural wisdom of the body etc. Then asked about
poetry. No clear answer . . .

So it seemed that matter
had been betrayed. What kind of thing
was that? Because
light would go on and matter would fall away

lamp of pity

something prior

2/25 Inverness

Dreamed my mockingbird had died beside the burner of a stove. I asked for
the meaning of the dream. I recognized it had died for a good reason—
what was that reason? If the mockingbird for me was the multiplicity of
life, what was it.

The sense that
because she had died, because
matter entraps the light—so that's it.
Matter had been betrayed.

Something prior means derivation. Derivation bothers me.
cthonic priestess

Everything that lets go still
uses its memory of attachment

and everything that refused to let go
still had its uses

⑭

I went on living with force. It was exactly as she had said to do.

2/28

I like to study where the blossoms come from. It's the from that I want to
be inside . . .
To write poems only I can write.

Oh mockingbird—did I drive you away by talking back?

Very Precious Tools

I STARTED KEEPING A JOURNAL when I was very young and have written in
notebooks or journals on a daily or weekly basis since then. The journals
are extremely important to my writing process—indispensable. The passages I have typed are from pages of my handwritten journals, which are
often full of complaints and cries of the spirit; I decided that it might be
useful to see a few finished pieces and to note how the material made its
way from the journal entries. (I have included passages of poems, with
numbers corresponding to the references in the journals.)

From "First Tractate"

Tell now red-tailed hawk
(for we have heard the smallest thing cry out beneath you):
have you seen her?
(Red hawk) Thrush walking up
the ragged middle:

    have you seen her? Mockingbird with your trills
    and scallops, with your second mouth
    in your throat of all things
    tell us:
    where is she whom we love?

I closed my eyes and saw the early spring,
pretty spring, kind of a reward;
I opened them and saw the swirling world,
thousands of qualified
pinks, deer feeding
on the torn changes

and I wanted to go back 'from whence' I came.

Up the coast, along
sandbanks and spillways,
the argued-about bays, spring came forth
with its this 'n' that, its I can't
decide, as my life had
before she died: preblossoming:
cranesbill, poppy—

and I wanted to go back "from whence" I came.

. . .

I went out in the night, I called out,
I felt along the edges of the panel:

without her,
everything seemed strange to me in this world;
just the taste of oranges: imagine!

And all of this compared to her seemed bulky.
For weeks this was true.
As if only being dead were the right amount.
Only being dead were fragile enough
for what the earth had to say.
Clumsy. For a while. Clumsy. For a while
it was too much to go on living.
Roadside acacias—
I could not bear them. All unzipped,
like meaning.
The ostinatos of the birds.
Magnolias—dogs'-tongues—curved
to spoon up rain. Too much shape.
Even that which was only suspected
of having it: the iris
that lay in the ground with their eyes of fate.

Near Jenner

I asked the mind for a shape and shape meant nothing;
I asked the soul for help, and some help came:

some wedding-band gold came around the edges of a sunset,
and I knew that my bride could see forward, behind it;

and all the women I had known
came back from their positions
where they had been hanging the silk
laundry of heaven
upside down by the elastic;

they'd help me find her

though they looked slightly faded from being dead,
as the first wildflowers here—
radish, and the ones they call 'milkmaids'—
look faded when they appear on the shoulders of the Pacific—

From "Visiting Creature"

—You think about a poem too much.
Like Spanish moss,
it starts killing the tree!

Look: Berkeley spring. A mockingbird
has chosen you. Try to follow his new
short songs: buree, buree, cheat-sheet, and the one
that sounds like maybe I
will and maybe I won't do any such thing.

From "The Panel"

So you thought of the moment of death
as a kind of panel or screen
behind which she might
join the watcher

and the watcher
did not change. Phenomena
streamed by in circles,
and the watcher did not change—

From "Possible Companion"

The mockingbird stayed for months in the legustrum—
blips and screams,
I couldn't get a thing done;

From "Split Tractate"

Help, mockingbird! don't say no!
Maybe she has forgotten us,
she has given us this priceless gift, ⌐ ①
she has let us go.

　　. . .

Spring could let go couldn't it.
Vireos hung upside down from the cottonwood.　⑫
The old calm towhee at the feeder—it did on tarry.

Beautiful, average mornings: the scattered actual: grief
changed them only slightly.
Mornings waiting for the triple A,　　⑩
of neighbors standing by their cars and chatting,

one pink kleenex　　　　　　　⑦
in the street—or is it a camellia—

From "Finding Her"

And out in the night
where the ragged patches converge:

everything that lets go
still has its memory of attachment　　⑭
and that which refused to let go
still has its uses.

I had a lot of trouble beginning the poems for *Death Tractates,* and these pages are some of the entries that helped me start that project. If I were to be teaching the poems in relation to the journal entries, I would note how an observation makes its way onto the page in a very different form from the final poem. There are perhaps a hundred relevant journal pages, far too many to type here, so I chose only a few entries from the month after my friend died. I did not begin most of the composition of the poems until about a month after that, so there was a lot of note taking about springtime, death, writing, and the soul and its travels. I would not have written *Bright Existence* or *Death Tractates* had it not been for the journal entries I raided at the time of drafting the poems.

I have enjoyed the notebooks and journals of Plath, Valéry, and Seferis. I like Cheever's diaries as examples of struggle. My favorite journals or notebooks are those of Gerard Manley Hopkins. I feel a close kinship with his style of notebook keeping.

I would advise all writers to keep journals, but not all writers are compelled by the necessity; one of my poet friends said, "I don't know how to keep a journal; I don't know whom I'm talking to." A novelist friend said, "It takes so much time to write a novel, why waste time taking notes?"

My journals are very precious tools to me. My experience is that a journal entry provides at least three kinds of tools. One might be an image that comes freshly and immediately, and may be lost soon thereafter if it is not recorded. Later, in drafting the poem, I comb the journal for the usable image. Secondly, it is a blank tablet for ideas. I like to make long lists of titles and ideas for poems. I tend to go through periods of psychological and philosophical agitation over an issue of perception or behavior, and these take years to work through. The other use—this is really the most felicitous—of the journal is as a musical score wherein one can write the whole musical line as a given, just as it is received in the brain. I hear whole lines and race to record them.

I have recently realized the limitations and dangers of putting some material into print, and I am reminded of the value of the private world of the journal. Those of us who use journals for our diaries as well as our writer's notebooks run the special risk of hurting people. I feel compelled to "vent" in my journals, as well as to record interesting private moments. I have little desire to re-read the venting sections for artistic purposes, but when I am troubled, it helps to re-read those sections to confirm a condition. I do feel that diary/journal combinations show a writer at her best and worst. In thinking about how to handle the problem of literary use and privacy, I have decided to edit sections of my journals for occasional publication but am not sure whether I will destroy the originals or not. Perhaps I will seal them so they cannot be read for a while . . . I certainly will do something about them in the next few years, because there are many of them (nearly 100) and much of the material I do not feel should ever be read by others, though I want to have access to the work until my death.

Finally, I feel writers should keep journals because when we begin to lose a sense of private pleasure, the assurance of a sacred space exists in a journal. There is only the purity of unstudied thought.

Israel Horovitz

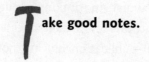ake good notes.

*I look out of my
window at a city
full of playwrights*

*looking
out of
their
windows.*

The thought of Paris haunts me—why must my gladdest memories plunge me into sadness? It seems cruel, this, too cruel!

The thought of seeing Beckett's grave cannot compete with the old thoughts of seeing Beckett—of planning each question, and guessing his answer.

We'll spend 5 weeks in Paris, where I'll pretend to be the writer I once was—it's all too sad. No wonder we die at 80; our spirits die at 50—30 years of withering without hope, without mystery—only worry about safety—watching children grow less and less connected—wondering why all that time was spent preparing them for such painful independence. No other way.

I had hoped my first entry in this lovely book would be a joyous thing—

Perhaps something laughable.

Perhaps, tomorrow.

9.1.93

NYC 20.1.95

He leaves a trail of bloody dental floss.

He lays on his belly at the curb,
forcing the kneeling bus to kneel.

Questionnaire

WHEN DID YOU START keeping a journal? 1970s.

What are your habits in keeping it? Sporadic.

How have the particular excerpts you contributed for this book shown up in your published writing or been helpful to it? Keeping a journal allows me to fool myself into thinking I've been writing.

Who influenced you in keeping a writer's journal? Beckett, Ionesco

Whose published journals have you read? Camus

What lessons or suggestions might you have for those who want to keep a writer's journal? Take good notes.

Pam Houston

These letters contain most of the significant incidents, real and imagined, that make up the fabric of my life. Like a journal, they are an invaluable reference source and precursor to my fiction and non-fiction projects, but unlike a journal, they have an audience, and when I have an audience, I'm far more inclined to excel.

Here are three examples from my collection of love letters, each of them roughly a year apart, that serve as my journal.

Dear G—,

It is, in fact, called "breaking horses," and the reason it is called that is because the term was invented by a man. The man believed, wrongly, that he was capable of breaking the horse's spirit, of removing all that was wild from her, and he also believed, even more wrongly, that breaking her was the only way he could hold her, when of course, exactly the opposite was true. That man would be the first to tell you that the horse was only valuable to him when she was strong and free and responded to him out of respect and love and dedication. The minute he "broke" her, he would say (though he'd be wrong, she allowed herself to be broken . . . which is really like saying she broke herself) he lost interest in her and turned her into a dude horse that old ladies and kids could ride. But of course you know all this.

Let me tell you what happened today. C— was bent on going riding, and even though this is the city, it is also Texas, so we looked in the phone book and found a dude ranch and signed ourselves up for a three hour ride. C— rode a feisty little quarter horse called Charlotte, and I rode a big rangy thoroughbred/Tennessee Walker cross named Paul. Our wrangler's name was James and he was young and just about as Texan as you can get. And of course we signed papers and everything that said we wouldn't run the horses, but I know C— better than that, and we weren't twenty minutes into the ride when James made the mistake of going around a different side of a little stand of pines than we did and C— seized the moment he couldn't see us and belted her horse and we took off at a flat gallop across the top half of this four hundred and some acre cattle ranch.

A quarter horse is the best horse to have on a trail because she is strong and smart and basically willing to do what you ask her. What a thoroughbred is good at is putting his head down and running for the finish line, throwing care and caution and sense to the wind, setting his jaw and running, through or around or over whatever might get in his way. It's not his fault. We've bred him for it. And there is nothing I've ever done in my life that is as exhilarating, nothing that is so equally and completely frightening and magical than being on the back of a thoroughbred when he's in turbodrive. It's as smooth as a Cadillac convertible and much faster. It was the first recreational bargain I made with death, and one of the few I hope to keep making for as long as I live. But I've gotten off track here.

The day went a lot like that. Ten minutes of walk/trot pleasantness and then C— would bring Charlotte up to where I was and our horses would start bumping shoulders and I would turn and look at James and catch just the hint of a smile or a shake of his head and that was all we needed to be off again. Anyway, what I wanted to tell you about was the training, the lessons that took place between me and . . . Paul. The first time Paul took off on me, I was really scared. He took off like only a thoroughbred can, and I didn't know him, or the tack I was using, didn't know the terrain. I tried every trick I know to stop him (and I know them all). Constant pressure, intermittent pressure, I tried to turn him hard in a tight circle, tried shouting whoa whoa whoa at every possible voice level, tried even to kick him to attention (very poor horsemanship), and finally, after crossing three stream beds, clattering over two very nasty rock outcroppings, and shaving off about fifteen tree branches with various parts of my body, I found a big canyon wall to run Paul into.

"Don't let that horse put his head down on ya," James said when he caught up to us that first time. "That horse puts his head down, and you're just fucked." The second time we took off I played it a little different. I let him run as fast as he wanted until we got to a place that was steep and rocky. And then I hauled back on the reins one time, said Whoa once loud and sat back hard in the saddle. Paul stopped on a dime.

After that we came to a big open meadow. James said we

couldn't go down there because it was the horses' winter pasture and they would get a little crazy in it, and I asked if I could go down for ten minutes by myself and work with Paul. I went down into the meadow and galloped him around in tight tight circles, but every time he'd stop fighting me, I'd drop the reins a little, and let him make the circle just a little more wide. I talked to him with my legs the whole time too asking for the gallop, and then asking for control (not my control, of course, but his, asking him to control his own gallop), showing him that asking for the speed and asking for control are not opposites, that they can be the same question asked with one movement of the leg, and you see that's why the legs are so important because in the same movement they ask for something from the horse, they also make a promise. They say you can trust me. They say I'm asking you to gallop with me, but I'm also telling you at every second that I'm right here with you to help you have the courage to gallop. The horse holds the rider up, it's true, but the rider holds the horse . . . in, or together. This is especially true when a horse and rider are out alone, because horses are herd animals and they need that constant contact of the leg then much more than most riders know.

Before too long we were galloping big circles around the whole meadow. C— told me that the whole time we were down there James was saying "Any second now Paul's going to come flying over that hill dragging Theresa behind him." And I did let him out as we ran the last length of the field back to where C— and James were standing. But I wasn't hanging on for my life anymore. I was flying along right with him.

It was, from then on, one of the best rides ever on a horse I didn't know. And we did give James a really big tip.

And of course we are talking here about the ability of the trainer to teach, and the horse's ability to learn, as well as the trainer's ability to learn and the horse's ability to teach, and that is what makes horseback riding different from tennis or skiing, that there are two wills constantly engaged and those four learning situations are always and must be at every moment inextricable.

And of course a horse tests his trainer, he tests her every minute, he reads her fears straight through her body like no human being ever could, he senses any momentary inattention and capitalizes on it. He sometimes pretends to be much less intelligent than he is, he walks into a hole or gets caught up in barbed wire, and I don't know why exactly. Maybe he likes watching her hands gently separate the barbs from his fetlocks . . . maybe he recognizes this as a tremendous act of love.

And of course they talk to one another, and most days they reach an understanding, and he becomes more human and she more equine, which doesn't take all that much becoming, because if she didn't have an equine spirit she wouldn't have become a horse trainer, and if he didn't have a human sensibility, he wouldn't be her chosen horse. And she does get tired, but not of him, or even of the training, but of falling down all the time in the same place. And though he's been tricked (not by her, but by something bigger, some universal law of order questionable but stronger than them) into believing that she's the one who's holding the lunge line, the simple laws of nature are that because of the different ways they are put together, one well enough placed kick can break her arm into nineteen pieces. And the one thing he really understands about her (and it's both the reason he sometimes bucks her off, and the reason he'll walk through fire for her) is that what she wants most of all, what all the years of training have shown her, is the possibility of never again needing to use the whip.

Did I tell you that Jerry Jeff Walker signed my blonde leather coat? Did I tell you about Gruene, Texas and the oldest dance hall in the state? Did I tell you that in everything I see that moves . . . me . . . in the young girl at the grunge bar with magenta hair and ten nose rings, in the tall young blues singer in a band called Joe Teller who wailed into the microphone and wrapped his arms around it like an invisible woman and then walked off stage saying "I hate this fucking six string, I hate this fucking club, and I hate all you fucking people," in the third verse of Mr. Bojangles, in the deep set lines on Jerry Jeff's life-worn face, in the paler lines of clouds in *the sky last night behind a lone Texas windmill, in the scrubby cedars and naked grey rocks of the canyons of the triple creek ranch, in the first surprise of speed in sixteen hands of horseflesh underneath me, in the slowing of that same horse, in the giving in. In all of these things and at every moment, I see my love for you.*

    P—

Ohhhhhh S—,

    I am living today in some other reality. Some half lit space of fever and hallucination and flu. I'm unsure whether it's day or night, in my head, you know, but all I need to do is look out the window and see that it's day. I read the script of the Good-bye Girl . . . and this I hesitate to admit even to you . . . cried continuously from about page 68 on. Nothing like snappy, overclever, utterly unbelievable dialogue to really open me up, heart and soul.

    I pause here, unsure what to tell you next. Do I begin by describing the writing I've been doing, by telling you what pure unadulterated pleasure (and of course the necessarily accompanying pain) I have found these last weeks reimmersing myself in writing according to no one's agenda but my own, remembering that process from years ago where I sat down and just wrote the thing . . . the story or image or scene or thought that I had to write, and then just sat there to see what happened then, how the seeing what happened became what was thrilling. That's what all the nonfiction has taken away from me, the screenplay too . . . they have their own variety of seeing what happens, but it doesn't touch the freedom of this other project, that can go anywhere and do anything and be any length and shape itself into any form it likes; poem, letter, chapter, story. It asks so much more of me, demands it, and unlike the others, I have to enter it not knowing if I am up to the task, not knowing whether or not I will succeed, whether or not I will, God forbid, waste time.

Or should I begin by telling you I spent part of today with one of the most delightful human beings I've met in recent memory . . . he was articulate, gentlemanly, quite handsome, and four years old. Maybe, the most wonderful thing on earth is introducing a child to a horse for the very first time . . . and in this case it was doubly wonderful, because not only was Deseo Sam's first horse, but Sam was Deseo's first child. His mom, L—, is one of my students, and he and I hit it off instantly when he came racing into class one day, skidded to a stop in front of me, looked me up and down and said, "No way Mom, she's not a real teacher." To say Sam and Deseo delighted in each other would be a tragic understatement.

Deseo was soft and encouraging and precisely the right amount of playful. . . . Sam was . . . well . . . soft and encouraging and precisely the right amount of playful. And the two moms, pride running off of us like water . . . we scarcely needed to be there at all.

Or should I begin instead with you and what's on my mind today concerning you, which is how very happy I am that you know me, as well as you seem to, that you know what my mind does with the things you say as well as I know exactly where Deseo's mind goes, not during, but in the few seconds after a mountain bike passes, and you know how to wrap your arms around that space, exactly how to rub its neck.

Or should I begin with my sighting of this bumper sticker near the Oakland Airport: Visualize Whirled Peas.

I think so often . . . too often, about the night that man, M— F—, said to me, "I can't remember the last time I spent three hours with someone who was less interested in me," and then I got hit on the head with the rusted pipe. Well there's more to that story than I told you that night, not a lot more, but since you do know when I'm telling the truth and when I'm embellishing (though you would not profess to) I'll fill in.

When he said those words to me we were standing in the hallway of his apartment building (his apartment was upstairs) and after I sort of bumbled around apologizing for a couple of minutes trying to explain myself he tried to kiss me. Kiss me! And I said, out of what I first thought was confusion, but now understand was more like rage,

"I'm really a little left behind by the turns this evening has all of a sudden been taking and I'd like to go home."

He said nothing, I left, and, two blocks later got thumped on the head. I got home about one, I think, sleeping out of the question, and the phone rang at two. It was M— F— wanting to tell me that I had made him want to throw out the window everything he thought he knew about women. (You might wonder how I managed to do this, since all I did according to him was talk about myself.)

I ended the conversation as quickly as I could. I'd been crying, and didn't want to discuss that with him. He called a few more times after that, but talked only to my voice mail . . . he always said he'd wait to hear from me, so I thought the best thing to do was to not encourage him. I heard nothing these last two weeks until yesterday when there was a message on my voice mail asking me to return a book he claims he lent me, which, of course, he did not.

This is not a particularly interesting story . . . another crazy person living alone in the city. I find it mildly interesting that the person who suggested we meet, a woman, is about as exciting and quirky as Wonder Bread, but only mildly. And after L—, M— F—'s craziness seems minor league, and happily, he doesn't know where I live.

It would be easy to dismiss him as crazy and stupid and wrong on all counts, but the thing that haunts me, the thing that I can't let go of, the thing I was thinking about when I got hit that night was the kernel of truth in what he said . . . which is that I don't ask questions . . . I've been trained not to by my father, by my mother, my teachers, and by all the men in my life who wanted so badly to hide. And you want to hide too sometimes . . . we all do, but not always. And when you ask me to come out of hiding it is such a strong and fine thing. . . .

I feel right now how I feel when I'm in front of a room of four

hundred people, and someone has asked me a question and it has
somehow launched me into some long complicated and well told
story and I get to the winding up place, where I'm going to bring it
all ever-so-elegantly back around to the question and I have no idea
what the question was . . . no idea, as I look out into the crowd,
even who asked it.

What are you saying, Pam?

Just this:

I love knowing you. And I want to know everything you want
me to know, even if I don't have the sense, or the strength, or the
grace to ask.

I described our conversations to H— the other day in a manner
that I thought you would appreciate, because I know you know this
feeling well. I said our talks held in them a similar pleasure as when
I am walking in a vast and varied foreign country with no map or
guidebook, only intuition and faith, and I am feeling it, breathing it,
taking in every bit I can of that strange landscape, when I round a
corner and everything has gone suddenly familiar, and I don't know
if it's a function of time spent or knowledge or karma or past lives,
but when it's happened to me, as it has in Georgetown, and the
Ardeche, Alaska certainly, even the Amazon, almost instantly at the
ranch, I understand it for the gift it is. And that's how it is when I
talk to you, the undiscovered and the familiar bumping against each
other like the knees of teenagers at the Pizza Hut after the basketball
game, unchaperoned for the very first time . . . . (Oh my God
she's off again)

I'll miss the Fed Ex man if I don't stop now.

P—

_____

B—

It's Tuesday night . . . late, I don't know what time, and I'm
supposed to be writing the lecture I have to give tomorrow. I'm
feeling more and more like I'm in solitary confinement here, though

I've made some connections with some wonderful people, and my students are pretty good and pretty smart. It's the no phone/no mail thing, and the scarred walls and the horrible bathroom with its horrible shower curtain that's hung in such a tight circle I can't take a shower without the slimy thing draping itself all over me like something out of a bad film.

Last night I stayed off campus in a crazy lady's gypsy caravan. Her name is E— and she gave me a pair of earrings she made, a moon in one ear and a star in the other. She grows flowers and garlic in her garden for money and is in love with a Polynesian man named H— who drinks too much beer and then gets mad. He left last night, before I got there for dinner, so we had several hours of good woman talk, she and her daughter, T—, and I, and then I went to sleep in the caravan in their yard, with lots of candles burning and Robbie Robertson playing on the stereo. Candles and music were just the ticket after sleeping in this sterile place all these days. H— was home by morning, everything patched up by the time I left for school. She's got a horse she wants me to ride that she says is real skittish. There's a beach you can ride to from her house that's covered, at low tide, with every color of sea glass. I'm gonna ride out there Thursday afternoon if I can take the time away.

This is the wrong place for me to be now. I just want to be still for a little while. To sit on the porch and just lean up against you . . . or like we did on the Divide, remember, I just want to lean up against you and have you tell me things. . . .

———————

Hello again. It's Thursday night now, about midnight and there's a party going on next door with some kind of loud awful music playing, so I'm gonna finish this letter and then go back to E—'s and crawl in the caravan again. I snuck away for a few hours this afternoon and rode her crazy horse, Apollo, about ten miles down the beach. We had a little rodeo action more than once but he wasn't really committed to getting me off his back.

There's something pure magic about galloping a horse next to the ocean . . . even when what I am most of all is scared. I didn't quite make it to glass beach, but on the way back I wrote the beginning of a poem about not making it, so I guess that's almost as good as getting there. I was nearly there, I think, but there was a big log across the thin strip of beach there was. The tide was coming in and when I asked Apollo to go in the water he did a pretty firm 180 on me with a couple of crow hops, and sometimes it feels like wisdom to just let the horse win. E— and I are gonna get up at five tomorrow morning and hike into glass beach. I've got to be back here to teach at nine.

E— told me the story today of how she and H— got together. They'd been high school sweethearts, had lost touch for 25 years when she started dreaming about him. In her dreams he was always sick or dying, in some kind of terrible trouble that in the dream she couldn't prevent. Her husband had walked out on her after eighteen years of marriage. She was trying to manage her farm on her own. But the dreams continued so she called a number she had long ago that belonged to his sister. She was more than a little surprised when it was H— who picked up the phone. The first thing he told her was that he was a junkie, that he'd spent most of his life in prison, the rest in Vietnam. She asked him if he looked the same and he said yes but his hair was silver. The silver fox was his nickname in prison. They made plans to see each other later that year. When she went to southern California they had less than 24 hours together to see what was between them. She was raising two girls, was concerned for their safety if she brought him around. He said he'd come help her with the farm, and if she wanted, he'd trade beer for drugs. She spent two months in the deciding, unlike her, she said, not to know right away. She was driving home one night from work, thinking she'd go mad with indecision, begging the universe to give her a sign. A silver fox sprinted across the road *in front of her vehicle. She called H— and told him to come the next day.*

　　　You can see why I like her. You can see why she found me. I met H— today, finally, and his magic is evident. They have a yard full of red and white gladiolus now, taller, even, than you.

　　P—

In Service of the Next Step

I HAVEN'T KEPT a journal for many years. The last time, in fact, I was only a girl, and the writing was so horrendously stifled and self-conscious that I have every reason to believe it would be fruitless to try to keep one again. But a few years ago I realized that I never wrote more fluidly, more excitedly, more directedly, and more honestly than I did when I was writing a love letter. And since I seem to be always in love with somebody, since I am driven in my life and my work most strongly by desire, and since I can scarcely tell the difference between desire for the word and desire for the one, I began writing letters at the end of most days to some named beloved.

Sometimes I send the letter to the person whose name is on the top of it, and sometimes not. Sometimes the events I describe in the letter have actually happened, and sometimes not. The named recipient is most often real, though occasionally imaginary, and he is almost always male, because when one woman writes to another, she is able to leave so much out.

These letters contain most of the significant incidents, real and imagined, that make up the fabric of my life. Like a journal, they are an invaluable reference source and precursor to my fiction and non-fiction projects, but unlike a journal, they have an audience, and when I have an audience, I'm far more inclined to excel.

The letters sometimes delight, more often confuse and almost always frustrate my friends, who wish, for my sake and theirs, I could get a better grasp on the whole fiction/reality thing. Often by the time I speak to them about the letter I can't remember which things actually happened and which things only happened in my mind. It doesn't matter to me by that point; by then I am wholly in service of the next step—the story—and truth has enlarged itself to mean something else entirely than what happened where and when.

Fenton Johnson

I was engaging the rhetorical . . . style of my Southern, white male upbringing: assigning to my imagined reader opinions counter to my own, then arguing with myself while my reader listened. Writing, after all, is about constructing identity. For me, a journal never provided the necessary reality check—or the sense of an audience before which and for which I'm performing.

7 December 1989

Dear N.,

*. . . Today is the memorial service for a good friend of mine . . .
he died, of course, of the Big A. We'll all gather in some all-purpose
room somewhere and there under the fluorescent lights we'll mark the
occasion of his passing, with little ceremony or ritual.*

*There's something about seeing, actually <u>viewing</u> a corpse that
brings home the fact of death, I think; "closure," a Californian
would say, which is ironic, since it's been more or less Californians
who have eliminated funerals from the cultural scene. . . . It will
seem odd, the bunch of us gathered without our friend himself, dead
as he might be, as the focus of our gathering. One believes and hopes
that his presence will be there, and after all there are plenty
(including my friend, from what I knew of him) who would find the
presence of a body gruesome. And yet to me this underscores the
necessary and vital fact of death in life. One could make the
argument that in some measure our lack of respect for the living
earth—for its resources, for our place among them, for life itself—has
its roots in our lack of respect for the dead, since it is from among
the dead that we rise up.*

*Some time ago, on a late-autumn visit [to Kentucky], I took a
car into the hills, looking for the gravestone of one of the men killed
in the sporadic wars between the hill families and the state police. I
went to Holy Cross Church, where I'd never before set foot, no
matter that it is ten miles from where I grew up.*

*Holy Cross is the loveliest of a series of lovely, early-nineteenth-
century churches that Catholic emigrants from Maryland built in this
small valley. The church sits on a slight knoll, raising it above the
surrounding fields—site of the first Catholic church west of the
Appalachians, built in 1787, according to the historical marker; the
present church dates from 1825.*

*Unlike most American churches (but like many European village
churches), Holy Cross Church sits in the midst of its graveyard. It's*

built of red brick, in the simplest of cruciforms, decorated only by curving lines of brick laid into the masonry facade. These curves are echoed in the curving lines of the wooden bell tower, painted white and topped with green shingles. The effect is that of an American primitive architecture, created by people who had no formal architectural training but who were first-rate craftsmen and who, in their simple way, took time and patience to create something beautiful and in harmony with its surroundings—the brick was fired in Kentucky, from the same kind of clay that underlies this churchyard. Looking at the church, it's easy to see how it's of a piece with the land on which it sits.

The churchyard was filled with black walnut trees, which on that early winter afternoon raised bare branching silhouettes against the sky. Spongy black walnut shells were scattered among the tombstones, leaching purple-black stains onto their limestone and granite. From the churchyard I looked down to the hamlet's single intersection (the "holy cross"), where limestone rocks unearthed by the thrifty gravediggers have been used to build retaining walls and a shrine for a plaster statue of the Virgin.

As I stood in the churchyard amid the graves of families whose names I'd never even heard, in the graying winter light, with the black branching limbs of the walnuts and the gray-bleached bones of an abandoned farmhouse silhouetted against the steel blue of the surrounding hills—a sense of sadness, of loss pervaded everything.

Years later, sitting in the Sinai Memorial Chapel in San Francisco, listening to an elderly tenor sing a pure, haunting kaddish, I thought about this: What happens to all that energy of grief when people have no way to give it voice? Where does it go?

12 December 1990

Dear J. & J.,

. . . I was reading through Samuel Pepys' diaries—he lived in London at the time of the plague—the "Black Death" of 1655 . . . What's remarkable about his diaries is his attitude toward death— his supposition that it may come at any time, and is handed out by a capricious and not necessarily merciful God (an attitude much closer to that of the ancient Greeks than to that of contemporary Americans). Pepys is never far from an acknowledgment of the mystery of things, and the ways in which all things, but most especially his health and prosperity, are dependent on the will of God. These days we would mock that as naive at best, and at worst an embodiment of Calvinism's so convenient dictum that material success is the best evidence of God's blessing. But in reading Pepys' diary his forthright and trustworthy voice comes through, and one understands the depth and sincerity of his belief in his absolute dependence on the whims of circumstance.

. . . I keep searching for some letter from [my lover], some piece of writing that says, "I know you'll be reading this after I'm gone, and I want to say to you that I'm still here." I go into his room again and again searching for that letter and it's never there. I know of course that it wouldn't make any difference, I know what I know and I know, or at least suspect, the ways in which he is with me now and will always be with me; and yet, and yet. I write this not by way of being maudlin but of bowing down before the mysterious fates, which allowed us the three-and-one-quarter years together that we needed to say everything that needed to be said, once, and we said it, once, and once it was said that was the end of it all. For virtually the entire relationship, he said to me, "I'm so lucky," again and again. A week before he died, I turned to him in the courtyard of the Picasso Museum, under a dusk-deep sapphire sky and said, "I'm so lucky." And it was as if the time allotted to him to teach this lesson, the time allotted to me to learn it, had been

*consumed, and there was nothing left but the facts of things to play
out. At the risk of being sententious I say: Think on these things, and
what they mean to you. All relationships are mortal, it's just that
most of the time we're too "well-wadded with stupidity," as George
Eliot would have it, or needing a gun pointed to our heads, as
Flannery O'Connor would have it, and we avoid thinking about it.
And then it happens, and it's over. There's no door more
unquestionable, more unanswering than death.*

———————

14 January 1991

Dear B.,

*. . . Grief is like any wound—there is some terrible pleasure in it.
It's better to need that wound, that terrible pleasure than to have
nothing at all. If love fulfills itself in companionship, grief fulfills
itself in solitude, for we grieve finally and necessarily less for the
dead than for our living selves, our aloneness in our survival, our
inescapable invitation to the dance.*

Ordinary Acts

BLESS ME, reader, for I have sinned: I have tried to keep a journal, and I
have failed. The reasons for my failure are many and complex; among
them may be laziness, but I think not. In my twenties, for something
like five years I kept a journal more or less regularly, during which time I
witnessed or read about events of great significance (e.g., the murder of
San Francisco mayor George Moscone and gay supervisor Harvey Milk;
the subsequent trial of the assassin Dan White, and the riots which

followed the verdict). I look back at those journal entries and find them so juvenile and self-conscious as to be unreadable.

In *The House by the Sea,* one of her collections of journal entries, May Sarton writes:

> I find it wonderful to have a receptacle in which to pour vivid momentary insights, and a way of ordering day-to-day experience . . . If there is an art to the keeping of a journal intended for publication yet at the same time a very personal record, it may be in what Elizabeth Bowen said: "One must regard oneself impersonally as an instrument."

My journal entries from the 1970s and 1980s were anything but impersonal—filled with polemic, directed at some imagined, recalcitrant reader whom I hoped to transform, through the alembic of my deathless prose, into someone exactly like myself. Looking back, I see that I was engaging the rhetorical style of my Southern, white male upbringing: assigning to my imagined reader opinions counter to my own, then arguing with myself while my reader listened. Writing, after all, is about constructing identity. For me, a journal never provided the necessary reality check—or the sense of an audience before which and for which I'm performing.

Letters were and are a different matter. Beginning earlier than my twenties—since I was old enough to write—I've used letters to record the passing events and impressions of my life. For me they present the advantage of engaging a known audience (my correspondent). The history my reader and I share lifts me out of myself; it reminds me that what I am about is not just expression but also communication. I write with intimacy because I know I am writing a friend; but I am bound by the discipline of letters to order my thoughts so that my audience may comprehend what I am trying to say.

Excerpts from letters which were written during my lover's illness from AIDS or after his death in Paris in October 1990 later became passages in larger, longer works. The letter of 14 January 1991 became the concluding paragraph of a chapter of my second novel, *Scissors, Paper, Rock.* The other letters became part of a memoir, *Geography of the Heart.*

As I write I am in motion—500 m.p.h. at 35,000 feet, a place and state of being I find conducive to writing; something about the stale, recycled air and the dog biscuit lunch, combined with that ineffable sense of being suspended in between, neither here nor there, the place where anything might happen even if it usually doesn't. I write in a Palmer longhand much deteriorated from the penmanship classes of my Catholic grade school days; letters which, on returning home, I enter into my laptop, print out, and mail to one friend or another, saving a copy for my own files. Passages from those letters frequently form the germ of a story, an essay, even a book.

Returning from the journey to France during which my lover died, I wrote his eulogy, an unbearably hard thing to do, in the form of a letter. In a paroxysm of epistolary love, Barbara Kingsolver and I wrote each other monthly for several years, five- and six-page, single-spaced tomes which covered everything from politics to literature to a mock marriage proposal which I accepted, and which I like to think remains in force in some polygamous, parallel universe. (Beware, however, of epistolary romances. A year later I carried on a similar, almost daily correspondence with a man who lived all of fifteen miles away, only to have the real relationship collapse the moment we had to communicate without cut-and-paste. Even so, at the risk of being thought crass I note that the romance served my writer's ends: It gave me the opportunity to record for a known audience my moment-by-moment experience of the world.)

In this difficult, overcrowded, complicated, troubled time, it seems to me that simply to endure without descending into easy bitterness, to sustain some kind of hope and faith for one's peers and for those who follow—this is an achievement, an ongoing act of courage whose magnitude we too often take for granted. Journals or letters—these are means (may they endure and multiply) for declaring the significance of the small thing: a record of the ordinary acts of life and love which bind us one to another, and which are our only true source of hope.

Maxine Kumin

*d*ream journals, journals
observing seasonal changes
on our own farm, journals about my,
and other people's, horses.

May, 1993

Pobiz is wondrous strange. On a free Sunday morning during an arduous gig in central Texas, Chester Critchfield, a retired biologist who bounces along jauntily on the balls of his sneakered feet, conveys me on a guided tour of the native flora and fauna. An enthusiast who would rather spend an hour watching a flower open than chase a golf ball across the ubiquitous greens, Chester is vividly at one with his environment. Behind his house where the land drops down to the creek he has excavated a sizable pond, lined it with limestone bricks and stocked it with Japanese carp exotically striped and stippled orange, black and white. Several ugly catfish patrol the bottom and a healthy school of tilapia rise to snap at the pellets he broadcasts over the surface. Tilapia, he informs me, are the biblical fish of the Sea of Galilee. He thinks they and the carp would do well in my sheep-pasture fire pond, a saucer some fifty feet in diameter, possibly eight feet deep at the center.

As we cross the adjoining meadow I see my first loggerhead shrike under Chester's tutelage: it's a savage little bird of prey that impales its quivering catch on thorns then retrieves and devours them at leisure. I had always expected a shrike to be bigger than a bluejay, at least. It makes up in ferocity for what it lacks in stature.

We drive out to a huge Thoroughbred breeding farm where Chester has made arrangements for a guided tour. Ken Quirk, the resident vet, is one of the most gracious hosts I've come across in these often sterile and forbidding establishments. We arrive at an easy rapport in spite of the hard night he's been through—a leased mare bred last summer and then sent home to her owner who failed to have her ultrasounded early in the pregnancy was returned to them a few weeks ago for supervised foaling. Last night she delivered full-term twins, in itself a rarity, as the mare's uterus seldom provides an eleven-month-long hospitable environment for twins. The filly is near death, sedated with Valium to control her seizures. She is a "wobbler" or "dummy foal," a condition caused by inflammation of brain tissue. They are trying to reduce the swelling with DMSO infusions, *but it doesn't look good. The colt has a better chance. He's been up, with assistance. He has a sucking reflex but is not yet able to swallow. Both are being fed four ounces of colostrum from the mother, milked out and delivered via stomach tube every two hours. The vet's heroic measures put our own dozen travails with dams and foals into perspective. Of course I am fascinated.*

143 bred mares here, the newest still in open pens under a high roof, which provides good ventilation. But with so many so close, there's a higher incidence of infection than, say, on the family farm. With us, pre-delivery precautions consist of taking out the old bedding down to sand and gravel, liming the area, and then rebedding. When the mare actually gives birth—or shortly before she does so, if we're alert to it—we switch from sawdust to straw, to reduce the possibility of a newborn inhaling dust particles and/or ammonia fumes from the urine. One of our mares, a greedy old lady, eats straw, which complicates things a bit. We've sat out a few tough nights with mares whose distended udders made them reluctant to give suck but we've never—so far—had a bacterial or any other postnatal infection.

It's still showery and cool here although spring is well advanced. The redbuds are finished flowering and are putting out new leaves. Older colts and their mothers are turned out on pasture in groups of six or eight. These oldtime broodmares coexist comfortably. 15 stallions cover this herd; retired stakes winners, sons and latter-day descendants of Seattle Slew and Native Dancer. The stallions' life is far from enviable, however. All of them are confined to box stalls as we tour, though Dr. Quirk says they are usually turned out. It's Sunday and Sunday is a down-day at this farm. One stalwart morose stud is wearing a muzzle. We can see where he tears himself up biting in frustration. He covered 80 mares last year, which seems an extraordinary figure. It would be a kindness to castrate him and let him have an outdoor life free of his gonads, but he's a money-maker.

They raise ostriches here too, but the birds are setting now and can't be viewed. A fertile egg is worth as much as $1500—so much for any fantasies of breeding ostriches! Tilapia sound more reasonable.

Two days later I am driven in a stretch limousine, complete with liquor bar and tv back to the airport for a predawn departure. A first for me, the limo, but I chafe, thinking how wasteful and ostentatious it is.

I loved the carp. They live, Chester told me, as much as 90 years. You too, Chester. Be well.

Like Five-Finger Exercises

I'VE KEPT A JOURNAL intermittently over the years, probably for twenty or thirty years, from time to time—dream journals, journals observing seasonal changes on our own farm, journals about my, and other people's, horses. Most of this is grist for the mill in one way or another. I had thought of perhaps doing an extensive article drawn from this and similar entries, but I fear the material is too technical and too specific to have much of a readership, so I'd have to say that I do this for my own enjoyment.

I've always been drawn to journals and letters. They feed the voyeur in me as I suspect they do in so many other writers. I am most keenly interested in women's journals and letters—Plath, Sexton, Louise Bogan, Woolf of course. But also John Cheever's, James Agee's, and so on.

Keeping a journal is a highly individual and eclectic occupation. I can only suggest to the would-be writer that it's a good habit to get into, like five-finger exercises at the piano.

Craig Lesley

Many writers like to keep a journal every day, but I don't. It's important to be excited about journal entries and have something useful to say. I don't want it to be a chore.

August 18, 1994

The tiny Steerman biplane bursting out of the plywood mill fire was a photo I hadn't expected to find in the old <u>Madras Pioneer.</u> Jim Mellenbeck took the photo the night the plywood plant and stud mill burned up. (Doc Mellenbeck's brother. All the fillings Doc put in my mouth have fallen out by now.) When the editor at the <u>Pioneer</u> told me the pilot Ace Demers was still cropdusting, I couldn't believe it. He must have several guardian angels—the oldest cropduster in Oregon. I'm thinking of replacing the novel's car salesman with a cropduster. That would bring in the agricultural aspect of the small town.

Where did Ace get the Borate to drop on the gasoline storage tanks? Ask him. I remember the firetrucks lined up along the irrigation ditch and mill pond sucking up water to cool those tanks, because if they exploded, most of Madras would have been lost. And I remember a couple of heroic firefighters climbing up on the tanks and tying off hoses to keep them cool. But I sure don't remember that plane.

The firetrucks were from Madras, Bend, Warm Springs, Redmond and Prineville. It seems funny that no one had ever heard of Prineville, but now after the Storm King Mountain disaster, everyone knows it.

Idea—during disasters like this fire, the whole community comes together to fight the disaster. Even people that hate each other and won't talk to each other under normal circumstances.

Waldon or Waldron was the chief of the volunteer fire department during this period. He's a Madras barber with heart trouble now. One of the Stewart boys fell through the skylight—ask Mike.

Idea—one type of hero emerges during disasters. Other heroes live day to day existences, paying the bills and putting clothes on their kids. Who was the baseball player who after the World Series said he wasn't a hero, the real hero was the guy that went to work everyday, took care of his family and paid the bills. Check on it. He played for Pittsburgh.

Think of the men who went down on the <u>Carl Bradley,</u> the big ore carrier that sank in Lake Superior around 1957. Maybe you can tie in <u>The</u>

Sky Fisherman with working on the Great Lakes. Where was the memorial service for the men who died on the *Carl Bradley*? It was either in Rogers City or Alpena. Write to Ken in Traverse City and find out.

Notes for tomorrow: 1) Meet Ace Demers at the Madras air field. Is he really still cropdusting? Ask him about accidents and pesticides. Does he have any side effects? Get his memories of that night. Where did he get the Borate? Why would he have it hanging around?

Try to capture the thrill, the shudder you felt seeing that Steerman burst out of the flames.

An Eerie Note

MATERIAL FROM THIS JOURNAL entry wound up in my novel *The Sky Fisherman* (Houghton Mifflin, 1995). The character of Buzzy was based on my interviews with Ace Demers and his experiences cropdusting and fighting the plywood mill fire. In earlier drafts of *The Sky Fisherman,* I had a car salesman as one of the "backroom boys" but liked the character of Buzzy since a cropduster is obviously a more glamorous profession and also highlights the agricultural angle. Buzzy also ties in the reservation with the town because he has been dropping Borate on reservation lightning strikes and slowing the fires from burning valuable reservation timber until the Indians can arrive with a ground crew. Ace told me he had Borate because he'd been trying to work out a similar agreement with the Warm Springs tribe.

The *Carl Bradley* sinking made the book too. In 1971 I was working for the Great Lakes Maritime Academy and we docked our ship, *The Hudson,* for a memorial service in Rogers City to honor the 33 men that went down on the *Bradley.* Twenty-three were from Rogers City and the rest from other parts of Michigan and Ohio. In the novel I was trying to celebrate the everyday dangers that working people face and how they are only one accident away from disaster. The men on the *Bradley* represent working people who face danger every day just providing for their families and loved ones. That's one kind of heroism. Another occurs when those same working people perform heroic actions during floods, fires, and other disasters.

I don't keep a journal every day, but I do when I'm working on a novel. I tried keeping a journal during the time I worked for the Great Lakes Maritime Academy on Superior and Michigan because Captain Mike Hemmick kept a journal and told me it was a good idea. I also longshored in Alaska for a while and always regretted I didn't keep a journal then because it seemed that summer would've provided ample material for another novel.

While working for the GLMA, I read *Shipwrecks and Survivals on the Great Lakes,* and much of that book contains entries from the captains' logs. I had some pretty good writing material during my GLMA days, but unfortunately one of my girlfriends burned my journals because she didn't like some of the entries.

Many writers like to keep a journal every day, but I don't. It's important to be excited about journal entries and have something useful to say. I don't want it to be a chore. This particular journal entry was extremely important as was the "trigger" of seeing the tiny plane sliding out of the inferno.

Here's an eerie note: my friend Ken Marek sent me materials from the Michigan Historical Society on the wreck of the *Carl Bradley*. The same day I rechecked the facts and sent some revised pages off to Houghton Mifflin, I attended my thirty-year high school reunion. On that occasion, I saw my old high school girlfriend (whom I hadn't seen for twenty years) and was astonished to learn she had married a man from Michigan who lost his uncle on the *Bradley*. That gave me more shudders than seeing the tiny Steerman.

Denise Levertov

*t*he value of the notebook is in the way writing such things down deepens our experience of them in that act itself—enriches our inner life, puts us in more intimate touch with ourselves. It may indeed happen later that notebook entries are incorporated in poems—but that is secondary.

9 December, 1994

Rereading <u>Emma</u> with such delight. It seems perhaps the very best of Jane Austen, even better than <u>Pride and Prejudice.</u> 'Mr. Knightly seemed to be trying not to smile; and succeeded without difficulty, upon Mrs. Elton beginning to talk to him.' In Volume III chapter iii she writes, 'Could a linguist, a grammarian, even a mathematician, have seen what she did . . . without feeling (etc.)? How much more must an imaginist, like herself, be on fire with speculation and foresight!—'What a wonderful term, <u>imaginist!</u>

10 December, 1994

. . . Richard Jones' good reading, during which he said he'd come to see that Rilke's 'You must change your life' was not about a once-and-for-all, romantic change but about the need for daily renewal and rebirth. Also he said, 'Poetry is my teacher,'—referring to the way that, once begun, a poem evolves its own story.

27 December, 1994, San Diego

Savoldo's <u>Temptation of St. Antony</u>—an unexpectedly Boschesque interpretation [for its period]. The 'temptations' in such pictures are not 'alluring' but rather are such symbols of disorder that I think the temptation is not so much a seduction as the magnetic abyss of a loss of faith in the prevalence of God's order, of justice and mercy—a loss of hope in Truth and Beauty. So it is very relevant to the contemporary—the terror that the horrors of the world are in the end what will prevail, 'more real' than anything else. The 'after the Holocaust, poetry is impossible' syndrome. St. Anthony resists, not without evident effort—asserting the reality of the ordered world seen at the left of the picture.

Granacci's <u>Stilllife</u> (sometime before 1681) with its symbolism—the lizard and cricket at the bottom, the raffia unwinding on the Chianti bottle, the scale of dull to bright in color of butterflies' wings, the triumphant uprising of the red carnations, the last butterflies red and gold . . .

A small 'non-Italian' yet wonderfully still and brooding Corot in which the architectural element grounds the silvery romance.

Reading <u>Voyage Round My Room</u> in new New Directions edition (refound my French one <u>just</u> before I received it, after <u>years</u>!) The French Sterne. Also <u>Raj</u>, Gita Mehta. And rereading Okamura's <u>Awakening to Prayer.</u>

27 March, 1995

Things I left out of <u>Tesserae</u> (maybe to do some other time?): Bishop Breziando and the monkey muffs. Robert De Niro in the playground. Governor Rockefeller on 34th Street. Langston Hughes at Muriel's. Sonny Rollins at SVA. Haile Selassie at St. George's. 'The Venetian'—and the old man recounting 'Mireille' . . . Arrival at Brunnenberg in that 3-wheeler. Normal McLaren on the beach (Puerto V., or Barra, or Puerto Rico?). Daddy and 'Sixteen Pounds.' Etc! Oh, Paris: the old Russian anarchist with the goats, the non-excursion to Versailles, the Céline-style job, the day with the Spanish anarchists . . .

(Early 1980s)

NYC cop explaining to BBC interviewer: 'Any overt action on the part of this feller and I'm gonna shoot him.' Sports headline in English newspaper: 'An academic exercise fluently accomplished by Middlesex.' A nice comment on U.S. and British language use.

(Around 1958)

Held a black broad-bellied lizard in my hand. It eats flowers (likes dandelions). Have to support tail while holding. Janet may bring a blue-tongued skink home with her soon—it eats meatballs. Also a potto!

The new paint—how it made other things look shabby, but made beautiful objects more themselves.

October 9

The shadows of the lamp in evening sunlight.

The colors of the Indian corn.

Dedication of new PS41. Why do tears always spring to my eyes when I see kids perform their rehearsed bits at some such function? The photo of the N. African workman learning to read—same thing.

The pathos of anyone actually applying themselves to something for which they're liable to be crudely ridiculed while practising. Sense of human courage.

October 16

To the Frick Collection with Mitch. The sharp blue sky and clouds in the El Greco Expulsion from the temple—something of hope . . . The almost tender smile of Christ as he confidently advances. Rembrandt's face, its

*wisdom, its almost-about-to-smile look alongside its severe, judging, well-
knowing look. The life coming from it, the awareness.*

To walk the road in the Theodore Rousseau painting!

January 1959

Wallace Fowlie on Claudel: 'The universe as a text, to be deciphered.'

1959

*Dream: the cowardly Seneschal, the Knight and his lady—they were
arranging for a feast and the Seneschal was comically eager to so arrange
that he had a place of safety and a possible way of escape if there was
any trouble. The Knight or Lord and the Lady knew him of yore and
exchanged mocking glances over his head. She wore a fur-trimmed robe,
14th century style. The wall—the great fireplace—the great door at the far
end. A strong sense that this was not a personal dream but a fragment of
the actual past suspended in time, into which I entered briefly. The
'handles,' so to speak, by which I got in, were the face of the blacksmith in
The 7th Seal, which resembled the Seneschal's, and the title of the
Fernandel film we didn't see, Seneschal the Magnificent. And of course Sir
Kay the Seneschal, who was a coward. Nevertheless, I have the sense that I
was eavesdropping on the psychic image of an actual 14th century
moment.*

May 5th

Brancusi, quoted in article in 'Arts': 'An artist generally has the attitude that he must stop everything and get to work, that work itself is something special, sacred, apart from life. On the contrary, a man should work as he breathes, as he sweeps the floor, easily and naturally, without thinking too much about it.' (i.e., without thinking about the fact that he's doing it.) 'In fact, I can think of no better way of getting to work than drifting into it after sweeping the floor and cleaning up. An artist should always do his own chores.' Also: 'One's salvation is decided within oneself. Those who allow themselves to be drawn into competition are thereby allowing a degeneration of their vital forces.'

May 29

The cat's broad neck and small head.

Enriching the Inner Life

I DON'T RECALL keeping a journal till sometime in my late twenties, but in my teens I did fill a couple of large hard-cover legal ledgers with copied-out excerpts from what I was reading, particularly poems.

At certain periods later on I kept quite voluminous journals, particularly at a time when, under Jungian influence, I was meticulous about recalling and writing down my dreams. Even so, there would be large gaps. And at a certain point I began to feel I was living in order to dream and record my dreams, so I gave up even intermittent regularity and wrote in my journal only when I felt a particular urge to do so. Sometimes, however, I again felt a need for more regular journal-keeping over a period of months. Often, when I'm traveling, my journal or notebook fills up almost exclusively with notes on paintings I've seen, since I visit art museums whenever I can, wherever I go; such notations help me revisualize what I've seen.

When I was doing the Ignatian Spiritual Exercises I kept a separate daily notebook in that connection, while at the same time maintaining irregularly an ordinary journal. But ordinarily, notes on spiritual matters go into the same book as notes on things seen (in nature or art), quotes from current reading, dreams, and often, the first drafts of poems. Unless specially memorable or important to me, any notations of public or private social events, movies or plays, or musical recitals (unless I have something very particular to say about them) and so forth don't usually go into a journal but may get a comment in my engagement book, like 'Wonderful!' or 'Very good evening.' But I do list what I'm currently reading and for this and other reasons I often berate myself for being so irregular in journal-keeping: it would make so much more sense to give daily, or at least weekly, time to such recollection. But though I sometimes miss out a whole series of important inner experiences, I cannot seem to find that time except in spurts.

No one in particular influenced me to keep such notebooks and I cannot recall many published ones that I've read. Rilke's *Letters* were very important to me from the time I was about twenty-one; and at times these are almost like journals—as are Keats' letters, which I first read in my early teens. Coleridge's notebooks, too, and Dorothy Wordsworth. Keeping a journal simply seemed a natural thing to do.

Over many years of teaching young writers I have strongly recommended that they form this habit and I've always specified that a writer's journal must not be a 'dear Diary' full of their youthful angst and self-'psyching-out' nor a 'Had pizza with Joe, Mike and Barbara. Joe is rather cute. Mike was disgusting and only talks about making the team. Got back too late to wash my hair' type of retrospective datebook. Keep those separate, I tell them. A writer's notebook is a way of keeping in touch with your inner life in the midst of the rush of daily preoccupations. Note things seen (or heard) that really grab you—sensory details, concrete experiences. Note down your dreams—they may be more inter-esting and significant than you think. Learn to remember them—it can be learned. Copy out lines or phrases that specially strike you—or if they're long passages, at least note the book and page where you found them, for future reference. If a word haunts you, 'out of nowhere,' or a whole phrase, write it down. Ideas, likewise. But keep in mind that the point of this is not to store up lines and images that may come in handy later. That's not the way good poems get written—they're not patched together from 'effective' scraps saved up for the purpose. No, the value of the notebook is in the way writing such things down deepens our experi-ence of them in that act itself—enriches our inner life, puts us in more intimate touch with ourselves. It may indeed happen later that notebook entries are incorporated in poems—but that is secondary. It doesn't really matter if one never rereads one's 'writer's journal.' Journals are essentially private and personal and so it is not easy for me to find sections I wish to share by publication. However, there a few selections that may be of general interest.

Phillip Lopate

I started self-consciously ... retooling the journal for later use. I was like a squirrel hiding away nuts for an older me who would raid the stash. The fact that I often forgot what I had written there made the occasional tasty morsel all the more pleasing a "find" years later.

Aug. 3 1988

Saw Father for dinner. I was planning to take him to the Film Society members screening of "Married to the Mob," but when I got there he was so sloppily dressed that I decided just to do dinner.

We went across the street to a new Italian restaurant. Since he seemed completely uninterested in asking me about myself, I decided to do a monologue in which I told him every possible thing that was happening to me. No reaction, of course. We switched the subject to the family. In talking about Mother, he said: 1) "I feel that I loved her more than she loved me." Undoubtedly true, I told him, and thought to myself that I had almost always contrived to be in the opposite position, following his example negatively. 2) "She always attracted dykes. She must have done something for that to happen." When the meal ended, he tried to get up but couldn't seem to rise, so I gave him a hand and walked him to the men's room, one flight down. "Why do they always put the men's room where you have to go up or down a flight?" he said. I waited outside the toilet door for 10 minutes. At first I thought maybe he had died there. "Pop, are you all right?" He grunted something, so I knew he was still among the living. "Can I help?" I offered.

"No." Ten more minutes passed. I called through the door again. Finally he came out. "I had an accident," he said. I noticed the tiled floor was smeared with shit. "I made in my pants. I couldn't get them off in time."

"Okay. . . . Let's get outa here." I helped him up the stairs with the idea of leaving quickly, before anyone could see the bathroom floor. It was their problem, I thought; I'll never go back to that restaurant anyway.

As it is, the waitress ran after us to bring my jacket and his hat.

As we were crossing the street, he said, "I'm sorry."

"It's not your fault, Pop. It's old age."

I was already thinking what I would do next: get him undressed and in a shower, and then leave for the later screening. I was in a very calm-patient mode, like the way I used to be with schoolkids. We got upstairs to his room and he sat on the bed and took his pants off, smearing the bedspread with shit in the process. I helped him off with his shirt and took him into the bathroom across the hall. I stood outside the door. Two minutes later, still no sound of water. "Pop, what's the matter?"

"I can't get my socks off."

"Oh, for Christ's sake," I said, sounding impatient with him like my mother. "The socks can get wet—they're dirty too! Just get in the shower!"

I pushed him in. "I can't get the water hot," he said. Now his total helplessness was beginning to get on my nerves. He had turned on the hot water, it just took a minute to warm up. Didn't he know that after all these years? I gave him soap and told him to rinse well and left him in the shower. Turned on the Mets game in his room, so he would have something to watch when he returned, and threw away his soiled underpants. The bedspread I stripped and put on the floor, hoping the attendant would deal with it tomorrow morning.

He came back. One of his legs was still covered with shit. I cleaned it off as best I could with toilet paper. Wiping off his ass and groin wasn't what I'd expected for the evening, but—all in the nature of reality. I said goodbye. I could have stayed longer but I didn't. He could have said "Thank you" but he didn't. Instead he made his usual grunt, probably expressing resentment that I was leaving him.

As I walked outside the building I passed a junkie vomiting against the door of a car. The Night of Bodily Fluids. I was too shaken up to see the movie.

My Writer's Journal

RECENTLY, I embarked on a long, ambitious, difficult piece about my father. As is my habit, I tried to get as far as I could on my own, then started leafing through the journals for any entries in which my father made an appearance. I ended up using, with very slight changes, a few recent items, dealing with my father in a nursing home, such as the one above. These journal entries were intended to be "witnesses," and, as such, they transferred fairly directly from private journal to published book *(Portrait of My Body,* Doubleday, 1996).

I have been keeping writer's journals ever since I was seventeen. They fill more than twenty-five notebooks of all sizes and covers, and every time I've moved I have had to lug around that pile, and find a place for them in my file cabinets or drawers. I never put them on my bookshelves, because I wouldn't want a visitor opening one at random and reading, perhaps, about himself. Recently I went back (painful as that was) to peek at my first "writer's" notebook: at seventeen, I was hardly a writer but was trying on the persona to see if it would fit. At the time I was reading a lot of Nietzsche and Dostoevsky and thinking dark adolescent thoughts. I may have also been influenced by Gide's *Journals,* since he was another of my college models. In any case, I note how quickly I was drawn to the epigrammatic form, which allowed me to see if I had any thoughts by daring me to express them as concisely and analytically as possible. Here are a few typically pretentious entries:

Self-hatred is essential to my writing. Self-hatred and self-love—the game the writer plays with himself.

The unreal feeling that people are doing things for effect, for my entertainment. People pass me and break into laughter at a dramatically opportune moment.

I view all girls as objects, not real human beings. Perhaps I view all people that way. The writer knows people less than others. He builds up an image of a person by painstakingly gathering psychological data and external data. Is this true? Is it only that the writer doesn't know people well, but he knows them more than anyone else? My friend Mitch's distinction between knowing a person and knowing about a person (the latter is tied to existing vicariously rather than living on one's own.) Mitch says:

Knowing another person is feeling another person. (But how? Be more specific.)

Odd how early one's themes are set in place. Particularly in the last entry, I see the naming of a fault, followed by rationalization and self-aggrandizement (it's because I'm a writer), followed by a bald assertion challenging popular opinion (the writer knows people less than others), followed by self-doubt, the citing of a friend's contrary opinion, followed by unease about my capacity to feel. After a while, these abstract probings into my psyche and the impossibility of happiness gave way to more anecdotal entries. There were also many "brainstorms" for novel or film plots which, fortunately, never got further than being jotted down. However dopey or vulgar the plot was, I still had to write it in my journal—if for no other reason than just to get rid of it. I quickly decided that judgment would be suspended while I was writing in my journal: here I did not have to censor myself or appear more enlightened or mature than I felt. As a consequence, I have often appeared more immature in my journal pages than anywhere else. I would complain, settle scores, be "unfair," have the last say. The journals are not an entirely accurate portrayal of myself, overemphasizing as they do my antisocial voice. Here I mutter things I would not dare say aloud. But are they any truer for that?

In the first few years of keeping these journals, I would often vent my feelings. But one day, reading over the journals in sequence, I discovered I was repeating myself, because I didn't have more than five to ten regular emotions. So I began "expressing myself" less and documenting more: I would write down whole discussions after the fact, or note the quirks of a friend's speech patterns, or describe the decor of so-and-so's apartment. This period corresponded with a poetry-writing phase, during which I was trying to force myself to Pay Attention, to Live in the Moment. I was schooling myself in the concrete. For instance, going out with a woman, I would note that she always kept cherry sodas in the refrigerator, partly in the hope that, years from then, when I came to write about her, this detail would jog my memory and bring back other oddities of that experience.

By this time, I knew I was a writer. So I started self-consciously retooling the journal for later use. I was like a squirrel hiding away nuts for an older me who would raid the stash. The fact that I often forgot what I had written there made the occasional tasty morsel all the more pleasing a "find" years later.

In 1968, I went to work for Teachers & Writers Collaborative as a visiting poet, teaching children and adolescents. One of the requirements of the job was that we keep a journal of our classroom experiences. Many of the writers tried to dodge that task by turning in perfunctory, minimal entries. But the poet Ron Padgett and I saw it as a golden opportunity to sort out the jumble and excitement of trying to reach a class full of kids and their teachers. We competed for who could write the longest diary entries. At this point, I was keeping two sets of journals, one for Teachers & Writers and one for myself (concentrating more on my private life). Sometimes it felt ridiculous: I was spending half my life, it seemed, writing about what I had done, instead of going out and living more. Still, I remain grateful for the discipline of keeping pedagogic diaries: they formed the basis of my first prose book, *Being with Children* (1975).

My next prose book was a novel, *Confessions of Summer* (Doubleday, 1979), which had some fictional elements but was more or less based on the woman who kept cherry sodas in her refrigerator. I went back over my writer's journals from those years and pulled out certain nuggets for use, particularly in the chapter called "Journal of Decrystallization." I still thought of myself as half poet, half novelist, when my literary career took a dramatic turn in the late 1970s: I fell in love with the personal essay. Since then, I have been increasingly identified with this form; and indeed, I think of myself today as a personal essayist above everything else. I have also found there to be a more intimate, direct connection between journal-writing and personal essay-writing than any work I had previously done in other genres. A paragraph entry might contain a voice or an insight that was the springboard for a later essay. In a pinch, with a deadline looming, I could even cobble together a personal essay out of several journal entries on the same subject. Both types of writing were nonfiction, often autobiographical, relaxed, conversational, reliant on unfolding thought processes. The difference is that you could get away with the fragment in a journal, while a personal essay had to add up.

I went through a phase when the prose in my writing journals seemed to me perhaps the most characteristic and fresh and honest that I had ever done. Generally, I wrote in my journals at the end of the day, when I was tired—too tired to bullshit, and I just wanted to set down the thought in the most direct manner possible. Certainly I tried out a variety of syntactical and tonal maneuvers in these pages—the writing journal is to the writer what finger exercises are to the pianist—but overall, I opted for the least self-conscious formulation of a thought. Then I began to wonder: What if all my well-wrought book prose were actually *inferior* to the quicksilver jottings in my journals? What if the most original me was only to be found there? I conceived a project of plowing through my journals and excerpting the best parts for a new book. But I did not get very far: I bogged down around the period of my early twenties, when I found I couldn't stand to listen anymore to the callow fellow I was then; and when I tried to jump ahead, I was again put off by a combination of self-disgust and boredom. It seemed these journals were not as densely packed with goodies as I had thought.

So I went back to raiding them in the service of whatever individual pieces I happened to be attempting.

Jaime Manrique

This year, in the fall, I'm going
to live in the woods in
Massachusetts. I've decided to keep
a visual journal, with a video camera.
I'm really eager to start this project. It
will be called "A Year with Melville"
(Melville is my cockatiel).

When I arrived at El Barranco de Loba, I walked about a mile to
the town. An old drunken man, a relation of my mother's (or so he said),
recognized me as "Chole's son." He walked me to my grandmother's house.
She was sitting in the patio, and she looked dishevelled, her feet dirty, her
clothes soiled. She looked very old and thin, and she has no teeth. A couple
of aunts and cousins came to visit me and then, as soon as they were out
of mama Fina's sight, they asked me for "alms." Judith's daughter, a young
woman who looks younger than her years, and María Moreno's daughter,
a 7 year old girl, walked me to El Salto, which is an arm of the river that
runs behind the town. There's a new bridge, and we walked on it. A
gallinazo fed on a dead black dog. The ataruya grew thick on the water.
We were there chatting about this and that when Filomeno, Juana Eparsa's
son, approached us. He's black, African, and he's my cousin. Judith's
daughter (I can't remember her name) told me she can't see at night. She
goes to high school and is in the 10th grade. I asked her if she had plans
to leave the town when she finished school. Sweetly, she said, "How?"
Then, accompanied by my relatives, we walked all over the town: past the
school, the aqueduct, the cemetery. We stopped at a tienda and drank
Coca-Colas. After that, we went by the mayor's house, the health center,
the church. Back at the house, I was served lunch: pork, rice, fried ripe
plantains. I was still full from breakfast but ate a bit. I was terrified to eat
the pork, which seemed fresh but undercooked. After lunch, I rested in a
hammock in the patio. A parrot and parakeet amused me with their antics.
Then my grandmother sat on a chair next to the hammock, and we
chatted. The man I met when I arrived in the town had stopped in front of
a house and said: "They lived here: Don José, Doña Berthal and the kids,
until the eldest son killed a boy and they had to get out of town." Then he
didn't want to talk anymore about it. So I asked my grandmother, and she

told me that my uncle X had killed a boy with a knife. After that, the family had had to leave town in a hurry. . . .

February 21, 1989

2:30 p.m.

. . . . For the past few weeks I've been thinking about starting a new novel. The idea first came to me several months ago, but now I feel closer and closer to understanding the story.

Here it goes:

I/Santiago/Jimmy go back to Barranquilla after an absence of 10 years. During those 10 years Santiago has been living in New York City. He returns to Colombia (the novel is narrated in first person) because his father has just died and left him a small legacy.

. . . Then he goes to visit his step-grandmother and his grandmother up the river. There he visits his cousins. It's during the trip up the river that he learns the story of the murder one of his uncles committed. Also, he learns that his uncle (whom he worshipped in his childhood) has made his money selling acetona *to the mafia to process cocaine.*

. . . This is more or less the plot. Now: where do I want to go with it? What is the story about? Why should I bother writing it? I don't have all the answers to these questions, but I'm going to try to answer them the best way I can.

The novel ("Counting Days") will be about the impossibility of going back home, the political and social situation in Colombia, the betrayal of blood ties for power and greed.

The main character (Santiago) seems to suffer from a certain malaise: He's homosexual and the death of his lover has crushed him; he feels that in a world of greed and competition there is no place for someone who is interested in spiritual growth. He's on a spiritual quest—he searches for a center, for meaning, for a redemption that goes beyond the personal, the selfish, the fulfillment of bourgeois needs and wants.

The story will have a vivid tropical background: the light, the vegetation, the local color. It will have the spectacle of the society as a background (it should be a mythical place—the atmosphere of the land should feel almost allegorical—a Garden of Eden seething with murder and rot).

These are, of course, just random notes. I feel, though, that they give me a story (with an incipient plot, a structure—4 parts, the arrival, the trip up the river, the return to the city, the departure), and themes: we cannot go back home again, money is more important than love or ideals; the land of El Dorado has become a land of death, whose citizens have turned against each other.

Why am I going to write this novel? I'm going to write it because I'm a writer and this must be a God given gift; and because I'm only happy, I'm only self-realized, when I'm involved in a writing project. If I didn't have these stories to create, I think life would be meaningless for me—there wouldn't be enough reasons for me to go on with it.

What I've just written down frightens me but it is the truth . . .

February 24, 1989

. . . Tonight I feel good: I've definitely started a new novel which I've tentatively titled "Counting Days."

October 2, 1993

TOSNOVÁN

I have written very little about Tosnován. Recently, in my poems and my fiction, and even my memoirs, I've begun to explore my mother's family—the only family I know. I remember that during one of my first trips to Tosnován the children of the farm started climbing the trees and screaming like monkeys when they saw us. The next day, I remember approaching one of the farm girls and asking her, "How are you?" Her reply—(I was twelve or thirteen myself) changed forever my perception of reality: "I was born the last time the parrots nested here." This little bit I should be able to incorporate into "Twilight at the Equator" (used to be called "Counting Days"). The next time I go back to that book, I hope I remember this line and retrieve it and incorporate it into that manuscript.

The other character I've not written about is my uncle Lucho. We used to call him Dracula because he slept all day long and only got up at night. Then, he'd leave the house and he'd return at dawn.

Five years ago, when I returned to El Banco, my cousin Manuel tried to explain why Lucho became the way he did: one day my aunt Emilia was coming back to El Banco from her school in Bogotá. The family had gathered for lunch and Lucho asked my grandfather whether he could go in the jeep to pick her up at the airport. Apparently, my grandfather punished Lucho, forbid him to go to the airport, and from that day on Lucho changed. This story is somewhat incomplete; there's something I'm blocking and I would like to see my cousin Manuel once more to ask him for the details. It occurs to me now that I do want to return to El Banco—not necessarily because I will find out any more stories. Now I know that so many secrets were revealed to me the last time I was there because I'm a writer and these people were trying to tell me all these terrible secrets they have been carrying with them all their lives. They wanted to confess to me as a way of expiating the guilt they had carried for most of their lives. They were somehow hoping that I would "deliver" them from their burdens; that I would make public these things as a way of atoning for the past.

For "Twilight at the Equator"
The uncle's monologue about the murder
Juan Jacinto was my best friend. His house was around the corner from ours. He was a year older than me and from the time we started school we were always in the same grade.

His family was very poor—they didn't have land or animals. His father made a living catching fish, turtles, alligators; and his mother made sweets, which Jacinto's sisters sold going from house to house.

My father had a farm and cows so there was plenty of food in our house: milk, butter, cheese, coconuts, mangoes, avocados, bananas. We bought fish from Jacinto's father, and sweets from his mother's kitchen.

People used to say that we looked like brothers. We'd go into the forest to trap birds: <u>mochuelos,</u> troupials, canaries; we loved going swimming in the river and the lagoons; we used to look for gold in the streams that flowed from the Sierra Nevada.

When we reached puberty, we started having crushes on the young girls of El Barranco de Loba. Jacinto and Leila, a neighbor, started making out in the woods. After school, instead of spending time with me, they would go off by themselves. I was hurt. I had lost my best friend. We continued to see each other but not so often. One day, we went swimming in the lagoon behind the town. We were both naked. We didn't have bathing suits back then. We were lying on the sandy beach talking after a long swim when Jacinto began to tell me about Leila and the things they did together and I noticed that his penis got hard. He asked me if I'd like to masturbate together. I had already begun to masturbate a year before, but it had always been a solitary practice. When he started doing it, and I saw his penis get huge, I got an erection. At some point, as I was nearing my climax and he was heaving, I reached for his penis and grabbed it. I don't know why I did that. I was so aroused I couldn't help myself. I had never held another man's penis in my hand. Jacinto ejaculated, and as he was lying there trying to catch his breath, he said to me, "I didn't know you were homosexual." I got very angry and called him a son of a bitch. Then we started fighting, exchanging furious blows. I broke his nose and when I saw him bleeding I grabbed my clothes and ran away. Later, the next day, I was walking down the street bringing water from the well, when I saw Jacinto and two other boys at the corner. As I passed them by, they called out "Where are you going, you little fag?" Another boy started shouting, "<u>Marica, Marica, Mariquita.</u>" I didn't react then. I liked Jacinto.

He had always been my best friend, but when I got to the house and poured the water in the tinaja, *I kept hearing their words ringing in my ears. Then a blind rage exploded in me. My mother was in the kitchen making a fish soup. I went to the kitchen. I was possessed. I saw the long knife my mother used for removing the fish scales and I grabbed it and ran out of the house, as I heard my mother's voice calling, "Where are you going, you crazy boy?" I ran out into the street. It was near noon and the scorching sun almost blinded my eyes. Jacinto was still at the corner with his friends. They just stood there waiting for girls to go by so they could say sweet nothings to them. What happened then happened so quickly that even now (almost 50 years later), I don't understand. I know I approached them running. I know I was surprised when I saw the knife dripping with blood. Then I heard the other boys screaming, calling for help. I found myself on top of Jacinto. He was on his back and I sat on his hips—and once, twice, many times (until we were separated), I stabbed him in the throat.*

Then I got up, the knife dripping blood, went home and locked myself in my bedroom, where I lay in my hammock clutching the knife.

October 6, 1993

. . . . "Twilight at the Equator" (in progress) . . . has evolved through my journal-keeping. Although it is a book written in a very plain style, it has been the most difficult to cough up.

November 4, 1994
10 p.m.

Since I last wrote in this book, I did a major revision of "Twilight." Kenny Fries read it and gave me fabulous suggestions. For two days I revised working long hours. . . . Yesterday I felt the most profound

happiness. I came to my bedroom after playing tennis with Victor Perera,
dropped on my bed, and was overcome with an extraordinary feeling of
accomplishment. It's been 7 years since I began "Twilight at the Equator."
When I started it, I had no idea what I was getting into.

Two Thumbs Up

EVER SINCE MY HIGH SCHOOL English teacher, Pauline Smith, told me that
keeping a journal was essential to a writer, I thought about it; but it
wasn't until Christmas 1980, when my then lover gave me a beautifully
bound notebook, that I decided to start keeping a journal.

At first, I doubted that I would really stick with it. But as the years
have passed, I've become more disciplined about journal-keeping. Sometimes I write every day for weeks or months at a time, sometimes as
many as a couple of months go by before I open my journal.

Journal-keeping is the closest I come to doing automatic, stream-of-
consciousness writing. I don't care how I sound when I'm doing it.
Although now I've been keeping a journal for fifteen years, it never
occurred to me that any of that writing (so raw, so unpremeditated, so
private) would be published in my lifetime.

I haven't read many writer's journals. But one writer's journal that
had a profound impact upon me was Katherine Mansfield's. I read it
when I was in my early twenties, and I was touched by her nakedness,
by the way her soul was stripped bare in those pages. It was then I
realized that a journal can also be a very great work of art and a spiritual
practice.

The excerpts I've contributed to this volume I've culled from the
many entries pertaining to "Twilight at the Equator," a novella I completed last year. Over the seven years I worked on this book (with long
periods of inactivity), I wrote often about my struggles with this work.
The uncle's monologue, as it was written in the journal (during a free

write with my Goddard students), appears in the novella with a few changes. It wasn't until I wrote this monologue that the book finally started coming together in my head and that I understood that character.

This year, in the fall, I'm going to live in the woods in Massachusetts. I've decided to keep a visual journal, with a video camera. I'm really eager to start this project. It will be called "A Year with Melville" (Melville is my cockatiel).

To writers who don't keep a journal, but who have thought about it, I say: Check it out; it might eventually be a helpful and rewarding practice. It's worked for me, it's changed the way I write, and the way I understand my life. I give it two thumbs up.

David Mas Masumoto

But do worms and metaphors belong on the same page? I've written some of my best stories about worms—but I keep a different type of farm journal in addition to my writing journal. No one said I couldn't have more than one.

The Shape of Trees   July 1994

I need help in shaping young trees.
Their young shape stays with you for years.
Mistakes are not corrected,
they plague me like a wound.

Not a scar but a living wound.

That's not quite true.
If they are a wound,
I would cut out the tree and start over.

They plague me with their history.
In their shape I see the past
and the effect on the present
as well as the future.

Young trees need to be trained with tight centers.

Their vase shape needs to be rigid and
much more upright than you'd expect.

The reason why is because over the years, possibly decades,
the weight of the fruit will gradually pull the branches downwards,
stretching the limbs downwards
and opening up the vase.

The tree maintains an upright structure,
not sagging limbs heavy with harvest.

That image is great for poetry and painting
but bad for farming.

Like stretch marks,
sagging limbs do not return to their previous position
after bearing a heavy crop.

They will sag and continue to sag the rest of their life.

I can rope them to tighten the vase
but the wood will never be as strong and sound.

I need to think: structurally sound.

Peaches and Prose: Keeping a Journal

March 8

A journal about keeping a journal. This could be dangerous, venturing into the private world of a writer and exposing a vein. But isn't that what journals are all about? Another danger lies in analyzing journalwriting—the writer becomes too self-conscious, overly critical and the words lose their freedom. For me, that's what keeping a journal is about: thinking freely.

I've read many types of journals. I've tried lots of ways to keep a journal. I don't have a favorite journal writer and some of the best material I've read is about keeping a journal—or as in Joan Didion's case, "On Keeping a Notebook" (from *Slouching to Bethlehem*).

Because I farm, my field work is often woven into my journals. But do records on when the peaches first bloom or the grape shoots peek out at the spring sun or the early signs of worms in my peaches—do they belong in my journal?

Yes and no. They are part of what makes a journal important—a documentation of where you were and what you felt at a specific time and place. But do worms and metaphors belong on the same page? I've written some of my best stories about worms—but I keep a different type of farm journal in addition to my writing journal. No one said I couldn't have more than one.

March 17

Journals capture my ideas, my emotions, the smell of the mowed grasses, the taste of a wildflower lemon stalk, the images from the farmhouse porch on a cool spring morning. My farm journals do the same; they record my feelings about a spring storm on peach blossoms or the fear of invisible diseases growing on my grapes.

Writing and farming share a common tie—neither is done well by using formulas. Good stories are not based on recipes, a juicy peach cannot be grown by following "how to" books. Nor does technology automatically improve my work. Riveting characters and moving themes are not created by word processors and new software; bigger machines and new chemicals do not equate to better produce.

So I write and farm drawing from experiential knowledge. I need to dirty my hands to write about farm work. I need to feel the tightening of stomach muscles when a dark storm approaches in order to understand a sense of helplessness as I bow before nature.

My journals take many forms. Some are scribbled notes I write while on a tractor and then jam into a file folder. Later I'll pull out the pieces of paper like leaves in a family album, each tells a story of a moment in time and the emotions captured in the words and shaky handwriting. I keep another journal of one-page entries with headings that sound like short story titles. Some will grow into manuscripts such as a journal entry entitled "Five Worms" that later became a story about the meaning of finding worms in your peaches and my learning to live with nature.

My journals allow me to integrate my ideas with who I am. My words are not removed from the real and everyday. And that is precisely what I strive for in my stories.

April 8

I do not write in my journal every day, though I am disciplined enough to write daily. On days where the words cease to flow or my thoughts are jumbled, I can return to my journals. They help soothe and calm and provide a forum to "think out" ideas and issues.

My journals often do not make sense. I have a rule: there can be no wrongs in my journals. I misspell words frequently, use wrong verb tenses, create sentence fragments. I can check the facts later, I can verify quotes some other time. Some thoughts ramble, others remain disconnected and out of place, I enjoy nonlinear thinking, jumping from idea to idea without worrying about how they may be connected and coherent.

What's important is to get it out on paper, to commit feelings to words, to write and capture the creative spirit. I seek a freedom of expression, for no one will read these journals verbatim, my words are not intended for writing teachers or editors. No one will ever write in red ink "Who cares?" over my words. I care and that's all that matters.

Journals provide me with the raw materials to work with. I'll write about the frustrations of farm life and the precarious relationship when working with nature. I'll write about screaming at a dark thundercloud as my delicate peaches hang on my trees. Does it help to shout at a storm? Yes, because when I write about it, I realize how silly I must have appeared while doing a farmer's antirain dance. I'll explore the amazing power of the human spirit to rationalize events. If there was no downpour, I'll claim my pleas worked; if it hails, I'll assume nature is merely teaching me a lesson about humility.

In my journals I explore everyday life. The entries allow me access into my thoughts and emotions. I increase my odds at successful writing by making myself available—my journals provide me with opportunity.

April 25

Poetry and prose.
Some of my journal entries are written in the form of single-line entries.
I like to think of these as poetic prose.
Like good poetry,
the single-line format invites reflection.

Here's how it works.
I begin with a single word or phrase.
Then I brainstorm and am soon bulging with thoughts,
I need to get them out before I lose one.
That's when the ease and simplicity of a journal shines.
My writing resembles a random list of ideas.
Some stand independent of each other,
some are clearly connected,
but they all reflect how I think at the moment,
complete with the excitement of creative energy.

Later I'll add more details
Some ideas blossom into longer stories.
Others need to be clarified,
I bundle the thoughts into a package
that I can ponder when I'm out in the fields.
A few remain loners,
I'll wrestle with them
and try to figure out why they were even mentioned.

I seek to establish a series of connections,
thoughts that relate to each other
and give life to one another.
I search for those meaningful connections.

April 30

I often reread my old farm journals, retracing my footsteps over familiar ground while renewing past friendships. The passing of time contributes to a refreshing perspective—I no longer have high ownership of my words and ideas.

Why was I so preoccupied about summer pruning of peaches in '92? Did it really make a difference when I found some worms in my peaches? "Where I was" helps orient me to "where I am now." Journals date me because my memory too easily lies.

Future stories often begin in the passages of my farm journals. An old neighbor drops by and shares his invention for drying grapes into raisins. My nine-year-old daughter drives the tractor by herself—my little girl is now big and strong enough to push down the clutch—a modern-day rite of passage for farm kids. We fertilize a young orchard as a family working together, we all have our jobs as we nourish life for the future. Raw ideas for good stories, like an artist's sketches.

In my journals I show what once happened so I can later reread the passages and learn. The bad writing will reek terribly, I'll be amazed I even wrote such garbage. The good entries will ring with honesty and they will be fun to revisit.

May 4

Why do I keep a journal? Partially for instant gratification. I like seeing my thoughts put into words, I enjoy the sense of accomplishment when I complete a good writing session. Occasionally the entry becomes an instant first draft for a manuscript.

Let me share two examples. First, my story, "Snapshot, 1944," began when I found an old photograph of my uncle's funeral during the relocation of Japanese Americans from their homes during World War II.

The first line in my journal became the first line of the story, "I stare at the silent and still faces, expressions frozen in a snapshot." The story grew directly from my journal as I explored the meaning of this photograph, trying to make sense of a moment in history when my family, because they were Japanese Americans, were uprooted and imprisoned for four years behind barbed wire. The raw emotions of a journal entry provides the underpinning for a story that won a writing award, then appeared in my collection of short stories, *Silent Strength,* and will soon be republished in a "storytelling" anthology.

Second, because I write mostly nonfiction, many passages evolve into essays and may find their way into newspaper op-ed sections. I wrote one particular piece about a wonderful-tasting peach that lacks cosmetic "good looks" and becomes homeless in the marketplace. This was during the middle of a summer harvest; I had lost thousands of dollars and thousands of boxes of these peaches sat unsold in cold storage. My essay, published in the *LA Times,* was based on my journal entry: "The flesh of my peaches is so juicy that it oozes down your chin. The nectar explodes in your mouth. The fragrance enchants your nose, a natural perfume that could never be captured . . ."

This story then took on a life of its own. From journal entry to the *LA Times* to now, a book entitled *Epitaph for a Peach, Four Seasons on My Family Farm.* Good things can happen with our journals.

May 21

Soon my journal-writing will become lean. Farm work takes center stage, 80 acres of vines and trees demand my attention. I am torn by the dilemma, to stay inside and write or to go outside and prepare for the harvests. A writer must do both, no? But like farming, my journals will be here for the next season and if I'm fortunate, for the season after that too.

Postscript: Every family needs a writer, a family journal writer. Who else can document and save family histories? Who else can pass on the voices and characters for the next generation? Stories honor the legacy of a family for an audience of the living and those not yet born.

William Matthews

Some writers keep their journals, or notebooks, the way a cook might tend a good strain of yeast or mother-of-vinegar.

A morally sentimental 1968 rhyme: Nazi/ROTC.

Is it more interesting to distinguish between different levels of evil than between different levels of good, or just easier?

As a boy, I thought "good" was monolithic, and so I remember vividly the first time I heard the phrase "too kind." Who spoke of whom? Where? When? I don't remember. But the monolith began to crumble. Some loose pebbles, some rocks, next boulders, and then an avalanche.

White southern women: "She's too kind."
Urban black boys: "He's bad."

Irony is not a defense against emotion. It's an emotion about the relationship between words and emotion.

But then, emotion is a poor defense against irony. "Only a man with a heart of stone could read the death of Little Nell without laughing." (Oscar Wilde)

German food critic: "The wurst is full of passionate intensity."
Of course it's a dumb joke. Are jokes about being smart? Are smart jokes about being dumb?

Sebastian has asked me to give—to reinvent—one of the traditional blessings for his wedding to Ali.

I who've blessed my marriages with divorce
as a man shoots a broken-legged horse.

An uncouplet.

I get #7, which lists the ten shades of joy. A thrilling phrase, "ten shades of joy," but how dull they turn out to be, striding up the ramp in pairs not to the Ark but to the Love Boat:

> bridegroom and bride
> mirth and exultation
> pleasure and delight
> love and fellowship
> peace and friendship.

The problem of course may lie somewhat in the translation. They make redundant couples, like legal phrases:

> intents and purposes
> will and testament.

Of course marriage and contract law are themselves a couple.

But where's the breathlessness, the giddiness, the risk, the thrill and terror of vow-making? Eclipsed by all those abstract nouns.

Re-invent traditional ceremonies and Who may wind up absent? The deity formerly known as Yahweh.

But here's the recurring problem poets face. The forms bristle with rust. Throw them wholly out and you've asked yourself to start from prose and make a poem. But if you're not suspicious of them and intelligently combative, they'll write your poem not for you, but instead of you.

The purpose of the forms is to raise talk above babble, and the purpose of "talk" is to tether the severities of the forms to the mess of emotional life. It's a two party system, and each party needs a loyal opposition.

Wouldn't it be easy to scrawl a journal entry in which I describe the relationship between "the forms" and "talk" as a mixed marriage, which would suggest why I, a deracinated WASP, will give the seventh blessing at a Jewish wedding?

Yes, as Nixon said, but it would be wrong.

Only a very great writer, Nabokov said in a related context, could resist such a temptation.

Well then, I won't do it.

The forms represent their own history and the "talk" represents this singular instance in the history.

Consigned to the Unconscious

"WHERE DO YOU GET YOUR IDEAS FROM?" a poet gets asked, and all too seldom answers, "From other people." The notion that everything is *fatta in casa* is a widely tolerated fiction, and may be the equivalent in creative life to the genial falsehood that all successful Ph.D. candidates have performed original scholarship.

From books, from other people, from every opportunism I can think of.

A reason to keep a journal is to stumble upon scraps long after one first meets them in their own contexts. It's easier to wonder "Now, what could I make from that?" if one can no longer remember very precisely what someone else had made from it.

And a journal encourages scrappiness. Things needn't be finished, just stored, the way one might "store" a $5 bill in a trouser pocket in the closet for two weeks only to discover it smugly the next time the trousers get worn.

And "idea" is too big a word. It's not scrappy enough. An idea might lead to another, and thence to the exposition of an argument, and from there to the discovery of an intellectual pattern, and thence to an article, which might, of course, be expanded to a book. Next thing you know you've got a specialty, and you're the helpless owner of a career. "Sweet Baby Jesus," you'll be muttering to yourself, "if only I had a really good, small, selective scrap collection."

Some writers keep their journals, or notebooks, the way a cook might tend a good strain of yeast or mother-of-vinegar. Roethke's notebooks, in David Wagoner's beautifully edited version of them, *Straw for the Fire,* were used that way. Apparently he'd weed them each year, throwing out what no longer sparked. A few entries survived a dozen or more such cullings before Roethke put them to some use we can identify from his poems.

Roethke's was not a "scrapbook," with its hope to preserve something of the past, but a collection of scraps that yearn to be changed from their illusory current form into something else, something future. They're not to be kept, but burned. If the hope a writer has for such scraps is that they might be changed, as fire converts matter to energy, we could imagine a kind of negative journal, a blank space into which no scraps are placed for fear that the shape those scraps are now in—or maybe we should say that those scraps *are* their shape?—will prove an obstruction to their conversion. They're deliberately forgot, consigned to the unconscious for their slow, unwatched reformation. They do their work like leafmold on the forest floor.

Then the bright, unmarred sheet of paper, which might otherwise become part of a journal, represents the future's blinding glare of potential.

Elle vous suit partout. One of Byron's seals bore this motto, an incised, one-sentence journal entry. Does it describe a curse? A comfort? Why choose?

Some writers don't need journals because they have wastebaskets.

I thought: "Ten Shades of Joy" will be ten stanzas, of course, of ten lines each. Pentameter, natch. Perhaps each stanza might conclude with a couplet as an instance of knot-tying. "Ten Shades of Joy."

The two lines I thought might become 1/50 of "Ten Shades of Joy" became part of an altogether differently scaled poem than the one I proposed to myself then:

The Bar at The Andover Inn, May 28, 1995

The bride, groom (my son), and their friends gathered
somewhere else to siphon the wedding's last
drops from their tired elders. Over a glass
of Chardonnay I ignored my tattered,
companionable glooms (This took some will:
I've ended three marriages by divorce
as a man shoots his broken-legged horse),
and wished my two sons and their families
something I couldn't have, or keep, myself.
The rueful pluck we take with us to bars
or church, the morbid fellowship of woe—
I'd had my fill of it. I wouldn't mope
through my son's happiness or further fear my own.
Well, what instead? Well, something else.

Kyoko Mori

Sometimes I think that there is a minimum and maximum number of words I can/must write every day. If I am working on a big prose project, I tend not to write so much in the journal—I'm saving up my daily allotment of words for the project. If I'm not, I have to keep writing in the journal to at least attain the minimum daily word requirement.

Tuesday, April 13, 1993; 10 a.m.; on a plane to San Francisco

About forty-five minutes to San Francisco. I am taking this unexpected flight, eventually to end up in Osaka at 3:30 p.m. tomorrow.

I got back from Madison around 3 p.m. on Sunday. Chuck [my husband] said, "Your brother called this morning. He had some bad news."

I said, "What?"

He said, "Your father died this morning."

I started laughing as though this was some sort of a joke. The last time I heard from my father, back in November, he said nothing about being sick. He wrote me a guilt-tripping letter about how he had sold his condo and moved into a rental apartment so that he and Michiko [my stepmother] could go to a nursing home when the time comes, since there's no one to take care of them; he complained about how my brother won't stay in one place for more than a couple of months; he asked me if I ever planned to have kids. I didn't even answer the letter. Only a few days ago, as a matter of fact, I was telling one of my friends about not answering that letter, and when he asked me "You wouldn't write to him just one last time to explain why you can't write to him? You don't want some kind of resolution?" I said, "No. I'm not that much into resolutions—or forgiving or letting go or any of that." As I walked from the living room to the kitchen to use the phone, I thought about that: how there will be no resolution now. I began to feel sorry for myself, in a way. I had just spent the weekend with Michael and Sandy and their two-year-old daughter Ellie. Michael told me that he would as soon lose his career than Ellie. I don't think my father ever felt that way about me or my brother, but still, there must have been a time when even he was happy that we were born. How did things get so screwed up that now, it's thirty-six years later, and I'm sitting in a foreign country feeling no real grief?

I did—and do—feel some sort of pity, of course. I vaguely imagined him dying at some hospital. Would he have wanted to see me? Would he have thought of me and if so, in what ways? He must have known how little my brother and I cared about him, and if he knew he was dying, he might have felt sad or lonely or generally bad. For that, I do feel pity. But it's pity I would feel for any lonely man on a death bed. It has more to do with the situation—this particular situation and the broader one of mortality, what might be called the human condition—than with him as a particular individual or the fact that he is, was, my father.

When I reached my brother by phone, he told me what had happened. Our father died of cancer spreading to his liver (it started with rectal/intestinal cancer, for which he had that surgery in 1990: at the time, he was told that the growth was benign. To the very end, the doctors never told him that he had cancer. Japanese doctors don't tell people that they have cancer, for fear that the patients would then lose heart and die right away). Father had been sick off and on since February and had a couple more operations. Jumpei [my brother] was not at the hospital when Father died; he was working at his retail shop in Karuizawa [a resort town several hours away from the Kobe-Ashiya area, where our father lived]. Then Jumpei told me something that added to my surprise. Our grandfather Mori died in February from a heart attack. My aunt Akiko tried to call me then but had the wrong number and couldn't reach me. Jumpei himself had been in South America and didn't know until two weeks ago, when he returned to Japan.

Hearing all this, I agreed to fly back as soon as possible though I would not be in time for Father's funeral. I would stay with my aunt Akiko and my cousin Kazumi. With two deaths in the family (which leaves Akiko and Kazumi and my stepmother Michiko—three women who have never really worked for a living), I will have some business matters to settle. I need to go there now, not wait till the school year is over in mid May.

Friday, April 16, 1993; Ashiya

Yesterday, at a coffee shop in Osaka with my brother and me, Aunt Akiko somehow started talking about Okiyo-san, my father's long-time lover in Mizushima [an industrial town a few hours from Kobe]. What she told us was a surprise and not a surprise. We have always known about this woman though not consciously, and some details about the story seemed utterly familiar, especially to me.

The woman is married to a sailor, who is always away on ships. In his absence, she lives alone and runs a small bar/restaurant near the Kawasaki office (where our father used to go on business). He had been seeing her since I was in elementary school, before he was seeing Michiko. He did not hide his affair from my mother in any way. In fact, he told all his co-workers to patronize Okiyo-san's restaurant when they were in Mizushima on business. "Give her some business," he would say. "She is almost like family to me." God, how embarrassing this must have been for my mother when these same people came to our house and she had to wait on them. Once, Okiyo-san's younger brother was in a traffic accident and had to be hospitalized. Hiroshi [my father] was at his bedside, taking care of him, and he told his friends, "He's like my brother." I do remember about that time, my mother began to be angry that Hiroshi was so cold and indifferent toward her brothers.

So, after he started seeing Michiko as well, he had two lovers while being married to my mother. When my mother died, Okiyo-san hoped my father would ask her to divorce her husband and marry him, but my father married Michiko instead. He couldn't save face if he were to marry a divorced woman who ran a bar. Upset, Okiyo-san called our house late at night and hung up (I remember that). If Michiko answered the phone, Okiyo-san said she was a ghost (presumably my mother's) and my father had a lover in Mizushima.

My father was seeing Okiyo-san and talking to her on the phone even after he got sick. The first time he was sick, three years ago, Okiyo-san sent him some pajamas she had sewn by hand. Though he was in the hospital, the package was sent to his and Michiko's house. Michiko opened the package, was very upset, and came to see Akiko. She sat in the kitchen weeping. "How dare she send things to our house," Michiko cried. "Especially such a personal item." To Jumpei and me, Akiko said, "What was I supposed to say? I consoled her a little. That's terrible," I said. "My brother is selfish to have a lover like that." But really, I almost wanted to remind her. "What are you crying for?" I wanted to say. "Don't you remember how you were in her position when Takako was Hiroshi's wife? She was my best friend. How can you come to my house and cry about this?"

After Hiroshi got better and went back to work, Okiyo-san kept sending him gifts. But she now sent them to his work address rather than to his house. (Akiko had talked to Hiroshi about how upset Michiko had been. Though he said, "But I had known Okiyo-san for a long time before I even met Michiko. We are all adults," he did ask Okiyo-san not to send him anything at the house.) Almost every year since they had first become lovers, Okiyo-san had sent him boxes of peaches and green grapes because there were many orchards near Mizushima. Now, my father had to even hide these boxes, which she sent to his office. He would bring them to Akiko and Kazumi and said, "I can't bring these home. You two should eat them." He had to come during his lunch break since Michiko drove him to and from work. He came, chauffeured in a company car. I do remember the peaches. Unlike Michiko, my mother had to accept them at home. My mother always insisted that whenever I ate a peach anywhere, I had to be extra careful about washing and peeling them. She said her older sister had died from dysentery (before my mother was even born) and the last thing she ate was an unwashed, unpeeled peach. I don't doubt this was true, but I finally see why washing peaches meant so much to my mother. She never was insistent about washing any other kind of fruit.

Sunday, April 18, 1993; 7:35 p.m.; Ashiya

Another weird day. When I got back from my run, the phone was ringing. My aunt was in the kitchen, so I answered it.

"May I speak to Hiroshi-san's sister?" a woman asked.

"Just a minute." I called my aunt and handed her the receiver. Because something about the woman's question seemed weird, I stuck around, listening. Soon my aunt was saying things like, "Thank you for everything you've done for him in his lifetime." She described the progress of my father's illness: his operations, how he took a sudden turn for the worse in March. Before hanging up, my aunt said, "Please don't take it so very hard. Try to cheer up."

Akiko and I walked back to the kitchen, where Kazumi was arranging some flowers. "That was Okiyo-san," Akiko said.

Kazumi stopped what she was doing and stared at her.

"She was crying a lot," Akiko said. "But here is a big surprise. Hiroshi called her on the Fourth of April."

"You mean, a week before he died?" I asked.

"I was telling Okiyo-san about how he got sicker and sicker in mid and late March. She interrupted me and said she knew. She said he called her on April Fourth, sounding very bad—he was panting, like every word was an effort."

"He was that sick and he still called her?" I asked.

"I guess so. He told her, 'I can't even walk anymore. My legs are swollen. I'm not going to live very long.' At least, that's what she just said. She cried."

"He could scarcely walk but he could still call her? What about my stepmother? Wasn't she around?"

"Your stepmother must have gone out to the store. He took that opportunity to crawl to the phone and called Okiyo-san."

"Actually," I told Akiko, "I knew something was up because the woman called my father by name. She said, 'Hiroshi-san,' not Mori-san, but she didn't refer to you by name. Did she tell you right away who she was?"

"She said her name was Miss Yamada. I wasn't sure. I never knew her last name. So she said, 'I'm the woman from Mizushima,' then she started to cry, so I knew who it was."

Kazumi shook her head and laughed. "She said, 'Hiroshi really liked peaches. So when the peaches are in season again, I'd like to send some. Can I have the address?' I wasn't sure which address she meant, so I said,

'You mean of his new apartment?' 'No, I'd like your address,' she said. Akiko paused and smiled a bit. "You see, Okiyo-san wants to send the peaches to me so I can bring them over to your stepmother's house and put them in front of your father's photograph at the Buddhist altar."

We all three started laughing.

"She doesn't want me to say who they are from, of course."

"So you are going to do it?" I asked.

"Well, I promised, so she would stop crying."

"How would you do it? What would you tell my stepmother?"

"I'd say, 'Someone sent me a lot of fruit, so I brought some.' "

Even as she was saying this, I knew it would never work. My stepmother would suspect who the peaches were from. I also know, though, that my aunt would try to do it. She is a woman of her word.

Like Running

I USE THE JOURNAL mostly as a source book. I want to record what I see, hear, think, etc., so that I can refer to the entries later, when I'm waiting for my poem or prose work to take shape. What I recorded in the above journal entries, for instance, helped me write the poem "Peaches," published in my book *Fallout* (Tia Chucha Press, 1994).

Peaches

Not a year before his death,
my father appeared at his
sister's door on his lunch break,
carrying a box of peaches
sent to his office. "I can't
bring these home," he said. "You
eat them for me." Outside

in the shade of cherries,
the company chauffeur waited,
his white-gloved hands on the black
steering wheel.
                    Today, a woman
calls my aunt and weeps. She
interrupts my aunt's account
of his last days. "I know," she sobs.
"He called four days before
his death, his breathing so
harsh he could scarcely talk."
Soon my aunt is telling her
to cheer up, go on, be happy.
"When the peaches are in season,"
the woman asks, "may I send
you some to bring to his altar?
He loved them so." My aunt gives
the address. What can she
say?
                    When she hangs up, we are
standing in the hallway where
late every night my cousin
arranges her flowers, bending
the stems into clusters of
needles, snipping off excess
leaves or buds, trimming back
thick branches of plums. My
aunt tells me how my stepmother
came to cry in her kitchen
during my father's first bout
of illness, when the peach lady
sent hand-sewn pajamas for
him to their house. "Who are
you to cry," she wanted to
say. "Once you were in her

position, when his first wife
was my best friend."
                    Only,
they were both in her position
for years when my mother made
me wash and peel peaches though
never pears or apples. "My sister
died from dysentery," she said,
"after eating an unwashed
peach." Why did she insist, I
always wondered, this sister
having died long before
my mother's birth.
                    "I told your father,"
my aunt says, "about your stepmother
crying. He said they were all
adults, he'd known the woman
since his first marriage."
Nothing else to do, we shrug,
laugh, almost.
                    In the story of
the Peach Boy, there is an old
man who goes to cut firewood
in the mountains every day,
and an old woman who washes
clothes in the river, where one day,
she finds a giant peach
floating downstream—and inside,
a boy who will grow up to
conquer the island of
goblins and bring back
a treasure hoard. Even
in stories about couples
too old for child-bearing, it
is the woman who finds the peach
and brings it home, as though

the man would have thought merely,
"What a big peach" and gone on
tapping the withered trees with
his axe.
　　　　　　　So in the world after
my father's death, I am
a woman inside a yellow-
pink peach. I am floating down
a stream toward my aunt or my
mother's best friend who took her
hands off the steering wheel of
her car parked during rush
hour to cry when I stepped
into the passenger's seat
after nearly twenty years.
I am floating down the stream
toward their waiting hands
which have washed thousands
of garments. I will burst
out from a fragrant thin
skin, full grown and even now
some woman's daughter.

I plan to look over my entries from the Japan trip, as I prepare for my next project—a creative nonfiction book about returning to Japan after my father's death, which will be a sequel to my first book of nonfiction, *The Dream of Water* (Henry Holt, 1995). Some of the details I observed about the peach lady also helped me write portions of my forthcoming novel, *One Bird* (Henry Holt), in which the main character's father has a mistress.

When I went to Japan in 1993, immediately after my father's death, I was very conscious of the fact that I would end up writing about the experience in more than one form. For that reason (and the jet lag that kept me from sleeping), I was pretty diligent about writing in my journal. For the seven days I was in Japan, I wrote every day, sometimes twice a day. A lot of things were happening all at once; I didn't want to lose any of the details that might become important to me later. I approached these entries as a visual artist might use pencil sketches or snapshots to get to know the subject, before beginning to work on a painting, sculpture, or mixed-media collage. I was doing some preliminary gathering and even tentative shaping of the material.

In a way, the entries from the Japan trip are exceptions. I am not always so certain, as I write in the journal, that the entries will lead to any specific project. Perhaps none of what I record will be "useful" in immediate and direct ways. Writing in a journal, for me, is like collecting beads. If I go to a bead store and see beads that appeal to me because of their color, texture, shape, I will buy them even if I am not sure how I will use them. Periodically, I will look over my bead box to see what I can put together with the beads I have. Once I begin to envision a necklace or bracelet taking shape from some (not all) of the beads, I will have to make another trip to the bead store to buy a few more things to add, to be able to complete the project—and while I'm there, I'll see some things that won't belong in that project, so I will buy those too, and add them to the beads that didn't go into the necklace or bracelet in progress. I collect details in my journal in the same way: sometimes deliberately, other times not, but either way, it's an endless process. Another analogy for the journal has to do with exercise. I write in my journal with some regularity (at least once a week) just as I run regularly (about six times a week). I need to write regularly to stay in good writing shape, in the same way I need to run to keep feeling healthy. Especially when I am not working on any big project, I tend to write more in the journal, just to keep the flow of words going so I don't fall out of practice. Sometimes I think that there is a minimum and maximum number of words I can/must write every day. If I am working on a big prose project, I tend not to write so much in the journal—I'm saving up my daily allotment of words for the project. If I'm not, I have to keep writing in the journal to at least attain the minimum daily word requirement. It's the same thing with exercise. When I was running competitively, I always cut back on my daily runs as the day of the race approached. Now that I am not running competitively, I take numerous easy runs.

I got into the habit of keeping a journal because my maternal grandfather and my mother both kept journals. Though they were not professional or published writers, they were the two people who taught me to appreciate literature, who encouraged me to write. I wanted to emulate what I saw as their discipline. So off and on through my childhood and adolescence, I kept a journal, to record my observations and thoughts, to help me think and feel better. Later, in college, I had a writing teacher—Vince Broderick at Kobe College in Japan—who required his students to keep a writer's journal. If there is a distinction between a journal and a writer's journal (in that the latter is more specifically designed to help the writer write), I would say that I started keeping a writer's journal in Vince's class, since that's where I started thinking of myself consciously as a writer, not just a person thinking various thoughts.

Though I have read some excerpts from the published journals and diaries of various writers (Virginia Woolf, John Cheever, Anaïs Nin, etc.), I have not been much interested in *studying* them at length. I find the short excerpts very interesting, but for long sustained reading, I think the journals are of interest mostly to the writers themselves. Unless it is a writer I feel some special interest in and want to study at length, I would as soon read the resulting novels, poems, etc., instead of the journals. To read the journals in addition to the poetry/fiction would be like examining the preliminary sketches for a painting or listening to a recording of a composer trying out a piece of music in progress. I find a lot of value in such studies, but I'd as soon have that in small and intense doses. I do advise all of my creative writing students to keep a writer's journal, though I do not require it, mostly because I don't have the time to enforce such a requirement. It is hard to recommend exactly what kind of thing each person should write in the journal, though, or how often, how long, etc., since we all work differently. Perhaps the most important thing is to write in the journal with some regularity (once a

week to once a day, depending on need?) but not get unnecessarily obsessive about it (because then, journal-writing eventually becomes a chore
to be dreaded). Journal-writing is a discipline that gives us a good source
book, that helps us keep our words flowing. We should take pleasure in
sitting down to write.

Naomi Shihab Nye

A few times on journeys . . . it seemed the abundance of sensory stimulation around us might make us expire. I wanted no more sounds or sights, no more flavors or fragrances. . . . I stared at single words for rescue. I wrote down single words as clues. Sometimes notebooks are our calm companions, but other times they serve as crucial sounding boards, balance beams, rudders, oars.

From notebooks:

The Length of Red Tape during & after IRS audit, 1987

> *Receipts for meals, every step*
> *taken in the line of duty,*
> *telephone calls, postage,*
> *record, record, record.*
>
> *How desperate*
> *she makes me feel*
> *when she enters with*
> *her little adding machine,*
> *her reams of paper asking,*
> *What did we eat in 1985*
> *that might be deductible?*
> *and the truth is I remember*
> *only one or two meals,*
> *one because I walked*
> *all over Philadelphia*
> *dizzy & pregnant*
> *looking for a sprig of cilantro*
> *and two, the artists in Memphis*
> *who barbecued a fish.*
>
> *Oh yes, and the Maine farmers—*
> *this was while on the job, understand—*
> *who served a bowl of steaming potatoes*
> *at every meal, I promise I went there,*
> *the tires rolled, the car ate gas,*
> *and we came back.*
> *It was a hard year. People died*
> *with loops of red tape*
> *encircling the legs of their beds.*
> *It reeled out of their lives noose-like*
> *into the lives of their neighbors.*

Start now, she says.
If this ever happens again
be ready with your cartons of receipts,
the little teeth of numbers all lined up
gnawing on your dream of a simple life.

Tonight I invoke Thoreau
and his list of monthly expenses.
I weep for his packet of bean seeds,
the handle of his hoe.
I want him to stand by me
in this tedious modern life ribboned by
red sealed by red
with red extending
outwards stickily into
all plans all future days.

Alpine, Texas July 11, 1987

Saved

Once I burned a man's letters
in a metal can
right in front of him.

It comes back to me
in the clear breath of mountains:
his rueful look, the flare of anger
that struck the match.
Nothing we'd planned to happen did;
we have all been saved so many times.

Why I should think of this
years later in such uncluttered air
not wondering what happened to him

or feeling any regret
but thinking instead
how the signs on abandoned motels
west of Langtry Texas

have faded more each year:
EXCELLENT BEDS
just a pale red whisper now

TILE BATHROOMS
ghost of a promise
receding into stucco wall
SLEEP WELL HERE

Jan 30, 88
On airplane San Antonio—Dallas

Sat across from 3 yr old Stephen w/ his grandmother traveling—
a neat little boy in overalls & black tennis shoes—his grandmother
fussed at him for fooling w/the windowshade
Swat—don't touch that! and I kept thinking
Gee I'd be curious too how neatly it slides in & out
he wasn't hurting anything & she took out of his little
suitcase his "favorite toy"—THE CRYING MONKEY—
a handknitted very peculiar toy w/ a plastic contorted face
& large tears coming from eyes & a hat that came off the head
like a hood & she said NO! don't take that hood off
He looks ugly he's so bald & the boy was rocking
his crying monkey while the grandmother told us
his mother died last July & she's been staying w/ him
ever since trying to figure out what to do w/ him
since his daddy's in the service & gone all the time.
"Thank God there's only one child" & it's so hard to find
reliable live-in help & Stephen was grinning at Madison
& me because we liked the crying monkey & he let us hold it

& examine its human-like feet & hands & play w/ it & then
the plump very conservative-looking woman next to me said,
"I'm on my way to Palestine (Texas) to visit my son who's in
prison there" & she said the thing that helped her survive
this experience was knowing that everyone in every prison
had a mother somewhere & the plane was landing the little
Stephen wanted to pull the window shade again & the monkey
was still crying.

Japan—Aug. 1994

Simple Tastes

They laugh at me
because I don't want meat
I don't want fishy aspic
or compote of shrimp

The shrimp have eyes
in their milky disgusting custard
I don't want any raw swimming things
sashimi sushimi sackatackatock
I mostly don't want eel or stinky soup

I want cabbage and noodles fried
They say
You're in Japan!

Go to China
for cabbage

Always Bring a Pencil

There will not be a test.
It does not have to be a no. 2 pencil.

But there will be certain things:
the quiet flush of waves,
singed paper from a child's firecracker,
ripe scent of fish,
smooth ripple of the wind's second name,
which prefer to be written about
in pencil.

It gives them more room
to move around.

Re: The Writer's Journal

AS A CHILD, I was fascinated by my mother's small red leather diary, which I had unearthed from the bottom of her drawer. She had written it when she was eleven and twelve. Although her penmanship was exquisitely and consistently slanted, a talent I did not inherit, she rarely wrote in complete sentences then—"Saw movie. Got new dress." I would have liked to know more. *What color was the dress?* I would beg, during our long, steamy St. Louis summer afternoons as she peeled peaches for cobbler and I lay on the floor thumbing through her early life. "I have no idea!" she'd exclaim. "You think I can remember everything?"

I started keeping my own notebooks because I wanted to remember everything.

My appetite for detail felt voracious. The dog that bit me under the eye—I wanted to remember his smell, in case I ever smelled it coming toward me again. The lavish vine wrapped around Norma Bauer's ga-rage; her mother's deft fingers as she turned a garment under the needle of the whirring sewing machine; our cat Puff, who froze in the snow one winter, whom we tried to thaw out in the oven; the fabulous bloodred stain of a perfectly ripe strawberry on my fingertips; the smell of the earth at Al Mueller's farm. These were my necessities. Let someone else think about futures and goals and professional lives. I would keep track of the ball of dust scuttling under the cabinet. Mark its progress. Vote for its long life.

I have kept so many notebooks that I can't keep track of them anymore. They are not chronological. Their dates and entries jump around from book to book. This doesn't bother me. I have always found it necessary to keep more than one notebook at any given time. Big and little ones both. For a while, I kept various notebooks for different things—dreams went into the odd Scandinavian one with wooden cov-ers, overheard remarks by friends and strangers went into the hand-bound notebook my friend Becky made. Extremely portable notes-on-the-run went into the miniature journals Kim Stafford folds out of typ-ing paper. He makes a cover of heavy stock and sews the binding with a thread. He puts a 1 cent bird stamp on the front. Then you're ready to fly anywhere.

It is heartening how some restaurants have begun distributing "scratch-books" instead of matchbooks—teeny-weeny notebooks with the restaurant's name on the cover. I have also long favored the common gray Jerusalem copybooks used by Arab students in schools—they are pliable, can be bent and stuck into a back pocket or purse. You can pick them up in the Old City stationery stores very cheaply. I like that the place for name and address is on what English speakers would consider the back of the notebooks. Frequently, though I write in English, I use the books from back to front, as an Arabic-speaker would. Strangely, this seems to offer more freedom. If we find ourselves getting tied in knots as we grow up, we need to discover ways to keep loosening them. I have not had particular luck with unlined pages, though many other writers I know have. I keep feeling they are a "thing of the future" for me. One day soon I will wake up and find myself unlined.

When I look back at the passionate, melodramatic notebooks I kept in high school, I feel they are a clear, definitive map of those kooky years. Memory alone offers slim tints and echoes. Notebooks fill in the whole rich body of the story. Some people don't want the body anymore. I certainly don't want to read it very often. But I like to know it's there if I need it.

As a frequent traveler, notebooks help me focus on where I am. They help me retain moments, details, accents, images. Without them, my head would be swirling. A few times on journeys—I remember this happening in India—it seemed the abundance of sensory stimulation around us might make us expire. I wanted no more sounds or sights, no more flavors or fragrances. On these days I dove into my notebooks as a drowning person might struggle up, gasping, onto a shore. I stared at single words for rescue. I wrote down single words as clues. Sometimes notebooks are our calm companions, but other times they serve as crucial sounding boards, balance beams, rudders, oars.

If you trust your notebooks, they will give you what you need when you need it. If you go back to them with curiosity instead of too much judgment—notebooks are definitely a place we should go easy on ourselves. I've heard someone say that notebooks are the kitchen drawers into which we place all the little scraps of things—bits of string, ragged recipes, nails and screws, half-used birthday candles, coupons. *Where is it? Oh, it must be in there. Where else could it be?*

Here is how "Saved," which appears in *Red Suitcase* (BOA Editions, 1994), turned out:

SAVED

Once I burned a man's letters
in a metal can in front of him

a wisp of that smoke returns
in the clear breath of mountains
his rueful look   the flare of anger
that struck the match

nothing we'd planned to happen did
we have all been saved so many times

why I should think of this
years later in such elegant air
not wondering what happened to him
or feeling regret but thinking instead
how the signs on abandoned motels
west of Langtry Texas have faded more
each year

EXCELLENT BEDS
just a pale red whisper now
TILE BATHROOMS
ghost of a promise
receding into stucco wall
SLEEP WELL HERE

Of course, most all my poems were little seeds in notebooks once. I find a phrase planted crookedly over by a margin and recognize it years later. *Imagine! That little scrap began a poem that changed my own life!* Most stories and essays began with dialogue scrawled down in a notebook. They always start with people's voices. I could trace everything back and back . . . but I'm not that organized. Sometimes a notebook will surface that I'd entirely forgotten about—the one written shortly after childbirth, for example, where the handwriting looks as blurred as my brain felt, when the hours blended together like drips of milk on a cloth diaper. I am reminded of the many seasons that go into this rich brew. Would I have remembered that first summer-of-motherhood specialized-brand-of-fear without reading it again? I would not.

I have read as many notebooks by other writers over the years as I could find, for sustenance. Two contrasting experiences: I read the notebooks of David Ignatow (edited by Ralph J. Mills, Jr., The Swallow Press: Chicago, 1973) and felt so warmly invited into the process of his writing that it seemed we might have lived next door to one another for years! I return to his thoughts and ideas, his honest revelations, with intimacy and gratitude.

I read some notebooks of May Sarton and couldn't believe how much she complained about her mail. Think how many letters she could have answered in the same amount of time! Isn't that what William Stafford would have called "a happy problem"?

Stanley Plumly

For many years now I've kept the record of rewrites of my poems. Why I'm not sure. Except that they represent less the record of my failures and more the reassurance of just how the wrong direction got straightened, the wrong language got transformed, how one odd piece of the evidence turned into something, something whole.

Ours is the moment everybody fears—
The journey home to habitual self.
You stood at his tomb

Keats in Burns Country Etcetera

I

For some writers journals are the necessary preparation—even competition—for their stories or poems, like wellsprings to deeper waters. But for me the very idea of the journal is a dissipation of energies better spent on the work itself. Journal-making, for me, is not perfectible. I've admired, in fact, writers who can do the diary of their more-or-less daily inner lives; and feared the danger that were I to try it myself I'd be writing the journal entry instead of the poem. I've always needed to let the well fill up.

Yet there are plenty of poets, like Dickinson, whose poems, poem to poem, read with the intensity of a journal; and others, like Whitman, whose many rewrites seem written toward a form as open as a journal. Coleridge's *Biographia Literaria* is a journal; Keats's letters are journals.

One narcissism may be as useful as another.

For many years now I've kept the record of rewrites of my poems. Why I'm not sure. Except that they represent less the record of my failures and more the reassurance of just how the wrong direction got straightened, the wrong language got transformed, how one odd piece of the evidence turned into something, something whole.

Every poem is the autobiography of the emotion, but finding the story—the form—that will best carry it into the world—that will make it, with luck, its own world—is a process; a process, at the least, of reconciliation.

What you don't want is for the process of rewriting—which is journalism of another kind—to become a trick of mere sufficiency. You don't want the process, like the potential journal, to become an end in itself, a surrogate success. The journal of the rewrites ought to teach us, with a little distance, the difference between what is achievement and what is only the information of a poem.

Here's an example:

//

A.

> *This is the moment everyone fears—*
> *The journey-home to habitual self.*
> *You stood at at his tomb*

B.   Like everybody else Burns died too young.
a year exactly after you were born.
He failed, like most of us, at everything
save one—failed at farming, fathering, failed
~~at~~ drinking, ~~dram by dram~~

> *1 L#*

Scotland seemed to him the hardest place he'd ever
been

> *2 L#*

C.   It wasn't so much that Burns, like the best
died too young   *1 L#*

Fact: that he was alive—
Burns' widow—
quote from the
first sonnet,
then note the
throw-away
sonnet

It isn't so much that Burns, like the best
dies too young, nor that he's buried among
Lowlanders, at the Borders, nor that in
eighteen eighteen Scotland, in spite of the
beauty, is still hard country, nor that
       presbyterian
the Kirk is a ~~sky of black~~ stone over

the Celtic soul, nor that the poverty
of the farmer, which Burns was and was
poorly, is medieval—it isn't these
hostilities so much as the fact of
Burns

It isn't so much that Burns, like the best,
dies young, nor that he's buried among
Lowlanders, at the Borders, nor that in
eighteen eighteen Scotland, in spite of
the beauty, is still hard country, nor that
the Kirk is presbyterian stone
over the soul, nor that the poverty
of the farmer, which Burns was and was
poorly, is medieval, nor even that
                    survives
Burns's widow ~~is alive~~ and haunts
the churchyard—it isn't these hostilities
nor any you can imagine so much
as the fact of Burns alive in failure.

*< only his poems
to compensate
for life*

Tom is alive as well, in Hampstead,
hanging on, younger than both of you will
ever be again. This is your epic
journey to the clouds and to the pillars
under them, mostly a ragtag walk
between towns in consumptive rain against
black
~~cold~~ wind, summer but one hour's paly gleam.
You think the tomb on scale though small
or too large for the spirit of the man,
depending how one judges poetry.
You write two sonnets, the first for Tom
the second for yourself, one at the grave,

(1 more line)

~~The~~ other at the house Burns was born in—

you can't make ~~up up~~ *your* mind, *up* how you feel
or what is true. His Misery is a dead
weight ~~upon the nimbleness of one's quill,~~   *(1 more line)*
you write to Reynolds; ~~From Dumfries to Ayr~~
     All is cold Beauty,

Poems / failure

pain is never done, you write for Tom.
       mortal
For yourself you toast the body/with such

passion ~~honesty~~ no one can tell for sure/whose
       the
~~mortality~~ smiles most among the shades.   *? whose face will smile*
Burns, you fear, is the future, so you throw
your poem away, something you have never
done/before. ~~Burns talked with bitches, drank with~~
~~with blackguards, died with passion.~~   *slumming*
     This is your first taste of whiskey.
O for a beaker full of the warm South.

       In Ayr

D.   It isn't so much that Burns, like the best,
    dies young, nor that he's buried among
    Lowlanders, at the Borders, nor that in
    eighteen eighteen, Scotland, in spite of   *dumfries*
    the beauty, is still hard, country, nor that   *gore*
    the Kirk is presbyterian stone
    over the soul, nor that the poverty
Celtic   of the farmer, which Burns was and was
    poorly, is medieval, nor even that
his   ~~Burns's~~ widow survives and haunts
    the churchyard—it isn't these hostilities
    nor any/you can imagine so much
    as the fact/of Burns alive in failure,
with   only/his(poems) to compensate for death.
~~passion~~

   his few good poems

Tom is alive in Hampstead hanging on,
younger than both of you will ever be

again. Scotland's your epic journey
to the clouds and to͜pillars under *the*
them, yet mostly it's been(a)ragtag walk
between towns in consumptive rain against
black wind, summer but an hour's paly gleam.
You think the tomb on scale though ~~small~~ *hardy not*
~~or too large for~~ the spirit of the man   *large white*
depending ~~how one~~ judges poetry.   *revelant*
You write two͜sonnets on the spot/the first *on the judgement of*
for Tom, the second for yourself, one   *it*
at the grave, the other at the house/Burns
was born in—you can't make up your mind   *English Cottage*

how you feel or what is true. All is cold
Beauty, pain is never done: then you toast
to Burns your own͜mortal body and the   *frail*
thousand days left until you smile among
the shades. This is your first taste of Scotch
~~whiskey~~, your first ~~real~~ taste of the barley-   *true (good) (real)*
bree of fame. Outside the ~~cottage~~͜windows .   *bruised birthplace*
the͜yellow fields are running under   *rape*
the rain-dark clouds ~~off~~ the Irish sea.   *bright (dull) (from)*
Burns worked and walked here, you are thinking,͜   *dun*
and talked with Bitches and drank with Blackguards,   *pled*
the intimate sublime of what he wrote.   *harrow'd had*
You are tiring and by the time you climb
the highest point in Britain you'll be dead.

and Talked and drank

E.   ~~Keats Near Ayr~~

It isn't so much that burns, like the best,
dies young, nor that he's buried among
Lowlanders, at the Borders, nor that in
eighteen eighteen, Scotland, in spite of its
beauty, is still hard-core country, nor that   *dirt*

his passionate poems

the Kirk is presbyterian stone
over the soul, nor that the poverty
of the Celt farmer, which Burns was and was
poorly, is medieval, nor even that
his widow survives and haunts the churchyard—
it isn't these hostilities nor ~~any~~ *those*
you can imagine so much as the fact
of Burns alive in failure, with only
~~his few good poems~~ to compensate for death.

words on paper

Tom is alive in Hampstead hanging on,
younger than both of you will ever be
again. Scotland's your epic journey
to the clouds and to the pillars under
them, yet mostly it's been a ragtag walk
between towns in consumptive rain against
black wind, summer but an hour's paly gleam.

Highland the heart

You think the ~~large white tombs on scale though hardly~~ *cold strange marble*
~~relevant to the spirit~~ of the man *tomb's on scale*
nor ~~the silent judgments of poetry.~~ *the perfect*
You write two cottage sonnets on the spot, *heartbreak nothers*
the first to Tom, the second to yourself, *of his poetry of the*
one at the grave, the other at the house *(half perfect) spirit*
Burns was born in—you can't make your mind up *of the man*

how you feel or what is true. All is cold
Beauty, pain is never done: then you toast
to Burns your own frail mortal body and
the thousand days you ~~have before you smile~~ *You think you might have left*
among the shades. This is your first good taste
of Scotch ~~warm Scotch~~

malt
bree

whiske~~y~~, your first real taste of the barley/*bree*
of fame. Outside the birthplace windows
green
the bright fields run to yellow then to ~~shade~~
~~under the belltower clouds of the Irish Sea.~~ *off*

Burns worked and walked here, you are thinking,
and talked and drank with those he loved and worse
~~the intimate sublime of what he wrote.~~
~~You are failing by the time~~
You are tiring, and by the time you climb
the highest point in Britain you'll be dead.

[handwritten margin, left: soon dark / an intimate — / old-age at / thirty-six]

[handwritten margin, right: This is your first / taste of whiskey, your / first real taste of / the barley-bree of / fame]

F.   KEATS IN BURNS COUNTRY

It isn't so much that Burns, like the best,
dies young, nor that he's buried among
Lowlanders at the Borders, nor that in
eighteen eighteen, Scotland, in spite of its
beauty, is black granite country, nor that
the Kirk is presbyterian stone
over the soul, nor that the poverty
of the dirt farmer, which Burns was and was

poorly, is medieval, nor even that

his widow survives and haunts the churchyard—

it isn't these hostilities nor those
you can imagine so much as the fact
of Burns alive in failure, with only
words on paper to compensate his death.

Tom is alive in Hampstead hanging on,
younger than both of you will ever be
again. Scotland's your epic journey/to the clouds
and to the pillars under
them, yet mostly it's been a ragtag walk
between the towns' consumptive rain and chil-
blain wind, summer but an hour's paly gleam.
You think that Burns' white marble tomb's on scale
though nothing of the spirit of the man

nor the half perfect heartbreak of the poems.
You write two cottage sonnets on the spot,
the first for Tom, the second for yourself,
one at the grave, the other at the house
Burns was born in—you can't make your mind up

how you feel and what is true. All is cold
Beauty, pain is never done: then you toast
to Burns your own frail mortal body
and the thousand days you say you still have left.
This is your first warm taste of whiskey, your
first real taste of the barley-bree of fame.
Outside the birthplace windows the bright fields
run to yellow then to shade then open
north to the bedrock-covering of mountains.
Burns worked and walked here, you are thinking,
and talked with Bitches and drank with Blackguards,
the intimate sublime of what he wrote.
You're failing too and by the time you climb
the snow cloud of Ben Nevis you'll be dead.

III

In the late spring of 1818, exactly a year before the great Keatsian odes, the three Keats brothers are each planning trips "abroad"—journeys that will further fragment their orphan family. George, the second brother, is to marry and emigrate to America, where he intends to make his fortune; Tom, the youngest, is thinking of Italy, where, at eighteen, he hopes to grow wiser and healthier; John, the eldest, is determined to trek, with his friend Charles Brown, two thousand miles through the Lake District and Scotland—"clamber through the clouds"—where he hopes to earn the experience and inspiration for an epic poem.

George, within a year, will end up in backwater Kentucky temporarily bankrupt. Tom, within weeks, will end up in bed, too ill to travel anywhere. And John, already complaining of a chronic sore throat and barely five weeks into an optimistic four-month tour, will catch a boat back to London, exhausted, wasted, ill, and permanently frayed at the edges.

There is something in the dissonance between the "best laid plans of mice and men" aspect of all this and the actuality of what happens that appeals to my sense of how we succeed more often than not in spite of ourselves—how our best plans fail in favor of our real successes.

All three brothers will die of tuberculosis—George in his early forties, Tom at nineteen, and John in his middle twenties. And they will die, befitting the theme of journeys, in different countries. But George will have succeeded, finally, in finding his fortune in the making of a good family. Tom, the fatal brother, will find his future in the deeper resonance of John's poems. John will fail at epics and become the greatest of lyricists.

Each of their stories is really John's.

By the end of June, they are brothers in departure, an emotional fact that has only begun to burden Keats as he heads north from Lancaster with Brown, who must now act the role of a brother. Keats was ever a young man in need of brothers.

Even in the relatively short time Keats travels with Brown he manages to fill his eyes and heart and report the richness of his encounters in long impressionistic letters to Tom, whose health is much worse than anyone suspects, and who will never leave Hampstead. The most fundamental encounter of Keats's five weeks in "mist & crag" country—including later among the clouds of the Scottish Highlands—will be his moments at Robert Burns's burial and birth places, in Dumfries and Ayr respectively.

Keats's identification with the fatalism of Burns's short life is complex, uncanny, and total. He sees in Burns the vulnerability of the struggle of the individual against poverty, convention, and the machinations of poor health (in Burns's case, rheumatic fever, exacerbated by a penchant for Scotch). He sees in Burns the price of poetry, the cost of ambition, when one isn't a lord. And he sees in Burns the reality of personal failure—a mortal body left a thousand days.

His letters to Tom are primarily travel literature; in the sections on Burns, however, Keats warms with whiskey and anxiety:

> His Misery is a dead weight upon the nimbleness of one's quill—I tried to forget it—to drink Toddy without any Care—to write a merry Sonnet—it wont do—he talked with Bitches—he drank with Blackguards, he was miserable—We can see horribly clear in the works of such a man his whole life, as if we were God's spies.

Burns dies at thirty-six, condemned of and by his passion, in a Calvinist world. Keats speculates on the size of Burns's tomb compared to the size of the life—he speculates the meaning of a life's work.

Burns proves a warning come too late. When Brown and Keats leave Burns Country they head straight into the worst of Scottish weather: first the bone-wet chill on the Isle of Mull, then the ice-cold bitterness on the highest point in Britain, Ben Nevis, where the snow and gravel cloud are practically, and constantly, ontological. In some essential way the days spent among these island and mountain isolations will tax Keats's body close to breakage.

By the time he limps home to Hampstead he sees in Tom's wasted condition the destiny he intuited in Burns. In nursing his brother to an easier death he'll commit himself to his own. In the meanwhile he'll write his great work.

IV

In my poem I quote indirectly from the travel letters as well as the poems Keats wrote at both Burns's burial and birth places. His diction against mine speaks for itself.

I suppose through this experience of Keats in the presence of Burns, with all the emotional and biographical baggage attending, I thought to evoke the ways accident and inadvertence control, perhaps transcend, intention and desire; the ways that the situation itself usually takes over in ways we don't recognize.

The changes I make, the rewrites, the editings, they are my journal . . .

David Reich

*t*he disciplines of carefully
seeing and hearing, and
carefully writing what we see and
hear, have become so natural through
repeated practice that we forget
ourselves and the mechanics of our
note-taking and give our attention
over to the person or scene in
question in all its peculiarities.

[In Managua]

Bus driver Efrain w/ Che Guevara T-shirt and Cincinnati Bearcats cap.

Palacio Nacional—blue janitor uniform with machine gun.

Catedral Metropolitana—clock stopped forever at 12:31—Earthquake killed 3 kids next door to Pedro. Grass, litter, faint barn smell, steel rafters, cracked frescoes, crows flying around inside. Dried wreaths. Plants growing out of cracks in marble altar. Empty frames for stained glass, glass pieces scattered.

Park—refreshment stands scattered amid rubble of buildings. Piles of bricks for new construction. Slightly ragged kids w/ milk crate "cars." Jim takes their picture. Kid wearing "<u>pirata</u>" (paper replica of pirate eye patch).

<u>Centro Cultural</u> to be built in ruins of the Gran Hotel—home of <u>chicos plásticos,</u> whores, entertainment of diplomats.

Somoza tanks/trucks wrecked in lot. [Anastasio Somoza was the dictator overthrown by the Sandinistas in the 1979 revolution. His followers were known as *Somocistas.*]

US Embassy—concertina wire.

Disconnected barrios [due to large parts of the city leveled by the earthquake and never rebuilt].

Billboard: <u>Al manejar, la irresponsibilidad puede convertirse en homicidio.</u> [Basically, a safe driving message.]

Packed Mercedes buses.

Soldiers lounging by roadside, unarmed, unclear what they're doing.

Monument to Heroes and Martyrs on precipice where the Guardia [Somoza's National Guard] *used to drop bodies.*

[The Road to Estelí]

Billboard: Usted paga córdobas. Nicaragua paga dólares. Ahorre energía. ["You pay cordobas" (the nearly valueless local currency). "Nicaragua pays dollars. Save energy."]

Pan Am Hwy. Scrub land with a few pigs and cattle lounging by side of road.

Then kids driving herd of half dozen brahma cattle.

More toward Estelí neater brick houses w/ tile roofs, windbreaks of palm and sahuaro.

Sébaco—onion center of Nicaragua. Only soldier since Managua.

Construction everywhere—food processing plant being built—financed by Bulgaria—Tile being laid over tin roof—rice fields. Trucks w/ cement bags. LADA (small Russian cars). Lots of truck traffic. Rice plant (coop?) School girls in uniform. Campesino/ox/plow. [*Campesino* translates roughly as "peasant farmer."]

[Arrival in Estelí]

Estelí—dinner at old woman's house—3 portraits/photos: [Cuban revolutionary fighter] *Camilo Ciefuegos + Lenin + inspirational Jesus like portrait of Che. Also 3 romantic 19th century landscapes.*

Welcoming ceremony at church hall. Welcomed by young leader as people of Walt Whitman who <u>cantó la naturaleza</u> [sang nature] and Martin Luther King. Nicaraguans a people joyous in the middle of war. Computers, laboratories of death, can't change our resolve. The word "foreigner" doesn't exist in Nicaragua.

Family of pigs rooting in ditch.

[More Images, Etc., from Estelí]

15 yr old Antonio (brother-in-law of man dead in ambush) tells me proudly he's signed for draft and will serve in 1986 or earlier if necessary.

Looking for Ann at house of her host family. "Is Ana at home. Is she inside?" "Sí." Then Ann comes in from outside. Desire to keep guests? To give you what you want?

On Sandinista radio—Michael Jackson—Lionel Ritchie—"El ex-Beatlay Paul McCartney"—Madonna—Stevie Wonder—Requests from various barrios—Melachrino-style arrangement of Beatles tunes.

Stay here for rest of life. [This is my shorthand for an incident wherein the father of my host family fixed up a special room for me and another of the volunteer workers and then put his arm around me and smiled at me and said, "Now you have to stay here for the rest of your life"(!)]

Radio news item re: "marginal" barrios of Jinotega whose residents wrote to CDS [the Sandinista neighborhood and block committees] complaining that road was so crappy that taxis can't get in and that they've been complaining about it for years.

Walls [in the small house of my host family]—*various diplomas
(prerevolution confectionery school, family health, director of literacy),
family and baby photos, sentimental Jesus pic. w/ backdrop of stylized
cedars, Jerusalem, DaVinci Last Supper, dogs of various breeds w/ human
clothes and props (glasses, cigar) play pool above primitive oil painting
that from a distance appears to be a rural landscape by a Sunday painter
(fields, trees, a fence, a brick arch at the entrance to a long country drive)
until you notice that slightly to the left of the arch is burning tank
surrounded by dying Somocistas and across road in foreground, 3
Sandinistas w/ guns (1 in beret and hair and 2 in fatigue caps), ceramic
wall plaques of birds. Poster for "La Voz del Campesino" (farmer's radio
program) over a church calendar.*

*Middle-aged bespectacled Juanita w/ huge cross one day and yo voy con la
frente* [pro-Sandinista] *T-shirt next.*

*Pekinese-like dogs. 1st sentence (TONE) = There are a lot of Pekinese dogs
around here, which is somehow an odd breed for a supposedly fanatical
communist country fighting a war vs. bourgeois imperialism. One of the
three in the house where I'm staying bit me on the thumb the other nite, at
which point Carmen rushed me into the kitchen and cut a lime and held it
there as if to draw away a poison.*

*Sandinista radio plays from 6 am to 10 pm: Mexican ranchera and
mariachi #s, Latin romantic and pop #s, an occasional religious #, and a
fair amount of salsa. Also "la música del alma de los negros"* [black soul
music].

*Meet guy in middle of countryside—speaking English—"You're from
Estados? You are good people."* [One of the U.S. volunteer workers
says,] *"Sometimes"—i.e., when we're not causing wars in impoverished
third world countries. Nic. guy shakes head and wags finger: "No no."*

Thought I had met my 1st pro-Contra, but no: "Your govt is bad, your people is good."

Graffiti in front of bookstore <u>"Daniel un soldado del Pueblo/Sergio un intelectual del Pueblo"</u> [Daniel Ortega and the writer Sergio Ramírez were the Nicaraguan president and vice president, respectively. The graffito says, "Daniel a soldier of the People/Sergio an intellectual of the People."]

Dora says she teaches at Catholic school where tuition so expensive only rich kids went. Now kids of all social classes. Though school is under state, 9 of 12 nuns remained, and director is still a nun. 2 hours per week of religion class.

More radio: Mick Jagger, "el conocidísimo Cat Stevens" [the super-famous Cat Stevens (!)]. *Revolution w/out Puritan Soviet joylessness that makes rev. so unappealing to Westerners. Like walk to Masaya—festive.*

Carmen re: attitude of CDS to people who (my words) "don't support the [revolutionary] process." "Impossible that everyone would want to be integrated, and if they don't, they're left alone," she says.

Graffiti across from cathedral: 1) <u>Cristianismo y revolución son iguales</u> [Christianity and revolution are the same] *2) <u>Carismáticos/fariséos/traidores del pueblo</u>* [Charismatics/Pharisees/betrayers of the people].

Aid from Cuba—doctors and teachers. Australia—powdered milk for war orphans. France—wheat!

[Rolando]

Conversation w/ Rolando—middle class store manager. During <u>Somocismo</u> [the Somoza dictatorship] *people living "in the road"—cf. conversation*

with Carmen on US homeless people. Economic effects of Contra War 1)
campesino can't produce 2) young people fighting for 2 years and possibly
killed who might become doctors, engineers, agri specialists needed for
development. But people understand it's not fault of govt.

Rolando's conversation w/ farmer—bean prices up—New breed of beans
" '79" presumably named after year of Sandinista "triumph" [over
Somoza]. Tasty thin beans, tender. During Somoza's time much landholder
land out of production. "I want it for my son," though son may end up
being engineer or other work.

Rolando says Reagan a "maniac"—Hitler, too--->Started World War—But
all people want to live---->Hitler's (and presumably Reagan's) ultimate
defeat.

Q. Differences in your own life (as a result of the revolution)?

A. Health care is free, son of campesino can go to school. . . .

Q. But you are not a campesino.

A. Obviously, but now my children can go to university, a campesino's
children can go to university, a worker's children. This is what is known as
equality.

Proud of govt. Didn't vote in Somoza elections because no one to represent
his interests. All representatives were rich landowners who campesinos had
no access to. Now there are representatives of all groups incl. women,
workers, campesinos, professionals.

"A man will defend his home."

"Revolution like a river—impossible to stop."

"Revolution is not war and combat but changing lives of people. A revolutionary sees injustice and says 'I don't like this, this has to change.' Of course there may be obstacles—as in building a road, there may be trees in the way and you must sweep them aside."

[Chepe, a poet in his late teens or early twenties]

Chepe—Friends waiting for brother. Later found out he'd been taken out by <u>Somocistas</u> *and shot. Chepe's role in revolution---->getting powder, making bombs at age 15.*

[One Last Image]

More kids' toys—wooden tops, old tire detached from toy truck. Kid throwing 50 centavo pieces in the dirt and letting them land and singing.

Notes on Notes

I WRITE MAGAZINE and newspaper feature stories, a genre so traditional it's petrified, like a prehistoric ant preserved in tree sap. So it's probably strange that the main inspiration for my note-taking and journal-writing comes from a couple of eccentric little articles by the highly untraditional novelist Jack Kerouac—author of *The Subterraneans* and other Beat Generation classics. So be it. "Essentials of Spontaneous Prose" and "Belief and Technique in Modern Prose," Kerouac's two articles, counsel writers to be "submissive to everything, open, listening" and to write with the same concentration on a subject and attentiveness to particulars as a visual artist sketching a scene or a bowl of fruit.

Now, this is tricky advice. On the one hand we're being asked to put ourselves in a "semi-trance" (Kerouac's term) and on the other to remain alert for the useful and ideally the resonant detail—what Kerouac calls "that which finds its own form." But in practice it makes sense. It's like

Zen archery, where you learn to hit the target dependably only after the mechanics of the bow and arrow are so natural to you that they're transparent, like breathing. In the "semi-trance" Kerouac is recommending, the disciplines of carefully seeing and hearing, and carefully writing what we see and hear, have become so natural through repeated practice that we forget ourselves and the mechanics of our note-taking and give our attention over to the person or scene in question in all its peculiarities.

But what I like best about Kerouac's method isn't so much this mystical notion of the semi-trance but the common-sense idea, or metaphor, of sketching, of arriving on a scene, as we reporters do, and compulsively taking down any image that might possibly help me tell a story—landscapes, architecture, home and office decor, elevator music, cooking smells, odd bits of apparel, regional pronunciations, facial tics and blemishes. . . . I try to take it all down and weed out what I don't need later.

This said, I must admit that in the entries I selected for this book, I "sketched" as much from memory as from life, often at the end of a day of hard work, and I based them not on formal interviews and close observation, like the writing I make my living at, but on my casual day-to-day experience and conversations in the month I spent as a volunteer construction worker in Estelí, Nicaragua, in 1985, during the so-called Contra War between the country's mildly leftist Sandinista revolutionaries, who controlled the government, and the U.S.-supported counterrevolutionaries ("Contras"). Before I went to Estelí, I had read up on the country and its politics, so that I brought with me some facts and figures that seemed to me to argue for the Sandinistas and against the Contras and the war. But when I returned home and started to write about the country and its predicament, I saw that the best thing I had to offer was not information I had gotten from books but my own sense of the place and people. If I could convey these to a reader, I'd have a better argument than I could make with statistics or history out of a history book.

The article I put together (published in a literary magazine called the *North American Review,* December 1985) relies heavily on notes from my journal, as well as images and incidents I didn't write down but luckily remembered anyway. The article begins with a polished and re-polished version of a journal entry about Pekinese dogs, which, bizarrely, it seemed to me, were the Nicaraguans' pet of choice. Even at the jour-nal-writing stage, I thought the image of the Pekineses (and my own getting bitten by one of them) would make a rousing good opening— first because, by painting myself as the victim of a tiny domestic animal, I hoped to show my readers I could take a joke, and thus to gain a little of their goodwill at the outset, something a writer should never underes-timate the value of; also because the image was so darned *resonant* (a word I used above), suggesting the grotesque irony of a nation full of owners of miniature, upper-middle-class-identified pets being attacked— rhetorically and with bombs and bullets—as dangerous subversives by the truly dangerous Ronald Reagan and his murderous lieutenants (and lieutenant colonels).

For those who would like to compare finished prose with the journal entry it was based on (and get a hint of how much of the work of writing involves figuring out, through much trial and error, how sen-tences and paragraphs fit together), here is the passage on the Pekineses from the published article:

> The most popular dog here is the Pekinese, which strikes me as an odd choice for a country full of Marxist outlaws, bent on destroy-ing our way of life. My own house has no less than three of the Pekes, and one of them bit my thumb last night, though luckily his teeth didn't break the skin. But Carmen saw the whole thing (all I was doing was trying to pet the little monster) and rushed me to the kitchen and cut a lime, which she held against my thumb as if to draw off a poison. Carmen is the same one who irons my socks and underwear with her 1930's vintage iron when I'm off at the construction site and can't do anything about it.

Again for comparison purposes, here is a passage from the published article about my conversation with the businessman Rolando, which is based on another of the journal entries in this book:

"What is the effect if the mercenaries come out here and burn some crops and kill some *campesinos?* To begin with, the people leave the land and nothing is produced. In a country that depends on agriculture, this is a disaster. If nothing is produced, then where do we get the foreign exchange we need to fund development? In the second place, our youth have to join the army and fight for two years and possibly die instead of training to be doctors, engineers, agronomists, which we also need for development. As if this were not enough, the government is forced to put its money into arms instead of schools or medicine or housing. So the war creates hardship and suffering, but the people understand that is isn't the fault of the government, and they're ready to do whatever is needed. Reagan is a madman, an addict of power, but Hitler was a madman also, and the people of the world defeated him. People want to *live,* and this is a desire you cannot crush."

After gathering some mangoes for Rolando's wife, we start back down the covered path. "I talk about fighting, our willingness to fight, but please don't confuse revolution with war. Revolution means changing the lives of the people. A revolutionary sees injustice and says, 'I don't like this, this has to change.' Of course, there may be obstacles. When you want to build a road, there may be trees in the way, and then you must sweep the trees aside."

At the end of the path, we stand in the house of one of the tenant farmers. Rustic wood siding with the bark still on it In the front room a dirt floor, some woven hammocks, the inevitable holy pictures. Rolando and some farmers talk and smoke. Chickens run around the floor, under our chairs and between our feet, until a small girl in a long white dress chases them off with a heavy twig broom. A woman brings in coffee, and a middle-aged man in a baseball cap discusses the hike in the price of beans, which he seems extremely happy with. The conversation turns to the city of Masaya, where recently the government, after weeks of demonstrations and demands by landless campesinos, redistributed some large plots of idle land. Everybody in the room agrees it was a good decision. Rolando: "How are we supposed to feed ourselves? So much of the land has been out of production. A rich man will say,

'I am saving this farm for my son to work,' and then the son will
go off and become an engineer or lawyer."

A few more explanatory notes: Most of the wreckage depicted in
the Managua journal entries resulted not from the war but from an
earthquake that leveled about a quarter of the city toward the end of the
1970s. In addition to the Pekineses and the Rolando dialogue, the background material on the Catholic school (which I eventually was to visit
and wrote about later from memory) as well as the short entries on
political graffiti and on Nicaraguan radio programming found its way
into the finished article, again in somewhat more careful prose. Many of
the notes I took reflect the eclecticism (including heavy Top-40 and
Hollywood components) of Nicaraguan culture, people's commitment to
the revolution, and what I heard one Nicaraguan call their joyousness in
the midst of war. Like the little scene with the Pekineses, a lot of what I
took down responded to the relentless, moronic drumbeat of anti-Nica-
raguan propaganda in the Reagan-era U.S. media.

Lisa Shea

The journal allows me to bring ideas that are submerged to the surface and address them in a formal, expressive way. It is a quarry for everything else I write—fiction, nonfiction, and poetry—and it is a shelter from those other works, no less from the world.

March 4, 1995

When I came across the word *lovage* in the newspaper this morning, in an article on English herbs, I thought of two other words—*love* and *age*—and right away I knew I wanted to write about these words, to put down something of their meaning, to see what I have learned from them, taken together and apart, in the eight months since my second marriage ended.

I want to know where I am with love, and with age, and what is the proper fit of my heart, and how I will go on out of that need, out of all the knowing that I do not yet know.

Love first. Because it is harder, more ineffable, bigger, dumber, more wondrous, harder, truer, falser, faster, slower, not at all, harder, softer, softer, softer; it is unreliable, less and more, and never enough and baroque and italianate and South Brooklyn and Northampton and Washington and all in the mind and in the heart and especially in the groin.

Love is barbarous and cruel, chivalrous, utterly civilized, capable of killing you and you it. Love is backward, forward and I don't have to tell you it is upside-down. It is sincere, a sham, shamanistic, solipsistic, scruffulous and smart, stupid and shocking and still-born and somnolent and sublime.

Love is a lie. It is pure truth. It is a sickness, and in perfect health, till death do us part, partake, take apart. It is a small green park, a moat, a chimney, a purple rock. Love lies there, seducing you with its gorgeous hair and eyes, its muscled back.

Age. The thing we wear, our first skin, and into it and out of it we shrink and expand, elongate and contract, shrivel and stretch. Age carries us on its back, as we carry our children, and they us. It is newborn and unborn and reborn. It is the color of nails and eyelids and teeth, of the planet Saturn, of anything homemade, of wariness and pleasure and beat-up hope.

Age bears down as it flies up, coming round like sniper's fire and feathers, like olives and old underwear, touching our ear lobes, our ready loins. *Age takes us and gives us back, always different, always the same. We can't walk away from it or toward it but only with it, as it stays and stays, making us real, forcing us with its brilliant, bullying, buffoonish ways to be who we are, and only that, thank God and Goddammit.*

So there are love and age, and how they separate and combine, mysterious herbs in a strange garden, the worlds of these words dehiscent as I read in the paper of lovage and borage and fire and frost, as the days accumulate away from an ending that was large and long, full of love's terrible labor, the gorgeous, grotesque garden of our making and unmaking.

A Repository of Secrets and Experiences

I BEGAN KEEPING a journal in the eighth grade, as a record of my preadolescent pains and fixations and, especially, of increasingly sexual and subversive thoughts. I have continued to keep a journal, with some lapses, since that time.

My journal-writing has served primarily as a repository of secrets and experiences, a place where observations and opinions, feelings and facts intersect and entwine. I have used the journal to record daydreams and nightmares, wishes, fantasies, cruelties and conundrums, to relax and to scrutinize. It is where I tell the truth, and the place where I fashion lies.

One of the many uses of the journal has been as a companion, a silent listener, an "other" to whom I can reveal myself without constraint. As a child, growing up Catholic, I went every week to confession. I think the habit of journal-writing is, for me, connected to this early ritual act.

The entry I chose is essay-like but unrevised, and is one kind of writing that shows up in my journal. In this case, the excerpt is a meditation on love and age in the wake of my marriage having ended eight months earlier. The journal allows me to bring ideas that are submerged to the surface and address them in a formal, expressive way. It is a quarry for everything else I write—fiction, nonfiction, and poetry—and it is a shelter from those other works, no less from the world.

I have read and been influenced by the diaries of Virginia Woolf, by F. Scott Fitzgerald's *The Crack-Up,* by Anne Frank, the Brontës, and Jim Carroll, among others. The published letters and occasional writings of some authors have a journal-like quality to them: Flannery O'Connor, John Cheever, James Joyce, Simone Weil, Samuel Beckett. One of the pleasures of reading other writers' more personal works is that they reveal the writer's habits of mind, allowing the reader a window onto the writer's less guarded—or more guarded—thoughts. I am voyeuristic in my own thinking, and so journals and letters are very appealing in that sense.

Keeping a journal is a form of mental and emotional exercise. It helps keep the mind limber and the soul supple, the better to get at the root of your own curiosities and obsessions as a writer.

A year ago, I wrote an essay for a magazine about my life-long reluctance to smile; how smiling felt unnatural to me, forced, the facial equivalent of a push-up bra. Some time earlier, I had made notes, or observations, on my habit of not smiling, in that rather free-associative way that marks much of my journal-writing. When I began in earnest to work on the essay, I went back to the notes and used what I had written down as a guide into the published piece. I think, more importantly, that the journal gave me a kind of courage to even write on such a subject, because they were made privately, without deliberation, without self-consciousness, without the expectation of being worked into something formal and subject to scrutiny.

If you do not know what engages you, deeply and unreservedly, how will you ever write deeply and unreservedly, making every mistake, taking every risk, to tell the one true story, and the next one after that?

Kim R. Stafford

Because the language is alive, moving and trembling like a river around me, that twinkle is always there, beckoning daily for my listening. Collecting from this abundance and recording what I hear in a pocket notebook makes life a random richness.

Some random lines from the book in my pocket:

—a crow listens to its name in all languages
   —"Why I came to Vladivostok? To see the sunrise in the east
      water."
—rain and river
—dream: "cold hands, warm heart, dark window"
—essay: "Greensleeves," the language of courtesy through
      centuries, syllables
—a midsummer night's dream for Oregon
—what is the structural or aesthetic principle common to Oregon
      native plants?
—could you feel the raindrops so completely you would polish
      them?
—how to teach a class: laughter, then tears, then anything we
      want
—a student reminds me I said once: Why defer the pleasures of
      preparing to die—prepare by doing the things that lie
      before us?
—I will put down my wine & be drunk on sorrow.
—a great tree in a gentle rain—one leaf touched here, one there
      (how the mind thinks in tranquility)
—Patrix the male cradle of becoming through mind alone
—Freud's patient afraid her personality would be dispersed if
      anyone had her signature
—some people will be at the christening but not at the funeral
—we could have been given thirty years of unmitigated light
—dream: "ad-verse birth" (commercialization of childhood and
      poetry through advertising)
—dispersed harmony, close harmony, figured harmony (one voice
      moving, one still)
—forgetful grandmother asks her grand-daughter "Did I have a
      husband?" And the child tells her again the story of her
      life.

Heart Pocket Book

WHEN I WATCH a great beech tree in a gentle rain, one leaf twitches alone, then another leaf swivels in the great stillness, then another. Looking up from inside the green dome, I begin to learn how my own mind works. One thread of thought wakens, then another, and far away another. There is great reach between glimmerings. How do they find each other? How do they gather, and recognize their kinship, these ideas? They find each other during those stretches of writing time that come to me, when I can sit still long enough to invite the full spectrum of the possible. And what about most of the time, in the daily rush? My writing would be doomed if the act of writing were limited to long stretches of solitude. But this good luck comes to me also in sweet morsels of tranquility lasting only a few seconds. My life of writing is rooted in meditative rain, not great rivers. The whole world will co-author my story, gradually, as long as I can read the language of the random fragment.

There is a kind of figured harmony in life, when the bass voice of the subconscious is joined by the moving trill of sensation. This means all coherence in my writing begins in the little notebook I carry in my shirt pocket. Because the book and pen are always there, and because my memory is weak, I take dozens of moments each day to jot phrases from the flow of life. I take down a conversation overheard, a sweep of fragrance, an idea that brims up. During a faculty meeting, I take dictation from my daydreaming mind to catch a few quick connections in a story I started last week. While I'm on the phone, I hear myself reporting a remark by a student that will not leave me, and flip open my book with one hand to remember it. At dinner, it comes to me I have been trying all day to record a dream. I put down my glass, take out the book, and get the key phrase stored for later. And sometimes, just before sleep, as the busy buzz of daylight loosens its grip on my mind, I heave my body upright, turn on the lamp, and pour a few hazy words onto the little page. Coherence begins in randomness. Memory begins with releasing my attention from the official task at hand. The palm-sized book folded open is where every piece of writing has its birth. Some small twinkle in the language around me makes me raise my head toward the east and find first light. Because the language is alive, moving and trembling like a river around me, that twinkle is always there, beckoning daily for my listening. Collecting from this abundance and recording what I hear in a pocket notebook makes life a random richness. The intrinsic electricity I feel in this collection results from the diversity of the fragments and their longing to enter into conversation with each other.

At the feast, all flavors yearn to join. When I really sit down to write, I do not start with an empty page. Instead, I sip from the many flavors clustered here in the little book. Or I comb through a half-dozen notebooks for some constellation of points that might collectively inhabit a story, an essay, a speech. The matrix or cradle of my experience in writing is thus the constellation of gifts from the world. I would have to invent the word "patrix" to identify invented wisdom that might come from mind alone. Mind alone would spin too weak a thread for me.

Perhaps because of my habit of random hospitality in the notebook, my finished pieces tend to develop some kind of honeycomb structure. My novel consists of fifty interconnected monologues: "I will put down my wine and be drunk on sorrow, sorrow of a vintage rare . . ." I call my essay collection, "Eight American Journeys," eight cells for collecting small jewels from the world: "A crow passing through Europe will hear its name in many languages, most of them harsh. . . ." Poems often begin with a line from the notebook that has heartbeat in it, a particular rhythm and warmth that wants to stay small: "Did I have a husband? / Where have you taken my rings? . . ." And when I am asked to speak to a charitable foundation's meeting, I decide to begin with a phrase from my notebook—"a midsummer night's dream for Oregon"—and follow with a series of compact local discoveries which have appeared recently in my notebooks: "It's all rain for the river now. . . ."

What if I want to write a long piece structured by a single, evolving idea, a formal piece of exposition? I did that once, a 316-page dissertation designed to fit a schema not native to my daily experience. The experiment earned me a degree, but did not feel like honesty. As my advisor put it, "This may be a block of the most turgid prose ever penned." And I believe it was. It was dense, an unwavering pursuit of proof. I heated rooms with my concentration. And during that period I survived by pushing aside a volume of medieval criticism to jot stray lyric impulses on the 3×5 bibliography cards in my pocket, which then became folded sheets of typing paper as I neared the end, and later evolved into the little books I now sew together half a dozen at a time.

My high school English teacher invited us to begin keeping journals, but after a decade in that habit, I found them bulky and ostentatious. Working among others, I like something more the size of a grocery list. I like smuggling stray thoughts into daily office work. There is treasure there. If anyone has influenced my practice, it may be Dorothy Wordsworth, whose *Alfoxden* and other journals show the power of detailed, external observations to convey interior experience.

It struck me during a faculty meeting recently that we might have been given thirty or forty years of unmitigated light. Instead, if we are lucky, we are given seventy or eighty years of daylight punctuated by nights, years of satisfaction punctuated by surprise and grief—or the other way around. We live a sequence of discrete and compact sensations threaded by time into a longer curve of experience.

My father was fond of quoting from Nietzsche, as I remember it, "In our time of uncertainty, all sustained discourse is hypocrisy." Maybe my father liked that little manifesto because he had four children who made it difficult to enter the long trance of writing sustained discourse. He wrote poems before first light, and threaded them together into collections. I write sequences of short meditations and lyric stories pieced into quiltlike essays and fictional works. And the artesian source of it all is this trove of fragments in the tiny book I carry. If the house catches fire, it's already in my pocket.

Ilan Stavans

I want to think that corresponding with old friends and keeping a personal journal are similar activities, only differentiated by a degree of deep honesty. One's own voice, chaotic, unobstructed by artificial mannerisms, comes out pure and clear in a letter, but it has an even purer quality in a journal kept for nobody but the self—at least for the time being.

August 2 [1994:] Damn! A phone call from Cass. Has decided to postpone publication of The Hispanic Condition *until April of next year. Why is this book's appearance making me so anxious? It's certainly not my debut (even in the English language); far from it. Whenever I get my phone messages, Cass' voice makes me nervous. Well, what can I do? I guess I'll have to wait a few more months.*

In a few years I should probably expand the book. I've been rereading the proofs. It's insightful, lyrical, it has pathos—but I'm sure some of the ideas will take a different shape in my mind in the next decade or so. And what will the reaction be? I don't know. The literary establishment in this country is not only capricious but frankly antiHispanic. Its Eurocentrism makes it approach anything that comes from south of the Rio Grande either as deliciously exotic or as below the standard and thus not worthy of attention. Add the fact of my being Jewish, which places me in a strange position—a room of my own. Who remembers Pedro Henríquez Ureña in the U.S., in spite of the fact that he delivered the Charles Eliot Norton lectures at Harvard and was as prestigious as any Latin American intellectual can be? Nobody. Today the attention, if any, goes to Octavio Paz. . . .

August 13: . . . Scheduled lectures in Denver, San Antonio, New Hampshire, and Durham in the next few months. Have to find time to write. Alison will hate me for stealing my sleep hours, but do I have a choice? Week in Maine.

My beloved Josh brings me down to earth. While I sneak out at night, just as he falls asleep, and walk to the office, I cherish the moments spent with him in the afternoon. Perhaps cherish is the wrong word, I don't know. I guess what I mean is, without them I would probably lose my mind.

Funny how people perceive me as eternally relaxed, well-centered, bla bla bla . . . But inside I live like a caged beast—furious, impatient, sarcastic.

I've been reading Fernando Ortíz's Cuban Counterpoint: Tobacco and

Sugar, as well as other works of ethnography and anthropology. Purpose: selecting entries for the Oxford book of Latin American essays. Best stuff is still by José Martí, Borges, Paz, and Julio Cortázar. (Wouldn't be a bad idea to write something in the spirit of <u>Eminent Victorians</u> about twentieth-century Latin Americans.) Martí's piece about the Charleston earthquake is simply superb. . . .

Talked to Art Winslow at the <u>Nation.</u> He returned to my piece on Ricardo Piglia and wants a review on Julia Alvarez's new novel. Will talk about it in detail. Good old Art!

Thinking about a piece on Cantinflas for Skip Gates' <u>Transition.</u> Should write a synopsis and talk to Mike Vazquez.

Excellent review of <u>Tropical Synagogues.</u> Just wished another publisher had brought out the book. It lacks visibility!

August 19: More relaxed. Had lunch with Cass in New York City a few days ago. Couldn't stand him at first, but then things got better after a chat. Talked about future projects. He obviously trusts me and is betting on my marketability.

Tenure case on right track. Some external readers sent me a version of their evaluation. I was flattered! One called me "a dynamic, original mind ready to change the way America perceives Hispanics," and another referred to me as a new Edmund Wilson. Supposedly I should not read these letters, but hey, they sent them to me!

September 7: Had lunch at Pinoccio's with Jules Chametzky, who's on the faculty at University of Massachusetts. I profoundly admire the man. For me he personifies a Jewish wise man. His knowledge of American Jewish letters is an insatiable well. We talked about writers in the American city. He and his wife Ann had us for dinner a while ago and I had a wonderful time. (The chicken he made was marvelous, from an Italian recipe book.) Somehow, Jules' presence in town makes me feel secure. Even when I don't see him for several months, the knowledge that he's there somewhere, nearby, is quite comforting.

Being Jewish has become essential to my view of literature and the world. Every piece of fiction I envision deals with the subject, and I've come to understand translation and the act of writing as a struggle to insert myself in the chain of Jewish generations. But Amherst is far from an ad hoc environment. Too WASPy! I fear for Josh. I'm not religious, and neither is Alison, so will he end up marrying a non-Jew? My heart would bleed. . . . Curiously, Amherst does remind me of Mexico when it comes to being a Jew in these latitudes: once again and in spite of the considerable number of Jews in the region (some of them orthodox), I'm a minority and the environment sees us as black sheep—bizarre, ghost-like. To be honest, I often wake up hating this place. Was it the right choice to abandon New York and move into this small college town? Many advantages are given to us, no doubt, but I don't know. The future does, of course. Will I regret it someday? Yeah, somehow . . .

Corrected proofs of Cuentistas Judíos, an anthology of international Jewish stories that Editorial Porrua will bring out by year's end in Mexico. Its introductory essay, about memory and literature, makes me proud. I polished a few paragraphs and it flows with ease. That's how I should write non-fiction—in a direct tone, honest, very personal. (Will I ever accomplish the same in English? Yuck!)

Would like to teach a course on Jewish short stories. Students at Amherst College would love it, I'm sure.

September 8: Tenure case proceeding with ease. (Sometimes I think I should have made it part of my contract to come with tenure, but I wanted to give the institution time to know me.) Some two dozen outside letters are in. (Why so many, others ask; but I don't know.) People want me to be nervous, but I'm not; I have nothing to fear. Decision ready in early December.

Sent a couple of short stories out to quarterlies. Waiting for response.

Rereading Pablo Neruda's Memoirs . . . and Danilo Kiš' A Tomb for Boris Davidovich. Kiš died so young—the Kiš of death.

Liz Fowler can't sell my collection of stories and novellas. Keeps *sending me flattering letters from editors at Farrar, Straus & Giroux, Harcourt Brace, St. Martin's, and so on . . . "Stavans is original and insightful," "a meticulous craftsman," "his stories are genuinely memorable"; yeah, yeah, but nobody wants to buy the book because they don't think they will know how to market it. Or because delicate tastes don't make for a huge readership. Come on! It's bullshit—pure and bottled shit! If New York houses cannot be courageous, if they don't have the knowledge, then they can't be serious about the trade. And of course it's hard not to be disappointed and depressed with so many elegant rejections of my fiction. Being a young Latin American writer is tough, and even more so in A*M*E*R*I*C*A.*

As for the biography of Gabriel García Márquez I want to write, Liz has tons of interest. Together with Palmer & Dodge in Boston, she's orchestrating an auction. García Márquez, of course, means money—lots and lots. But I'm not sure; something about the project doesn't feel right. It can be a great book of course, but García Márquez is alive and that, ironically, is a terrible handicap for any biographer. He will want to control me! He'll want to dictate his own biography, the way Octavio Paz has <u>utilized</u> Enrico Mario Santí as marionette to shape his own intellectual biography, which Harvard contracted several years ago. (Paz is such a tyrant!). I would hate that—hate it till death! Have to remain independent.

Independence of mind is everything; the rest is just chatter.

September 9: A short dream, which I've had some four or five times all together in the last few years. I am alone in a frozen, crystallized forest. (The scene reminds me of a long, first-rate Russian film I saw decades ago, <u>Siberiad;</u> Who directed it? Konchalovski?) The air is stiff and I'm terribly cold. I notice water is covering my feet. I look up—the trees are bare. Shouldn't it be better to fly? I wonder. I climb a tree and, defying the laws of gravity, begin jumping at the tip of my toes on top of the forest. How can it be? I ask. I wake up after that but the moment I leave the bed, I have a peculiar sensation on the plants of my feet: I'm walking on top of a forest.

Let a psychoanalyst interpret it. Their brains are full of categories and are paid to say nonsense about one's imaginary life!

Talked to Marjorie Agosin; called from Wellesley. She asked me for a blurb to a memoir she wrote on growing up Jewish in Chile. Also suggested that I might want to show my stories to Dana Asbury at the University of New Mexico Press. I should, especially now that I've taken the collection away from Liz. I have bad luck with agents; she never sold it. And yet, I don't fully blame her. Selling fiction in the United States is like preparing oneself to be executed by a firing squad: you're an important voice, but you're always guilty of not having turned into Hemingway, Carver or some other classic—and hence, should die. It's obviously worse when you come from elsewhere in the linguistic stratosphere and English is your second or your third language. The consensus: too bad you're not one of us! Of course you'll be perceived as exotic, but exoticism isn't a ticket to success, especially after García Márquez has managed to monopolize all of it in the last couple of decades. The university presses have come to play a crucial role in disseminating important though non-mainstream writers. You never get the exposure of a New York house, but again, the dialogue with the reader is established. Literature in this country is equated with money: if it doesn't sell, it ain't worth.

A*M*E*R*I*C*A. I can't but think of <u>West Side Story</u>'s song about Puerto Ricans dreaming of making it in America. What a pity! I'll send them to Dana and we'll see. I guess she'll need to send the manuscript to readers. Who will they be? I don't know; I have total faith in these stories and am sick-and-tired of elegant rejections.

September 13: Spent yesterday in Manhattan, trying to sell the García Márquez biography. Met Fred Hill from Simon and Schuster, as well as Katherine Court from Viking-Penguin and a junior editor at St. Martin's. I've prepared a very solid proposal, and editors admire it. But I still have a gut feeling the volume is not going to happen. Will see!

Hill seems to be an incredible person to work with. He edited the Hemingway biography I have at home, as well as the multi-volume on

Nabokov. He knows Greg Rabassa; was his student at Columbia University. . . . We talked about a thousand things—he's perfect! Ending up with somebody else would be terrible. And if García Márquez is not the topic, would he be interested in something else? I certainly wish so. What a gentleman!

October 4: ¡Mierda! The whole García Márquez project ended in disaster. Simon and Schuster offered $105,000; I could have worked with Fred Hill, but I chickened out when I discovered that the reason García Márquez wasn't cooperating was that somebody else, a British academic, was "officially" doing the job. Why wasn't I notified? To hell with the project. Writing a biography of a living author isn't my idea of fun. Too bad, though, because Fred Hill seems to be a first-rate editor. Hope the future will bring us together again. . . .

October 8: Tired of Liz Fowler, her apologies, her mistakes. I've tried to be polite and cordial. I won't fire her; she will leave on her own. No doubt she's done great work with me, but was simply inexperienced when handling the García Márquez biography. Should I tell her that I need to move along? Truth is, with the exception of a couple of anthologies for Dell I've sold every single one of my books in English on my own. Do I need an agent? What's an agent good for? Dealing with numbers and handling editors. I know that without one I won't get the commitment from publishers that high-power writers do, but hey, my books will still get published. And what matters is getting in touch with readers, isn't it?

Finished a review for Nation *and another for* Washington Post*. I enjoyed doing them, although I'm getting to feel that my time and energy should better be placed in short stories and a novel.* TriQuarterly *is bringing out "The One-Handed Pianist" in the forthcoming issue. Exciting!*

Dana Asbury has been wonderful: she loved the stories I sent her and in a postcard said she would love to work with me. Outside readers still need to see the MS, though. . . .

November 12: Attended conference and delivered lecture on translation at Duke University. Met Ariel Dorfman, Alastair Reid, and Helen Lane, and saw again a handful of old friends, all well-known translators of Latin American letters: Suzanne Jill Levine, Fred Mac Adam, Edith Grossman, et al. Translators from Spain and south of the Rio Grande were also present. Quite interesting event! (Jules will like to hear about it, I'm sure.)

December 2: Writing for Época in Mexico is strange! I send them what I want and they publish it. Then a huge check comes. How long can this bizarre present last? It began about a year ago, perhaps less, but Mexico's economy will not be in a honeymoon forever. Salinas de Gortari seems to me a liar. Everybody loved him, up until the Chiapas uprising and the assassination of the ruling party's candidate, Colosio Murrieta (I like the second last name; it reminds me of Joaquín Murrieta.) And yet, I'll keep on sending them material. Good correspondence has come from it and an inflated bank account. Nothing illegal, just the happy times.

Wrote a couple of op-ed pieces for Boston Globe and Miami Herald.

Skip Gates and Greg Rabassa sent great blurbs for the cover of The Hispanic Condition! But Skip's might have arrived too late; Cass probably will wait and use it in the paperback.

December 5: Spent yesterday with Marjorie. She came with her family to visit. Had a long talk about books and political resistance. In a few days the semester will be over and I'll have time for myself. I have countless "pending" projects. Sometimes I feel awful having chosen academia. I want nothing but time to write, away from the noise. But here I am, receiving a monthly pay from Amherst College. It's good to know that my tenure case will be resolved soon. At least I'll know then that, if I want it that way, I can remain in this "monastery" forever. But I don't want it. I just want the security, the knowledge that I have it just in case. Of course Alison would be furious if she heard me say I want to leave the job. What will we do? she would ask. Will you support Josh though freelancing? Well, perhaps. Why not? My own father spent almost two decades of his life doing something else other than acting. He was a businessman and would go to the office from 9 to 5. But he had no financial vision and hardly managed to support the family until he found courage and decided to devote himself full time to acting. All of a sudden, opportunities began pouring in. I of course cannot compare myself to him. I've been successful as a writer even while keeping my academic career. But it's no secret that I nourish a hatred for mediocre academics and would do anything to avoid them. Why then don't I?

December 23: Tenure granted. Can Amherst be the place where I'll spend the rest of my life? I'll need to move on. Meanwhile, the future has begun.

I do have to thank Antonio Benítez-Rojo for inviting me to Amherst (back in 1992) in the first place; whatever happens in the next few years, life here has been good so far. I value his friendship dearly.

Read Antonio Skarmeta's <u>Burning Patience;</u> heard a new Italian film will reach the U.S. next year. (I've yet to watch the original Chilean adaptation.)

January 3 [1995]: Spent New Year's in Manhattan at the Park Lane, with my parents, mother-in-law and the rest of Alison's family. Next we went for a visit to the Holocaust Museum, Washington D.C. Its chambers were impressive, obviously quite different than what Yad Vashem is about. Even though I knew much of what was on display, there was still lots of room for learning. But the thing I'll remember the longest about the Museum is its basement bookstore: incredible stock! I found books I had never seen before, all about Jewish writers, not to mention historical accounts about . . . well, about everything imaginable. Jews write, that is a known fact; but only after spending a few minutes in that bookstore can one begin to grasp the size of such statement. I bought Danilo Kiš' first novel, <u>Garden, Ashes,</u> as well as one by Elias Canetti's late wife. I also bought various titles by Hannah Arendt (including <u>Eichmann in Jerusalem,</u> which I shall reread in the next few days); <u>How German Is It?</u> by Walter Abish; a Grace Paley's collected stories; and a bunch of other books. Amazing! One day my own novels will be there too! (Actually, somebody called me last week to say that <u>Tropical Synagogues</u> was in the bookstore at The Jewish Museum in New York).

Marjorie came to visit in early December; had a long chat on books and quilts. As agreed, I'll transcribe some of our dialogue; should do so this week.

February 2: Jaime Manrique, the Colombian-American novelist, has arrived. He'll be teaching at Mt. Holyoke for a semester as Visiting Writer.

Had a dream: I am at the lobby of a fancy hotel, probably in New York City. An elegant chandelier hangs from the ceiling, the carpet has taste, and sofas and chairs à la Louis XIV are lined in perfect square around the room. Rich people of all colors are seating and talking. I walk around behind their chairs and observe. At one side, I notice a beautiful young Caucasian woman talking to a man. On the other, what looks like a group of African royalty—a big chief dressed in suit and tie, several women, a bodyguard. One of his women is thin and is wearing a beige miniskirt and jacket. She has a purse from where she takes out a small, enchanting gun. The chief next to her smiles and she points the gun to the beautiful Caucasian woman—and shoots! Commotion in the room. Everybody is in shock. The beauty is dead and people are running from one place to the next, but doors have been closed and the police is expected. I ask myself in the dream: Why didn't I stop the African woman from shooting? Why didn't I scream? Should I go to the police and tell them what I saw? Could I recognize the assassin if she was wearing a different suit? Am I an accomplice for not having acted on time?

Now that I write, I recall reading in yesterday's paper about a shoot-out in a big city in which a young woman died while bystanders did nothing to stop her victimizers.

February 3: Got a phone call from Melinda Kennedy, editor of <u>Metamorphoses.</u> She wants an essay on ancient Nahuatl poetry. What do I know about the subject? But I told her I would send her something.

Perhaps this is the time to write about translation during the Conquest. Will see!

February 8: Dinner at the home of Antonio Benítez-Rojo. Months ago I got a phone call from an NBC reporter, Cecilia Alvear. (Or is it CBS?) A bunch of people are planning a glossy magazine in Los Angeles, devoted to Hispanic topics. Had a conference call and seems as if the project is moving ahead.

Had journalists and scholars from Boston and New York come to visit. Wrote a piece for Salmagundi *on Octavio Paz's* Vuelta.

February 21–22: Chat at Keene College in New Hampshire. My usual theme: "Lust in Translation: A Writer's Journey." Boring! Dinner with the trustees of Amherst College at week's end. Michael Dirda from Washington Post *called; he wants a book review on Octavio Paz's* The Double Flame *and an essay on the books I read as a child. Is this the occasion to write about Emilio Salgari, an Italian writer of adventure stories about whom nobody knows anything in the United States? Without Salgari, who would I have become? . . . A totally different person.*

March 13: Had lengthy talk with Ariel Dorfman on bilingualism and translation. I taped it with his permission and I hope to have the time to transcribe it soon. (Larry Goldstein, at Michigan Quarterly Review, *might want to print it.) Gone over the proofs of* Bandido: *its style is sincere, non-artificial. Am I finally making the English language a property of mine? I feel I can write anything I envision with assurance and clarity.*

March 18: Talk to Dana Asbury. What a charming, devoted woman she is; I'm very fond of her! Proofs of The Invention of Memory *should be ready in a month or so, but the publicity people at the press want to change the title:* The One-Handed Pianist and Other Stories. *Sounds fine with me. It took more than a year to place this collection of stories—too long! I can't believe it is actually going to be out. Dana promised it should be ready by* early December 1995. And we talked about the possibility of another book of mine: my best essays since I began writing in English in 1986. It's good to work with a university press: time is on one's side and money is not an issue. Should continue to do so.

April 6: Dana Asbury is very excited about Art & Anger: Essays 1986–1995 and so am I. She cannot send a contract until approval from the committee at the press is secured, but she assured me it would come by early summer. She has asked a reader to provide her with an evaluation. Tomorrow is my birthday; I'll be 34? Have I found the best of me? Am I happy?

Talked to Alastair Reid over the phone; discussed works by Alvaro Mutis. What a gentleman this irlandés is!

May 7: The summer is near. Have a thousand projects to finish. Among them, I'm thinking of writing a short story about a female student I once had at CUNY, incredibly bright, who decided to quit school in order to return to her hometown down in Mexico to kill the man that raped and tortured her mother. The idea crosses my mind almost every day; I'll stop its recurrence by putting it in paper.

July 2: Trip to Lake Ontario with Josh and parents. My mother is a pain-in-the-neck. Can she be quiet for more than 10 seconds? God, why have you forsaken me? Is there any Jewish mother in Dante's Inferno? Did the Inquisition ever consider the idea of torturing its victims by condemning them to eternity at their mother's side?

Wrote the story about the CUNY student. Title: "The Kiss." I think it will make a charming addition in the anthology I'm editing for Dell. The central character, Jovita, has now a different name from my former student; background is Mexican, of course, but quite different from hers. The final product is satisfying, although it makes me think of Lamed Shapiro's terrific story under the same title (I included it in Cuentistas Judíos), which of course is completely different.

Have been thinking about a novel that has as its protagonist a translator. Probably my experiences with James Sterling in New York City from 1985 to 1990 would suit it well.

July 9: Had a peculiar dream. What does it mean? I was in a huge lawn that looked like the campus of UNAM in Mexico's capital, where I used to play soccer and bike as a child. Alison and Josh were at a distance, busy collecting wild flowers. I had a feeling of happiness and tranquillity in me and spent some time walking around. At one point I discovered a huge entryway—obviously the door to an old, sacred building. For as much as I wanted to see what was inside, beyond the door was only darkness— heavy, impenetrable. There were three steps next to it, on which a very old man sat quietly. He looked to be an orthodox Jew not unlike the keepers of synagogues in Eastern Europe at the turn of the century. He was a hunchback and kept looking down, but when he heard me around he raised his sight and saw me. A long beard. A smile—I realized he has only a few teeth. I decided to enter the building and soon got the feeling I was at a yeshiva. A few religious men came toward me while discussing some midrash. They hardly noticed me. I continued to walk. Darkness was everywhere but I could notice a few classrooms, with teachers discussing the Torah. Then I got an urge to pee and looked for a bathroom, which a found at the end of a hallway. The bathroom was gigantic, like that at Amherst College's gyms—immense mirrors, common showers, innumerable toilets. I peed and proceeded to wash my hands when I heard whispers in my back. I turned around and realized two adolescent girls were kissing. When they saw me, they panicked and began to run. They were the first women I saw at the place. For some strange reason, I decided to follow them but soon I saw a couple of doors synchronically opening, as if their move had been staged by a Hollywood director. The girls disappeared and the only thing I saw were TV cameras and reporters pointing at me—or better, in my direction. I woke up with a pleasant feeling of accomplishment.

August 6: Josh has been asking about book reviewing. What is a review? How does one write one? Yesterday, he finally decided to write his first. He took one of his books and dictated the following to Alison:

Under the Water
Review by Joshua Stavchansky

> Under the Water *is about fish and divers and plants underwater. And sharks too. The sharks eat little fish and the little fish eat plants too. I like the octopus and the lobster because they can kill little shells, pointy fish and stinger fish. If my friend Brody wants to read the book I would let him read the book. I want to know how the underwater plants grow and how the fish get their stingers. How does water get islands? and fish, shells, plants? Where do shells come from? How do plants grow very deep underwater? How do birds that live in the water get their feathers? I like this book.*

Hiroshima, fifty years ago. Also, today's my mother's birthday; she turns 54. We're in Cape Cod for a week (Josh, Alison and my mother-in-law). A nineteenth-century house, remarkable but hardly functional. I picked up a novel by Graham Greene stored in the attic—The Honorary Consul. Published in 1973, when Greene was 69, it is remarkable in that it develops with ease, in an engaging fashion. Novels ought to be written the way Greene wrote them, if they ought to at all.

It's been raining outside. Stayed at home: cooked, played, read, ate in first-rate restaurants . . .

Greene's career comes back to mind. His was a careful art. Can a non-native English speaker achieve such control of Shakespeare's tongue? Perseverance, I guess, is the key. Bandido, my biographical inquiry, will be published next month. Early reviews have been extremely positive. Will people like it? Will my books be read in the future—someone finding them in bookstores and libraries, like I found Greene? Nothing else should preoccupy the writer but the desire to find balance between talent and vision. Vision, though, is as much a present gift as a bet on things to come. After Bandido come my stories from New Mexico: I'm very proud of them, but I know they will appeal to a very delicate, elitist taste.

Yesterday night I also finished reading 1920 Diary, Isaac Babel's personal scribbling that served as the foundation for his stories on and about Odessa and the Red Cavalry. Babel is a favorite of mine and his rushed, nervous prose ("urgent" I guess is the word) is simply admirable: it opens a wide window into his ambivalence as a Jew under the early Soviet regime. Ambiguity, of course, is what attracts me in his stories (particularly those set in Odessa), as does the same component in Kafka, Shultz, Danilo Kiš and even some of Phillip Roth's work. Does modern Judaism offer any other option but ambiguity? Perhaps, but not for me—and not for the "psychological Jews" (Freud's term) concerned with both tradition and cosmopolitanism. Babel's autobiographical paragraphs, in truth, inspired me when I began writing fiction.

Finally, a word about insecurity. I had closed the journal when the absence of such a feeling took over me. I should say that insecurity used to be my lot but in the last few months, particularly since The Hispanic Condition was published, I somehow seem to have left it behind. I feel I'm on the tight track, writing and reading . . . at least most of the time. My whole life has focused on the desire not to be a pariah, not to live on the margins of society. I have fought to have a place, to be taken seriously, and am now feeling I'm getting there. Switching languages was a risk. I don't think I was aware of its aftermath when I made the decision to become fully active as a writer in English. But here I am. Slowly, but I'm finding my center.

August 9: Cape Cod is dazzling! Colors acquire a special texture here— artificial, unexplainable—and everything looks cinematic. Hollywood is everywhere in A*M*E*R*I*C*A!

Talked to Dana: she's working on the cover of The One-Handed Pianist and Art & Anger; will be on vacation until September.

I just reread some of last year's events, as described in these pages. With all its ups and downs, what an exciting time it's been! Hurrah—no, shouldn't write that! Who knows what the next twelve months will bring?

Thinking of writing a short story about a rabbi found dead of suicide. Why? He had a dream in which God told him he didn't want him as intermediary. But rabbis are not intermediaries. So the whole thing pushes him to reevaluate his life. No, no, no; the plot still needs development.

August 28: I got an advance copy of Bandido today—what pride! To think that it took me two weeks to write it. Talked to Mike Vazquez at Transition. His mother died unexpectedly and he feels disoriented. Still, he's preparing the new issue and wants a piece on Subcomandante Marcos and an interview with the young Mexican-American film director of El Mariachi.

The issue of plagiarism is tremendously complicated in Spain and south of the Rio Grande, where newspapers reprint material from abroad without paying permission and where writers, since Colonial Times, were taught to imitate foreigners. That's why Borges' "Pierre Menard, author of the Quixote" is such a Hispanic story. I developed this topic in my essay "Translation & Identity," but it certainly needs other outlets. Ours is a derivative civilization, a culture founded on plagiarism—e.g. Columbus rewritten by Fray Bartolomé de Las Casas rewritten by Fuentes rewritten by me?

I will always live in translation . . . and shall die in translation too.

Where could my bones be buried? Terrifying question, not because death is frightening (it isn't really), but because I don't know where I belong. Or better, I do: my wish, let it be known, is not to be buried in A*M*E*R*I*C*A but in Mount Olives. I shall patiently wait there for the coming of the messiah.

And when he comes, which language will he speak? Hebrew, the sacred tongue?

Who cares since I'll be dead. Dead and buried.

A Confessional Silence

I BECAME INFATUATED with a writer's journal when I first read, in Spanish in the early 1980s, a three-volume set of Kafka's diaries. They offered him an escape, a chance for intimacy, a sense of self-sufficiency, a space for reflection and the articulation of inner thoughts. (Years later, after re-reading them, I wrote my short story "A Heaven Without Crows.") But my passion for the genre entails autobiography in general: I am a voracious reader of volumes of correspondence, biographies, and self-portraits, and have, next to each other in my favorite shelf, books by V.S. Naipaul, Graham Greene, Hannah Arendt, Mary McCarthy, Borges' "Autobiographical Essay," Isaac Bashevis Singer's *In My Father's Court,* Pablo Neruda's *Memoirs,* and Isaac Babel's *1920 Diary.*

I want to think that corresponding with old friends and keeping a personal journal are similar activities, only differentiated by a degree of deep honesty. One's own voice, chaotic, unobstructed by artificial mannerisms, comes out pure and clear in a letter, but it has an even purer quality in a journal kept for nobody but the self—at least for the time being. I have kept a journal next to me since the mid-1980s, when, at age twenty-four I began writing in earnest. (I have four or five volumes on my library shelves, two thirds of which were originally written in Spanish.) The ideas behind many stories and essays, from my novella "The Invention of Memory" to *The Hispanic Condition,* took shape in a line or two first drafted in its pages. My journal is me without masks. I generally open it at night, after a long day's work, when everybody is asleep and the house is overwhelmed by a confessional silence. In its pages I have written out important dreams (and an occasional reflection on their implications), analyzed my faith in God and society, described my relationship with editors and colleagues, played out my goals as writer, and, in general, discussed the day's or week's highlights—all of which make it simultaneously an agenda, a loyal therapist, a creative notebook, and a confessional pulpit. Rereading it makes me confront the past in ways I cannot evade.

Marianna de Marco Torgovnick

I use my journal to jolt my mind when I sit down to write particular chapters or sections. I also review all the entries several times during any project: to make sure I'm not forgetting something; to catch a contradiction that will refine an idea.

1. Crown Heights
   In Laws House
   symbolism of the house
   Ocean Parkway. What it meant

                                            Teachers were
                                            Jewish

upward mobility/ambition
              Sky King and Penny
              Amanda and <u>Bonanza</u>

         Long way from O.P.!

   changed after 60's counter-culture

   Dick Chernick
      material things
      casting away

2. Who are the theorists of ecstasy in the Western tradition?

   Christian mystics
      St. Francis
      St. Teresa

         imp. that ecstasy is <u>not</u> union. Essence is
         momentary transportation out of self.
         Suspension of will and sense faculties

in other words
surrender of individualism

# of patterns
    pain\bodily discomf
    cross-gender patterns
    extreme attachment to father\broken
    silence\mountains
    surrender
    lack of material goods
    instinct for Things as Holy

Freud: hostile to the oceanic
Buber: lauds it
Use surprise more: what does it mean that they wrote at the same time?

Jottings

I KEEP A JOURNAL compulsively. It's my "I'd better write it down or I'll forget" way of remembering. My journal takes shape as I drive, swim, brush my teeth, drift off to sleep. I grab whatever paper happens to be at hand and jot down some ideas, quickly, often using abbreviations and symbols. I have no dates for the entries above. They were both written on the back pages of a Day-Timer (a schedule book) that I always carry with me.

My current journal consists of a large box filled with sheets of paper ranging from the marginalia on checking account deposit slips (always handy) to pages ripped from my appointment book (also always handy) to pages of typing paper scrawled over by hand and some printed on my computer very neatly. I also have a pretty notebook that I bought at a museum which is now filled with random jottings. Some are for my recent book of autobiographical and critical essays, *Crossing Ocean Parkway;* most are for a book in progress called *The Quest for Ecstasy: Primitivism at the Millennium,* which probes connections between fascination for "primitive peoples" and oceanic or religious emotions. The journal helped me think about the two books together, which was useful, since both are in various ways about women, materialism, violence (psychic or real), spirituality, and the "I" versus the "We."

My journals tend (as here) to outline ideas, links, and connections that sometimes make it into my published work and sometimes don't—but are very helpful anyway. Often, as in the first entry, I'm working hard on organization, so my journal has lots of tentative outlines. Sometimes, I really do find an organization that works (this happened in the first entry, the basis for the title essay of *Crossing Ocean Parkway*). It took a while for me to realize that "Crossing Ocean Parkway" is about the image of Jewish people that I had had as an Italian American girl growing up in Bensonhurst. I married into a Jewish family living on the "other side" of Ocean Parkway. Once I began the essay with a description of my in-laws' house, I was on my way.

Sometimes, I hit on ideas that lead to key insights. That is the way the second entry worked for me, establishing some motifs that run through *The Quest for Ecstasy*. I had found myself drawn to readings in Western mystics. At first, I wasn't sure why. The entry I have reproduced was a breakthrough: in it, I realized that motifs which appear in mystics' stories (the patterns listed in the entry) also often show up in the lives of figures like Dian Fossey, Georgia O'Keeffe, and the genital piercers about whom I was writing in various chapters of the book.

I use my journal to jolt my mind when I sit down to write particular chapters or sections. I also review all the entries several times during any project: to make sure I'm not forgetting something; to catch a contradiction that will refine an idea. For example, when I first read Martin Buber's *I and Thou*, I didn't think about how it had been written slightly *before* Freud's *Civilization and Its Discontents*. When I put them together in my jotting, I realized two things: first, that many writers, other than Freud, were interested in the "oceanic" and had important things to say; second, that a major debate in Western culture about interconnectedness and relationship had been lost.

I've worked with journals by Henry James, Virginia Woolf, and other writers. I've always enjoyed seeing how ideas begin. But I don't really model my journal on any that I've read. My journal is more of a writer's working notebook. It's not a diary of personal experience—which for me seems like a different genre—except that the ideas we live with end up becoming part of us.

Kathleen Tyau

I've . . . found journal entries for characters I invented before I came up with the idea for a book . . . I just hadn't known what to do with them at the time. When something like this happens, I have to ask myself what else is lurking in my scribblings. For all I know, I've already started writing my fifth or sixth novel and just haven't noticed yet.

February 13, 1991

Little stories. Little stories for my nieces? Stories about family. About Aunty who ate chicken butts. About Uncle who painted wild women after his wife died. About going to the monster movies. About the air raid alerts. About growing up on an island. About Popo.

Enough to Convince Me

I FOUND THE PARAGRAPH above in my fiction journal while searching for an answer to the question people often ask about when I first began writing my novel *A Little Too Much Is Enough.* I haven't been comfortable with my reply. "A few years ago" seems flippant and vague. So I turned to my journals, thinking that the answer must be recorded somewhere in the many logs I've kept over the past ten years. When I came across these words, I wondered if the answer could in fact be as definite as this. This was all I had written in my journal that day. Subsequent entries dealt with other stories I was attempting to write at the time, as if I'd dismissed the idea of these "little stories." However, one month later, on a March afternoon, I started a new journal in a yellow spiral-bound notebook and headed it simply "Story about food." I wrote a two-page list of foods I wanted to write about. What follows is a partial list:

> *Poi brain/rice brain*
> *Noodles/saimin*
> *Eating watermelon*
> *Pupus/poker/beer*
> *Mixing poi, eating*
> *Crabs in the kitchen*
> *Eating soybeans*

Spam/gov't rations
The lunch wagon, plate lunch
Shave Ice
Pig/luau
Chinese nine-course dinner
Soy sauce
Tripe

. . .

Lap Ap
Mogan [sic] David wine
Food at cemeteries, funerals
Raw fish
Eating seaweed

. . .

Chicken butts
Sugar cane
Tea/Aunties
Lemon drops & cuttlefish
How to cook rice
Fish eyeballs

I recall how warm and sunny it was that day, how I sat on the front porch at a rusty metal table and wrote all afternoon. At the top of each page, I jotted down a food item or a title. Some of these headings later became titles for my chapters (looking at them now I realize how many of them didn't go anywhere, but at the time they made me feel like I had a great deal to say). I remember that I was reading Mary Morris's novel, *The Waiting Room,* at the same time (my daily journal confirms this fact). I read a chapter of her novel, which had absolutely nothing to do with food or Hawaii, wrote one or two pages about food, and then read another chapter of Morris's book. These are some of my journal entries which led to stories that became chapters of my novel.

I watch my uncle mix poi for a luau. He squeezes it with both hands. His arms are covered with poi up to his elbows. He grins. He is dark, brown, a dark rich cocoa brown. The poi is gray & bland next to his rich skin. He sweats from the work—the sweat runs down his arms and into the vat of poi. He grins. "Taste mo' bettah dis way," he says. ["Mixing Poi"]

I am poi brain from birth. By birth. From my grandmother who came from Niihau. Niihau is a forbidden island—an island forever surrounded by myth. We do not know anything about Niihau except that we cannot go there & the Hawaiians who lived there are crazy from intermarriage. Later I read about Niihau & discover this is not true, but it is too late. The Niihau of my memory is forbidden fruit. I accept the insanity of my Hawaiian blood—I accept the mystery because I know nothing of my grandmother. ["Poi Brain, Rice Knuckles" and "Watch My Hands"]

He was sent to China when he was only five—taken away from his Hawaiian mother and his Chinese father. He was sent to live with people he had never met—relatives of his father. They were short like his father—he had his mother's height. She was a tall, stately Hawaiian woman his father had met while building houses. . . . he was shanghaied—sent by boat to China. One day when he was playing quietly in the front yard, his mother screamed & cried as his father put him in the old Ford and drove off. The Ford was filled with trunks & boxes of food and clothing for the family in China. . . . He stayed in China until he was 18. He returned home a man—his mother wept again. . . . He spoke perfect Cantonese and carved ivory elephants and half-moon-shaped earrings. He painted watercolors, always with elegant women in them. ["Mixing Poi," "Family Shark"]

Although I didn't know what I would do with these "little food stories," I continued to write them until I had enough to convince me I was on to something bigger than I'd imagined. For me that's the real key to using a journal—noticing, paying attention to what you've already written. I actually began writing about food a couple of years earlier, but I didn't see connections until that spring of 1991. I've also found journal entries for characters I invented before I came up with the idea for a book—Mahealani's Aunty Lucy and Uncle Chin, for example, first appeared in journal entries for a short story that I never completed—I just hadn't known what to do with them at the time. When something like this happens, I have to ask myself what else is lurking in my scribblings. For all I know, I've already started writing my fifth or sixth novel and just haven't noticed yet.

Although I would never let anyone read my journals from cover to cover, I like to read my students some of the earliest journal entries for stories that were later published, so they can see how unextraordinary the words are. Why do we think published writers—including our favorite writers—got the words right the first time around? I know I'm guilty of this kind of awe. Yet, when I go back through my journals, what impresses me is the importance of naive and unbridled audacity.

I try to freewrite in my journal until I've found the heart of a piece, something I learned from writer Sallie Tisdale in a talk she gave at a Willamette Writers' meeting. I write about the same thing again and again until I feel something happen, and then I revise, revise, revise. I listen first for the voice and then look for the story, for the real subject. Then I attend to the language, images, and so forth. What's amazing to me is how far I can get into a piece in a quick journal entry. For this reason, I honor these simple beginnings for reminding me that good ideas may not require much time and that the end—the published work—may not be that far out of sight.

I keep separate journals for my personal life and for writing, although the two often overlap, as in real life. At first I wrote on steno pads and then in larger, spiral-bound notebooks, but now I use the Blueline series of hard-backed composition books made from recycled paper. These come lined and unlined and in different colors. I like them because the journals don't flop over when I put them on my bookshelf. The first time a writing teacher, Doug Marx, suggested I use a stiff-backed note-book for this simple reason, I balked, but I soon discovered how right he was. These books are also a good size (9¼″ by 7¼″) for stuffing in a shoulder bag or day pack. I can't write in beautiful, cloth-bound journals because I feel like I have to write perfectly the first time. Now that I know the value of journals, I'm more careful about keeping them and dating each entry.

I like to write in the morning, first thing, while still in bed, before I've had my bowl of granola and cup of tea, but that's usually wishful thinking. After meals seems to be more realistic. I start with my daily journal, and when the words start turning to fiction, I switch over to the other journal. And then I make another cup of tea and run up-stairs to the computer.

I also keep a journal on the computer, although this is not intended to replace the journal I keep in longhand. In my WordPerfect directory for whatever project I'm working on at the time, I create a subdirectory called "jnl." Sometimes I split the screen (Ctrl F3) and switch back and forth (Shift F3) between the journal and whatever I'm working on at the time. If I get stuck, I freewrite (and grumble) for a while in my journal and then when I get good and revved up and the voices start coming again, I switch back to my draft. Sometimes I block whole sections from my journal and move them over to the draft. Keep-ing a journal is one way of dealing with some of the internal dialogue that haunts (and taunts) me while I write. "Can I do this?" "Why am I writing this?" My journals have talked me out many dead ends and alternative careers, and every now and then, if I am listening carefully, I discover that I knew what I was doing all along. Maybe the correct answer to the question about when you began writing something—whether it be a novel, a story, or a poem—is not the precise date upon which you put the first words to paper but rather the moment you realize what you have before you, when you see that you have created language, characters, *lives,* which may thrive beyond the personal sphere of your journal.

Joan Weimer

When I wasn't travelling, I was too busy living my life—as college teacher, activist, mother, wife, friend, cook, and tennis player—to record it. Then a vertebra separated from my spine. The trauma of surgery flooded me with unfamiliar feelings and disturbing dreams. To clear my brain, I wrote them down. . . . My journal became a place to pursue a feeling or a dream instead of forgetting or evading it.

Cairo, December 27, 1972: Our guide Hassan lives with his wife and eight children in Mena village, at the base of the Pyramids. He says if he meets his wife on the street, he himself cannot recognize her through the thick black veil she always wears in public. It's true, he says when I ask, that flirtatious girls and unfaithful wives are sometimes murdered by their husbands or brothers, and in spite of protests by women lawyers, the courts never punish this "crime of honor." How can a society be so modern that women can practise law, and so archaic that men can murder women with impunity?

Cairo, January 2, 1973: We follow the sound of <u>bagpipes,</u> of all things, to see a wedding procession winding up the spiral staircase of our hotel lobby. Belly dancers in red and orange spangles and veils flounce up the stairs, castanets clicking. What are they doing at a wedding? Young men in the party invite us to come along, and upstairs we see the bride, hefty in white satin, holding a little boy on her lap. Beside her on the dais the skinny groom tries to make conversation, but she never responds or changes expression through any of what follows:

At the other end of the room, the belly dancer—young, plump, pretty in a snappy way, dressed in red bra and brief and net midriff and skirt— bounces to the hard erotic beat of the music. She looks more like a high school cheerleader—"Let's hear it for sex!"—than either a seductress or an artist. Then she climbs up with one foot on the chair of the bride and one foot on the groom's, gets the bride to clap a few times—and bumps and grinds right in their faces.

What's a belly dancer doing at a wedding in a culture that values a woman's chastity more than her life?

Life Stand Still Here

WRITING BY HAND feels to me like punishment, like having to write "I will not talk in class" a hundred times on the blackboard. That's one reason why I never kept journals until I began travelling in the early 1970s to what we then called the Third World. I wanted to use what I'd learned teaching Women's Studies to understand the lives of women struggling with war, poverty, and repression. I'd sit on a balcony watching *feluccas* sail up and down the Nile, or on a beach in Rio de Janeiro gawking at women wearing string bikinis, and write down my impressions and questions.

The scene at the Cairo wedding became the opening of an essay called "The Belly Dancer and the Virgin." Eight magazines rejected it. Each time it came back I rewrote it. Finally the *Southwest Review* accepted it, published it in their Winter 1976 volume, and gave it the John H. McGinnis Award for the best work of nonfiction they had published in 1975 and 1976. I like to tell that story to my students. Keep revising, I say. And don't lose faith in your work.

In later travel journals, I wrote about torture in Brazil, about bombings of clinics and day nurseries in Central America—all paid for by my tax dollars. My journal entries turned into published essays about links between *machismo* and torture, about women's roles as mothers and as revolutionaries. My journal was the repository of my outrage.

When I wasn't travelling, I was too busy living my own life—as college teacher, writer, activist, mother, wife, friend, cook, and tennis player—to record it. Then a vertebra separated from my spine. The trauma of surgery flooded me with unfamiliar feelings and disturbing dreams. To clear my brain, I wrote them down. Long months of convalescence with no guarantee of full recovery gave me, for the first time since adolescence, the leisure and the urgency to examine my life. Who could I be if I could no longer do the things that had always told me who I was? When I was finally able to mosey into the woods next to my house, I wrote this:

October 20, 1988: Radiant yellow leaves floating down from maple
trees, pine needles drifting down to carpet the ground. The "dying"
trees are just as much alive as the "evergreens." They have different
life cycles. That's all.

In some strange way, I'm more "alive" in this strange new
life—hibernating, horizontal, mulling things over, connecting by long
telephone lines to friends and family—than I was doing my stimu-
lating, pressured, gratifying work. Incredible.

My journal became a place to pursue a feeling or a dream instead of
forgetting or evading it. In my journal I could say "Life stand still here."
I'd never forgotten those words of Virginia Woolf's for what an artist
does. I knew I was no artist. I just wrote journalistic essays and literary
articles. Before my injury, I had finished the research for a scholarly book
about a brilliant but obscure nineteenth-century writer, Constance
Fenimore Woolson. Now I wasn't sure that I still wanted to write it:

November 7, 1988: If I do write my book on Woolson it's got to be
my book somehow, not a salaam to the authorities in the field. I
want it to be quirky, opinionated, eccentric, even. I want to look
with my own eyes, occupy my own space on the planet, speak in
my own voice.

What does my own voice sound like? I've certainly spent a lot
of time these last six months listening for it. I'm hearing other voices,
too. "Live all you can. It's a mistake not to." "I did not wish to live
what was not life, living was so dear." "Envy is ignorance, imita-
tion is suicide." Henry James, Thoreau, Emerson. Their familiar
words come to me now with stunning immediacy.

December 5, 1988: I dream that I meet Constance Woolson in a
crowded hall. She's slim and tall. I put my arm around her waist. I
want to be on intimate terms with her. (Sisters? Alter egos? Lovers?)
I tell her I've brought her stories back in print, and she's pleased
and surprised. I don't have a copy of my anthology to show her.

(Letting her down?) She's shy and quiet but agrees to meet me on Friday, a day I don't teach. (This is not going to be business as usual.) Will she show up? She accepts so few invitations. I'm trembling with excitement.

My time with Connie is used up by evading a man with a terrible cold I don't want to catch. I know who he is! The patriarchal critic who's after me to write his kind of book, to imitate him, write him into a footnote. He's getting between me and Connie. He saps my energy, diverts my attention. His cold really is contagious.

Now I find myself driving on an icy road dangerously close to a car in front of me. I should drop back, put space between us. If I don't, I'll wind up in a ditch or the hospital. (The dream is telling me to be original. It's risky, but so is conformity.) Emerson again: "Imitation is suicide."

I wonder if I could write my book as a dialogue with Connie. Her life and mine, her writing and mine. We both travelled to Cairo and wrote about it. In Oxford David and I lived just around the corner from her boarding house. We lived in Florence before I knew she'd lived there too. I did much of my research on her in Rome, where she's buried. My first sense of affinity with her came from identifying with her passion for living abroad. Amazing that we gravitated to the same places, a hundred years apart!

This is a book I want to write, can't wait to write, and only I can write it! Huge excitement, despite the uncertainties.

That dream became the germ of my first book, a very quirky and eccentric memoir called *Back Talk: Teaching Lost Selves to Speak* (Random House, 1993). If I could have sat at my computer and slogged away at my scholarly book, I would never have written *Back Talk*. But thank God I couldn't sit. Instead, I spent months lying in a huge electronic harness to heal my spine. The only way I could write was longhand in a journal. In its pages, I agonized over my disability. I puzzled over my dreams. I tried to reconstruct my younger selves. I began to hear Woolson's voice asking me hard questions about my work, my parents, my children, my body. I'd write her questions down in my journal, and try to answer them. When they got really painful, I'd turn on her: Why did *she* work all the time? Did she really fall out of that window, or did she jump to her death? Through our back talk, she became my collaborator, my sister, my mother, my muse. When I was finally able to sit, 500 pages spilled out of me, showing how Woolson's life helped me comprehend my own and what my own struggles taught me about hers. An editor at Random House found the manuscript exciting but unpublishable. She thought it needed a narrative. How about the story of my disability and Connie's role in my recovery? I couldn't believe anyone would be interested in my spine, but I pulled out the mountain of journals I had kept during my year of disability, and from them I wrote a long synopsis, reconstructing my growing intimacy with Woolson, weaving into it parts of my 500-page draft. Random House bought it. That was as much a miracle as the healing of my spine. The journals I kept only because I couldn't sit at my computer made me the writer I'd always wanted to be, a person whose words could sometimes make "life stand still here."

Steven Winn

Many of my journal entries are made with a breathless, superstitious haste, often when waking at night or early in the morning. My journal is a phantom catcher. Giving each entry a date and sometimes a setting is a way of trying to tighten the web, strengthen the net.

*August 22—Story idea this morning in bed outdoors, a story called
"The Skylight." It begins with the father seeing the skylight like some water
blister on the roof from far off in the orchard. Later the analogy of the
house to a child's space toy, a rough sort of graft on an old house.*

*It comes out that the father never liked living in that old house
anyway. He has all daughters except for this son—and at first getting the
son out of the new house seemed to get him a new daughter—the son's
wife. But recently the son has seemed more prominent. He notes the stitch
of love in his son's brow, like some tribal decoration.*

The Skylight

How CLEARLY I RECALL that August morning, and how strange my recording
of it in my journal now seems—how specific yet sketchy, prescient and
blind.

I did in fact write a short story called "The Skylight," later published in *The Indiana Review* (Vol. 9, No. 1), and it conforms to the
situation roughly envisioned here. The protagonist, a farmer in arid eastern Washington, has one son and a number of daughters. His complicated feelings for his son are worked out, as I sensed they would be, in
terms of their adjacent houses. In the older house, once occupied by the
father and now owned by the son, the son makes various improvements—including a bedroom skylight. The father, having built a new
house next door, watches the once-dreary old house transformed before
his eyes.

But I was "wrong" as often as I was "right" in this entry. The story
does begin with the father seeing the skylight from afar, but the water
blister image occurs much later in the narrative. Another image that gave
the story its first substance for me—the "stitch of love in his son's brow,
like some tribal decoration"—disappeared entirely in the writing. And

the third, the notion of the house as "a child's space toy, a rough sort of graft on an old house," turned completely opaque and inert. I cannot recapture what I saw, or thought I saw, as I lay staring at a Marin County sky that morning.

"The Skylight" was a visitation, an idea that arrived pretty reliably whole to me. The plot was still to be discovered, as were many other folds and shadows. But the story's life was rooted in the almost physical deliverance of the images, even if the water blister was the only one to survive.

The primacy of the images is the reason, I think (without thinking of it at the time), that I recorded where I was when the idea came—"in bed outdoors." The open-air sleeping arrangement became part of the story's spontaneous gestation. Many of my journal entries are made with a breathless, superstitious haste, often when waking at night or early in the morning. My journal is a phantom catcher. Giving each entry a date and sometimes a setting is a way of trying to tighten the web, strengthen the net.

In this case, I was housesitting for a Fairfax, California, couple I didn't know very well. Shy of declining their offer to use the mattress on a deck outside the bedroom, I slept outdoors. When I awoke, a tiny silver jet was crossing the sky, trailing an extravagant white plume. And there, in that silent blue morning, was "The Skylight." I got up from the dewy mattress and found the spiral notebook that goes wherever I do.

The detail of the airplane I didn't need to record, for whatever reason. But I remember it now, a sense memory that is as vivid as the water blister. A journal entry preserves an event—this time, the birth of more writing to come—in telegraphic form. Rereading old entries reconstitutes the cryptic jottings into fully fleshed memories. The airplane and cool mattress, though unrecorded, were indelible parts of that August 22 event.

The blister was the divining image of "The Skylight," as it turned out. Water pressed against a translucent membrane was somehow bound up with the swelling audacity of the son's home improvements—of which the skylight was only the most visible to the daunted father. What I didn't know, or knew only subliminally, was that water would figure importantly throughout the story. The climax of "The Skylight" involves a rush of water into a basement; another scene occurs with a long, brown tongue of water lolling between two characters as they converse over an irrigation ditch.

Only a tiny fraction of the entries in my journal lead to stories or poems or essays that actually get written. There is, as far as I can see, no clear pattern to distinguish ideas that work and those that don't. (Not that I use my journal only as a warehouse for future product; it's also a place to vent, rant and reason with myself about personal crises, my perpetual homesickness for the East Coast and milder matters.)

Many ideas for stories seem to have evaporated, if they ever truly existed, when I look back at my journal. Occasionally, if the entry is old enough, I can barely recall what I was thinking; the dots and dashes don't translate back into intelligible speech with a distinctive voice. The idea doesn't bulge into three dimensions, insisting it be written, when I read and re-read such an entry.

At other times I'll make such extensive notes for a story, either in a long single entry or in several over a period of days, that the story seems to get flattened by too much advance work. A story came to me not long ago with such detail, of action and character and even names, which are usually very hard for me, that I recorded as fast as I could in my spiral-bound notebook, as if I were taking some high-speed dictation. I wrote for pages instead of a paragraph or two, frantic not to miss a drop that came gushing up from wherever.

But I've yet to begin work on the story, which felt so urgent at its arrival. And I now think I'll work on something else instead. I hope I haven't killed the story by pouring too much of it into the journal. But if I have, I was powerless to do otherwise. I never audit or second-guess what goes into my journal. What may or may not come out in some other form is, or at least seems to be, beyond my control. Some phantoms refuse to be caught.

"The Skylight" apparently wanted to be. Emerging in my journal a single, tremulous bead, the story disclosed enough of itself to be frozen for a moment. And that, I believe, allowed the full, live flow that would come later.

Shawn Wong

When I was eighteen I started thinking about becoming a writer but as an undergraduate student and later as a graduate student in creative writing, I didn't really have a career as a writer so I wrote letters, sometimes as many as five or six letters a day. In looking back at the thousands of pages of letters, I realize those letters were how I practiced my writing.

April 2, 1974/New York City
Dear Rhonda,

    . . . I've been staying up late nights still trying to catch up on
the time, eating dinner around nine, then going out nights to check
things out. Then home again to work on a novel I've been writing
for a couple of years now. I've rewritten the damn thing five times,
each time it gets longer; now I think I've got the thing licked. I'm
convinced I got the last chapter in hand. The story about a young
Chinese American kid who suffers from dreams, dreams about his
father, grandfather, great grandfather. And in the end, Rhonda, he's
split up with his Indian girl friend 'cause he ain't no Indian . . . he
knows who he is now. He's down at the lagoon by the ocean
waiting for a train, that old night train that used to steam down out
of the Sierras to come and pick up the Chinese workers wherever they
are. It finds homeless men, picks them up, runs through America like
a ghost.
        That's what I'm doing now, waiting for that train to come and
pick me up. I'm thinking about that picture of my father taken when
he was twenty-eight years old. He's sitting in that wooden lawn
chair. He's relaxed and smiling as though he's celebrating something.
So that's why I'm down here at this small boat dock. I brought
down a wooden folding chair and a wooden crate for a table from
my uncle's house. I went back to the house for a cup of coffee and
some magazines. It will be four more years before I'm twenty-eight,
but I'm celebrating my twenty-eighth birthday today. I feel good
about this day and how it got warmer as it got closer to noon. I
read my magazines with my sunglasses on because it was one of
those rare sunny days out here on the lagoon. But it's not just my
birthday I'm celebrating. I'm waiting for that night train to come
around the bend up there where the beach turns to the north. My
waiting is a celebration. I've become a patient man like my father.

Dear Rhonda: The Letter as Journal

I DON'T REMEMBER Rhonda's last name, but I do remember we worked together for a while, we went out a couple of times, and we wrote a few letters. I was living in a small town on the ocean in Marin County. I wrote to Rhonda while visiting New York, after attending the publication party for my first book, an anthology of Asian American literature entitled *Aiiieeeee!* (Howard University Press, 1974), which I coedited with Jeffrey Chan, Frank Chin, and Lawson Inada. The excerpt from my letter to Rhonda was revised and inserted in my first novel, *Homebase* (Reed and Cannon, 1979).

I never had a teacher, from grammar school through graduate school, who recommended that I keep a journal. My mentor in college was the writer Kay Boyle and she gave me just two pieces of advice: "Writing is about belief" and "Write every day." Since then, I've always felt that it took the same discipline to sit down and work on a piece of writing as it does to sit down and write in a journal. So I never have kept a journal. But I am a great record keeper—canceled checks, receipts, letters, college *and* high school class notes, report cards, greeting cards, grammar school term papers, numerous versions of edited manuscripts, old address books, and appointment calendars.

My journal is my letters. When I was eighteen I started thinking about becoming a writer, but as an undergraduate student and later as a graduate student in creative writing, I didn't really have a career as a writer so I wrote letters, sometimes as many as five or six letters a day. In looking back at the thousands of pages of letters, I realize those letters were how I practiced my writing. In my letters, twenty plus years ago, I recalled conversations I had during the day and wrote dialogue, looked for teaching jobs, sent manuscripts out, described myself and my writing, wrote to other writer friends, and was sentimental and flirtatious with girlfriends. The letters to writers are particularly interesting because many of them were in the same early stages of their careers. When

I was a student at Berkeley, I remember thinking how it was strange that professors never assigned work by living authors, let alone Asian American authors and other contemporary American minority authors. So I set out to find them on my own. The community of writers that I found and worked with now reads like the table of contents from any American multicultural anthology of literature: Ishmael Reed, Frank Chin, Lawson Inada, Al Young, Mei-mei Berssenbrugge, Leslie Silko, Victor Hernandez Cruz, Jessica Hagedorn, Ntosake Shange, Rudolfo Anaya, Hisaye Yamamoto, Quincy Troupe, and dozens of others. We started literary organizations, publishing companies, journals, magazines, read each other's works, and wrote letters. Those letters serve as a valuable record of our beginnings as writers.

As I started publishing and having a career as a writer and a professor I wrote fewer letters and I worked out my fiction less and less in my letters. For the past ten years I have used the phone more, the fax machine, and now, e-mail. With the exception of letters sent on the Internet, I still save copies of my letters. I'm afraid my letters aren't as interesting, or romantic, or sentimental, or humorous as they were twenty years ago. For the most part, they're now instructive and informational. I can afford to dial long distance now, so I do. As a professor at the University of Washington for the past twelve years, I probably write more memos than personal letters (the verse form that begins with the stanzas "TO:/FROM:/RE:). The various drafts of my fiction and other writings are my journals. I still keep meticulous notes on my whereabouts, meetings, travels. For example, on April 9, 1994, I was in Bellagio, Italy, and had a lunch of chicken ravioli soup, duck with a tangerine glaze, cornbread, baked tomatoes with parmesan, and raspberry cake for dessert.

I was once audited by the IRS and I found that I could reconstruct my life from all these separate pieces of information. I remember the IRS auditor began his investigation as to whether my writing was a profession or a hobby by asking in a mocking tone of voice "It says here on your return that you are a writer. So, how many *books* have you written?" At that time I had written and published three, so I answered his question and handed him the books. He was so surprised that he stuttered and then asked permission to photocopy the covers of the books. As I went about my task of documenting the fiscal activity of my profession, I realized that in looking over my records I had to control my tendency to tell him stories rather than justify expenses.

Elizabeth Woody

feel best when I write poetry.
However, the stress to produce a
poem is often too "gilded" with effort.
The journal, in its immediacy, is a
release from deeper obligations, of
attempts to write in a "higher
language."

Traveling so much, home is inside my mind. Security is not in relationship to affiliation, but on observation of movement, searching, arriving and leaving. If left to settle itself, my own lifeline will lose its tautness. Travel is walking a tightrope between destinations. It requires concentration and an inner hum of balance.

October 18, 1993
Santa Fe

Articles of Memory

IN 1993 I wanted to reserve my energy for "serious" writing. The manuscript *Luminaries of the Humble* was in its final draft before submission. I was working part time, then rushing home to eat dinner, answer phone calls, nap, and finally settle in to an evening with a set of tablets. I would write page after page of material to shape into poems. These sessions often went on until two or three in the morning, while I filled sections of the manuscript with newer pieces.

I was also incorporating stories and narrative poems into the second section of *Luminaries of the Humble.* To process the intense involvement with the narratives, I needed to step back and recover. Lillian Pitt, my aunt, had given me a beautiful handmade journal and turning the pages into private writing clarified my intentions. I found that using it also helped me produce new ideas. The journal, as an instrument, became a container for personal information and investigation. This was not a novel process, since writers are famous for their journals. It was fresh for me. I had lived with memory stored in oral history. Memory triggered by an event or an article in the teller's present that sparked her to tell of the past as a "teaching."

As I wrote the preface for *Luminaries of the Humble,* certain realizations surfaced: Poems are devices to recall important information, much like the symbols found in beadwork or heirlooms that bring stories of ancestry into the present. My commitment to writing is strong, but most of what becomes public upon publication is no longer exclusive. I needed something for myself. Journaling was a means to stay in touch with my separate identity away from the poems. The journal was immediate and private. Although I did not use a rigid day-to-day process of entry, later I found out that each entry was a small investment.

There are times I give a journal assignment in my English Composition 102 course at the Institute of American Indian Arts. I tell the students to think of it like this: "A journal is a penny bank. You will bank your experiences to draw upon for essay assignments and it may even support the art work you produce." To illustrate this I provide two examples from a collaboration with Okanogan artist Joe Feddersen. For the Tula Foundation Art Gallery in Atlanta, Georgia, in 1994, we made an installation of unusual book forms. The works centered on issues of native identity using text, photographs of hands, photocopies, and mixed materials. In an essay "Recognition of the Maker," in an anthology titled *Everything Matters* (Random House, 1996), I talk of the journal and its relationship to the making of art:

> Throughout the year we talked of many things in the A.I.O. (Americans for Indian Opportunity) program. We had fierce discussions about identity, sovereignty, and blood-quantum. A topic like blood-quantum is controversial and influences our lives. In my private life, many new ideas were discovered. In my journal during the A.I.O. program I wrote about this part of the process as I began photographing the hands of the ambassadors for the Tula Installation. (1993) "I was thinking of what each person had said, more or less, about being an Indian, by looks, skin color and the psychic pain of identity and perception of themselves. That trust needs to be established to *reveal* oneself and also to see acceptance as a *given* or response to trust and honesty. The face itself can be used as a tool of deception whereas the hands can reveal character, by use,

hard work or vanity. The genetic code of dexterity or strength, the fragility and the blemish are not covered up as easily or altered. Except by time and usage or care."

While A.I.O. met in Washington, D.C., I wrote a letter to my collaborator Joe Feddersen of these experiences coupled with impressions of a recent trip home. We used this letter in our 1994 collaborative installation of texts and unusual book forms at the Tula Foundation Gallery in Atlanta, Georgia. This letter suspended in my private thought shaped in part by the Ambassador's program. Joe felt it described a sense of place and belonging while acknowledging our differences even in the differing eras of a similar people. I describe a family event in the letter that expresses how the art project caused a deeper examination into my own issues of identity and the sense of becoming mature: "One cousin said, 'Pray hard for everyone. If we get strong the world gets better.' The salmon, deer meat, roots, fruit, corn, potatoes and the meal shared renewed my strength. It's odd to be thousands of miles away and thinking of telling you this. As Jolene and I walked outside, we strolled up the road, the air was rich with the exquisite smells of earth, sage, juniper. We were cupped in the liquid sense of sky, the mountain in the distance, the ground. I wonder at times why I stay away so long. I guess because I would miss it, if I did visit more. Sometimes, the work, the work I do, doesn't seem to fit and then I know I'm gathering things, knowledge, ideas, meaningful images when I travel."

In August of 1994 I moved from Portland, Oregon, to Santa Fe, New Mexico, to teach at the school I attended from 1980 to 1983. (I do have a history with the Southwest—I was born at Ganado, Arizona, and my father, Guy Woody, is Diné.) The movement was a new force in my writing, and it was through my journal I sensed the change. October 23, 1994, Santa Fe:

I have a lot to learn about this place, as a place of people who have a great sense of pride, history and community. That would help me, I believe, feel better. I know most of the time I watch the land, more so than the people. It is frustrating the way things move here, but I know it is part of the way people feel and move. I also thought of Spanish as a language I could learn along with many other languages. It would be good to be multilingual, like most of the people here. In the film, shown at the Wheelwright Museum, an older Hispanic man was asked, 'What foreign languages do you speak?' He answered, 'I know only one foreign language and that is English.' Which made the audience (predominantly S.W.) laugh.

I was absorbing new ideas about language. I wrote on October 27, 1994:

In one of my student papers, he talked of how we have given in to a mundane relationship with language, not acknowledging the sacred life that emanates from our tongue. Another student wrote of healing and about restoration of faith and belief in his essay. That we allow the bad to enter our lives and we are initially unaware of it. We nearly lose our lives. The body is only an instrument to accomplish the tasks we are responsible for to serve the earth, the good. I am learning from the students, "a genius," as Barney Bush says. The students are geniuses in the thoughts made of their (native) language. [It is good] To have them alive and in this life, their dedication and loyalty to their people and life, in all aspects of it. It is a simple "natural law" we have. I am near the point of making those distinctions.

Imagery slipped into the journal entries in the free hand and eye roaming, without thought of making poetry. Almost word for word from a journal entry, in the same period, the poem "Horizon" arrived. The language in "Horizon" and in another poem, "Flight," is taken from the journal and is a language of essences, of the landscape's qualities. The poems took on a new character once I started a journal. In my newer work the landscape series stressed a nameless existence.

HORIZON

Horizon,
palm to palm, exposure f/64, tonal shades on glass plates.
Long exposure. This will continue. Pause.
The kissing mist. Tongue mixing teeth. Arcing neck

a bridge. Repetitious hands move lengths of hair,
back, smooth hips, shape pose.

Inside the orange meat of a yam is pale yellow.
It falls apart in its own juices.
The old hot plate, a blackened porcelain cube.
Music of an empty transistor radio, round dial frozen.
The eternal wop wop of the center-
unrecognized flexible spine, the eyes and the Eyes,
swaying ache of muscle.

Clumsiness is to tear apart coherence.
Peaceful, skin sounds in the grooves that play digital.
The hips continue in parting.
Spirals are for centrifuge.
It is no longer light. The dark recognizable
as a chamber of throat and chest.

Inside, a child is cupped in the lap space of happiness
hears music. It is more.
It is the shaking interior of seeds.

Interior of flowers. The legs are crossbones
and creation mixing. Mirror.
A thin black pane between perception and flesh

We are the sweet sweep of eyelashes.
We are more than water purged of anger.
Belly sinks into another belly.

White water movement of glacier-aged
water, rock resists and then moves
away in the washout currents. The image is in silt.

Inside dream as Dream, spine balances, loses center.
In the ears, in wind, water, all sounds level.
Presence changed into a canopy of noise
over the tangle, the dense rain heart
of noise, noise, noise. Hands groping
lost ground. Feet brace the perimeters of corona.
Skin over the aural heartbeat without the organ.
Shell without the pressure of growth.

On the tip of mountains there is a cold white light.

The dips are waterfalls. The sun, a warm rise of crown.
Of halos and the reach of ankles, the trees emanate sound.
Covering is a small event, unzipped and locking teeth,
buttonless and sewing on shells, layered with opulent pearls.

Inside taste is a dark definition of light.
The drum is the garment for speech.
Intoxicated on the breath. No breath on collapsing.
Breath in explosion.
Hands roll away like aspen leaves, all color,
still, only captured light.

The power of synchronous heat welds loosened complexity.
The body expands, has unfolded itself from a rusted trunk.
It does not cull shame. Absorbs several values,
the original caul of luck, without its face and extremities
overwhelmed, claimed by crystal apertures.
The rise, a nose, breasts, or the knee laying
over the other knees, hand on waist.

Excerpt from "Flight"

Light and the rivers spark
the canyon below, stream over mountains, pools on terraces of high
    desert.
Step into the white spread of ozone, between and on the verge
    of the fall's memory of gravity, vulnerable peace.
The strike's breaking crack upon mountain desert resemble smallest
    fissures.
The pattern similar to the canyon's wear from movement.
Rain bounces diamonds on Red Earth.

Aspen, as sisters, genetically one, lean in comparable angle.
Radiance overtakes the iris of their bark.
Heated rocks crumble from the maternal anchor and fall.
Between mother and offspring, rock and gravity,
core and circle, is personal distance.
The creek song is mingled filament and clarity.
It moves to the edge of crevasse with unclouded sentiment.

Four Corners and Shiprock are hazy and gray.
Lukachukai is not far. Chinle, another conception.
Canyon De Chelly is peach in twilight and then plum.
Circles of rock and hogan, a twirling skirt and the color is sunlight.

Thunderheads are obscuration of rain, a glottal stop,
an inflection saturates empathic attachment to language.
Land's articulation is in resonance with congruity.
In renewal of nest, the eagle's restoration is for progeny.
Cradle of sandstone is worn by wind and rock of boulder.
Cedar reds, the color of cradleboards, is in the canyon walls.
The wells of rain a pocket of musings.

In the Cascade cinder fields of volcanic pasture,
a desert waits for the rain to jingle the small glass pockets
of obsidian. The sharp angles of smoky memory.

The cool temperature of absent fire.
Glassine windows into depth and night.
Black as burnt wood, rust, and snowflake.
Mountains, guileless and placid
in pearl casings rejuvenate the white water tentacles
reach to the rivers' meeting at lowland.

Water talks of its past in amplified song
which is loud and simultaneously soft.
In the south the language stops itself abruptly. Repeats itself softly.
In the north, songs rise and fall the scale of water tones.
From the river to the mountain,
the span in essence is descent and ascension in one body.

I feel best when I write poetry. However, the stress to produce a
poem is often too "gilded" with effort. The journal, in its immediacy, is a
release from deeper obligations, of attempts to write in a "higher language." I dip into the well without taking too much time away from my
daily obligations. I can remain ambivalent, strong and energetic, and deal
with the day-to-day issues of academic life. There are times when the
journal is the only writing I do.

When I have the space, I look to the journal to make artistic form
out of the words. I sense a particular memory in the pages of the journal
coupled with the present. Thoughts in a private context travel the fluid
path of language. I take the next step, the tightening up of the content
and intentions in creative activity. It is much like looking at my grandmother's beadwork, knowing her story is there and her creative self fills
the room with evocative memory. Once the habit is strong, the poems
are triggered from investments made in the pages of interior history.

Al Young

After all, with myself as the targeted, presold, fully subscribed audience for those pages, how could I possibly lose? . . . Discovery, excitement, the unchartable high of monkeying around with time and traveling through it—these were the rewarding facets of journal-keeping . . .

3rd April 1986

Driving into Santa Cruz and back, making that a full day's project isn't sitting well with me right now, back at this desk at almost 6 pm, almost suppertime in this land of such cold, hilly weather, perched and ready for the woman journalist who's doing a story on Carl Djerassi for San Francisco Focus and, according to Sally, might want to drop into some of the artists' studios to have them talk about their work and the placement here at the Foundation, and such. If I survive this lost day of poring over mss. to select students for the so-called advanced fiction-writing course I'm doing at Uncle Charlie's Summer Camp [University of California Santa Cruz (U.C.S.C.); a student-generated nickname] then I'm gonna spend the evening finally getting straight with SEDUCTION again; keep writing more pages, writing faster than I care to edit—and haven't yet sent a single page off to Joye Crespo, my typist and friend who's been waiting so patiently and generously to see what happens next. I've backed myself by now into a lot of corners that I'm going to have to just plain be bold to bust loose from. My sense is that solving the problems of the trunk and what's in it, handling Inspector Beaumont, bringing in Kendall and Sneaky Pete (who might very well be in cahoots with one another), working out the Benjie/Tree/Nomo thing, and possibly the Nomo/Danielle and/or the Chance/Danielle/Maxine rub. And what do I do about Mamie Franklin and Harry Silvertone now that they're back up in each other's face, however momentarily? And does it have to be momentary? And here you've gone and dragged poor youthful Theo into the picture to further aggravate matters. And what about Nixxy Privates and Charlean who're waiting in the wings, and the Fifi Prince/Privates connection, and Angelo Zelti (related to Zaccharetti?) and Crime and Punishment and Natasha Spellbind and Chance in Morocco? Can I keep all these balls up in the air, or should I start bringing them down one by one at once? And what about that scene with the hired servant and furnishings and all the excitement that Benjie, Nomo, Tree and Mamie generate around it, then they go back and see how *it was all a hired set-up, now broken down like a stage set? You gonna manage that? And soon?*

So now you see the problems and problems of writing a novel. You get all this stuff going and then figure out a way to make it make sense. It never was easy. But it does become more exciting as I get bolder about letting God or letting intuition, whichever you wanna call it, come in and fill out the empties and light up the corners and sand off the rough edges. Thinking this morning as I drove into Santa Cruz, towards Santa Cruz to be more accurate, on Hwy 35 then cutting over via Hwy 9, I was thinking about how it must feel to totally surrender; to let go with such faith and carelessness that you cannot help but land on your feet like a cat dropped from a hundred feet in the air. When you think about it the way Ann Hinkel's taught us to think about it, and the way Paramhansa devoted his entire life trying to get us to see clearly, then there is nothing else to conclude but that it must be more or less like going home. There's the ancestral sphere of infinitude you walked away from in your rebellion how many aeons ago? There's all the Mother or Father you'll ever need, right there inside you, playacting all your roles and roulettes, and everybody else's besides. There's the very thing—love—waiting to fill; that unfathomable hole you've got in your consciousness that can't be satisfied by anything but everything, all-out joyfulness forever amen. "I'm in this for keeps" would be a good answer to any question anybody asked about the spiritual life. FOR KEEPS. The only thing that seems to keep forever is forever. I love every bit of this journey and the force that's journeying with me, that is me, that is the journey, that is the is. Oh, language just doesn't get it the way you'd like it to—but that won't always be so.

Now it's hungry in the world time; no Michael here because I've goofed the time in Santa Cruz getting stuck in traffic and am gonna register with him again as a no-show. This, Thurs. night, is the only one he has free in this vacation of weeks, because tomorrow he goes to Tommy's for an overnight, the following day and evening will be spent at Great America, and the night after that is Sunday: time to start getting back into a school-going mode again. And me? Next week, just a few days from

now, April 9th, I take off for Chicago to give the Keynote address at the
Associated Writing Programs. The same day I take off for Nashville to do
the gig at Volunteer State the following day, spend the night in Tennessee
State, zip back over to Chicago. And we're talking about $500 for the
AWP, $1200 for Volunteer State, and probably as much as $350 laid out
for transportation via Republic Airlines from Chi to Nashville and back. So
what's that make for bring-home? Coming in at a little over a grand, yes?
That'll do. Feels odd not having any journalism assignments hanging
overhead at this very moment; miss those extra checks coming in. But it's
book or bust at this point. I'm sure it will start piling back up again the
minute I whistle the signal. Depending on the Creator for my income makes
it so much simpler than it used to be when I tried to shed headaches by
getting out there and forcing the economy. Simplification, that's the goal.

5 November 1986

It's funny how time works these days; every moment is accountable. I
suppose it was always so, yet now that I nakedly have no one to blame
for things that don't get done, I look at the passing of so-called time
differently; it's all blossoming out of me and my on-goingness. For example,
this weekend was spent in Los Angeles, where I continued to hang out with
Gary Larson, the cartoonist I'm writing the profile of for the New York
Times magazine. Larson was giving a talk at UCLA, so I thought this might
provide an excellent opportunity for me to look at him from another angle:
in a setting outside the privacy of his home in Seattle, which is where the
previous weekend was spent. Monte Kay has invited me to stay with him
and his wife Roberta for a night before moving on to the Sunset Marquis
Hotel for the following night. At the last minute, though, his plans have
changed; he and his wife can go to dinner with me, but the futon I slept
on last time is now in his daughter Susie's room and Roberta's son is
visiting. Anyway, the guest room scene has shifted and, besides, they're just
back from a Caribbean jazz cruise and so they're still catching their breath.

So what do I do? I pull an Al Young; that is, I land at Burbank
Airport, rent a Chevy Nova, drive around looking for the first motel that
looms in view, and end up at a place called the Bali Hai out in Sepulveda
in Van Nuys. It's $30 a night, but it also turns out to be a <u>low</u> dive; a
rendezvous joint for hookers and their johns and their pimps and male
prostitutes and probably dope traffic too. While I'm getting ready to take
an afternoon nap after check-in, I hear a soft knocking at my door but I'm
too weary to answer. Later that night the Kays treated me to a yummy
Mexican dinner at the Border Grill (where chile relleno with beans and rice
and salad tallied in at $14.50 and where the waiters and waitresses all
looked like Martin Mull or Farah Fawcett) on yupscale Melrose Avenue.
You talk about fern bars and trendiness! So after I've collapsed for the
night back at the Bali Hai, I'm awakened at 3:30 in the a.m. by what
sounds like a party going on in the parking lot beneath my window.
Pulling back the curtain, I peep out and see a couple of the women
chatting good-naturedly with their men while engines are idling and people
are patting one another on the butt and—well, there you have it. The next
morning right after meditation, I check out, drive down to the Santa
Monica Pier, gather a batch of screenwriting class assignments from the car
and go sit on the beach in the sun to do papers.

It always feels like Nathanael West's <u>Day of the Locust</u> whenever I'm
in L.A. Even the people walking past or jogging past my bench on the pier
seem like extras, like either they'd been famous long ago or are straining to
get discovered somehow. It's nerve-wracking. But there was a rather
remarkable thing that happened after I packed up and left Santa Monica
for Hollywood. No sooner have I driven the couple of miles up the Coast
Highway to Sunset than my attention is drawn to a hitchhiker right there at
the intersection with her thumb out, looking every bit like one of the
students I teach at Uncle Charlie's Summer Camp (as the kids call UC
Santa Cruz). At great peril to my health and the rented car, I pull over and
she hurries in. She's 22, blonde, impeccably dressed, very pretty and British;
Scotch, really, but quite the Anglophile. Her destination's Beverly Hills. Our

talk while I forged through murderous, smoggy midday traffic up sunset goes something like this:

"I know it probably seems odd," she says, "for someone like me to be hitchhiking, but I'm broke and don't have a car and this is the only way I can get around."

"Where you from?"

"Scotland, but I know my accent's English.

"Been in California long?"

"Two years."

"Like it?"

"I really do. My parents think they're going to lose me to Southern California. I would like to enroll at Santa Monica College next year and study business, brokerage in particular. And you, what do you do?"

"I'm a writer."

"Oh, really! What sort of thing do you write?"

"Novels, poetry, articles. I'm down here now doing a piece on a cartoonist, Gary Larson, who does 'The Far Side.' "

"How exciting! Yes, I'm familiar with that strip. I just finished a book myself."

"About what?"

"About my walk across America. It took 151 days. My name's Fiona Campbell, and my walk across the States was sponsored by the Campbell Soup Company—there's no relation, however."

"Did you make the Guinness Book of World Records?"

"Yes," she says, clearly delighted. "I'll be in the next edition. Writing is difficult, isn't it?"

"Do you have a publisher yet?"

"Not in America, but in the U.K., yes."

On it goes in this vein, with Fiona advising me about which lane I should be in and how I might want to snake around this car or that limousine. It's Indian summer with a vengeance; hot, actually in the 80's and still November, can you believe it? Palm trees are swaying and people seem to be generally in elevated spirits; at least drivers aren't honking or cussing at each other much.

At the mention of <u>Seduction By Light,</u> Fiona practically squeals with excitement. "What's it about?" she asks.

"Well, it's actually set right here in Beverly Hills and Santa Monica. She's a domestic who's also psychic and has an illegitimate son by a previous employer. She senses that she isn't going to live long, so she wants the boy and his father to get to know one another, and—"

"Oooh," she says, "it sounds a bit like <u>White Banner!</u>"

"Like, what?" I say, the title suddenly drowned to me in the unexpected tartness of her English tones and traffic noise.

"<u>White Banner</u>," she repeats slowly. "It was published around 1942, and it's also about a domestic who's psychic and who's had a son out of wedlock by a previous employer."

"You're kidding!"

"No, not at all."

"Where is it set?"

My heart is beating, even though I know the book can't possibly be anything like mine. All the same, I've made up my shocked mind to track the thing down.

"I'm looking for a job," Fiona tells me after I've recovered.

"Anything in particular?"

"About the only kind of work an alien like myself without papers is qualified to do: work as a domestic."

"Can't you be an English nanny?"

"No, and fortunately that sort of thing has gone a bit out of style here. I'm glad because I couldn't do it anyway. I find the idea distasteful."

And so I let her off someplace around Sunset and Rexford—which isn't far from where Poitier lives, I recall—in Beverly Hills, and I drive to the Sunset Marquis, where rooms let for $150 a night, check in, plunk down my Visa, and disappear into the world of doing school papers, going down for a Jacuzzi, then spiffing up for the meeting with Larson's publisher, his syndicate publicist and Larson himself that night at UCLA. Afterwards *we go out for dinner and it's already past 10:30, joined by Melanie Kirsch, sister to the publicist. And Melanie's got a book newly out about drugs that's got a lot of bread behind it; she's going on all the big TV shows like Donahue and David Letterman, and such. She turns to me in the back of the car and says, "So it looks as if I'm going to make a lot of money." Larson's coming down with the flu and can't wait to get away. I've got to teach in the morning and so I'm eager to get to bed.*

     By the time Vicky Houston drops me and the publisher George Parker off at the Marquis, it's almost one in the morning I pack up, as you might've guessed, and sleep like concrete, rise at 5, shower, jam down the elevator, settle my bills, hop in the Nova, remember to get gas before I get back to the rental site, dash into a 7-11 out near the Burbank Airport for coffee, which I snap a lid onto for drinking while I finish up my papers on the plane, but it's too close to take-off time, which is 6:53 a.m., so I end up leaving the coffee at the ticket counter, make the jet by the skin of my minty teeth, land in San Jose and hour later, find my Tercel, stuff my belongings inside it, motor to Santa Cruz and on it rolls like a dream.

     But imagine the chances of picking up a hitchhiker who'd read such a book as White Banner? *That's the kind of thing keeps me on my inner toes.*

Moments Noticed

LIKE COUNTLESS OTHERS, I began keeping a journal in my early teens, chronicling my daily impressions in one of those page dated, nominally lockable dimestore numbers that Tristine Rainer wrote about so unforgettably in *The New Diary*. It didn't take long, though, for me to grow wise to the limitations of jotting down my morning-to-night doings in the absurdly straight-ahead, ho-hum format the cramped design of those pocket-sized diaries dictated.

     My early teens coincided with the early 1950s, a time when I was devouring books from the Detroit Public Library and buying with money earned from shining shoes and janitoring downtown at the Sidney Hill Health Club—cheap, keepable paperbacks. My reading included such thrillers as William Saroyan's *The Twin Adventures,* Albert Camus's *Journals,* and Knopf's two-volume edition of *The Journals of André Gide.* The Saroyan book especially intrigued me. It combined the text of a novel, *The Adventures of Wesley Jackson,* with a charmingly chatty journal of equal length that the author, an American G.I. stationed in London during 1944, had kept while writing it. Characteristically, Saroyan had knocked out both manuscripts in a mere thirty days.

From such books, I gradually got the idea that keeping a diary or journal gave you the freedom to write (or not write) anything you damn well pleased. That you were also free to make entries anytime you wished gave me a curious little rush. I reacted quite differently, however, to Saroyan's seemingly informal "record keeping" than I did to Gide's or Albert Camus's, or to most of the other literary journals I had begun to study and comb. When I read even the childhood diaries of those larger-than-life literary Frenchmen, I could tell right off that their meticulous, delicately phrased entries represented something else again.

To whom had the ten-year-old Gide or the twelve-year-old Camus been directing their largely intellectual reflections, observations, assessments, and asides? Decades later I would conclude that these men-of-letters, even as children, tender prodigies, knew all about critical literary audiences and formal journal-keeping, to say nothing of posterity. Saroyan, on the other hand, gave every appearance of writing largely for himself, for the sheer fun and hell of it.

Quickly I lost interest in what a journal or a diary was *supposed* to be; instead I became absorbed with discovering or fashioning doors and windows that opened right up to me when I playfully hurled myself or tiptoed into my own unsupervised journals. After all, with myself as the targeted, presold, fully subscribed audience for those pages, how could I possibly lose? Mostly I wanted to get down something about the crazy turns and bends my days and nights had taken, something I imagined I'd find fascinating, gripping, or, at the very least, *useful* at some distant time—moods, thoughts, mysteries, illusions, passions, changes, the works. Discovery, excitement, the unchartable high of monkeying around with time and traveling through it—these were rewarding facets of journal-keeping that stunned and stimulated me then fully as much as they do right now.

MOMENTS NOTICED was the title I gave to a massive, three-ring bound journal kept between 1983 and 1986, and from which I've pulled the accompanying pages. Looking back, I can see where there had been so much boiling and bubbling in my troubled life at the time that journal-keeping became a crucial, obsessively therapeutic outlet. My mother had just died of cancer, my marriage of more than twenty years was faltering, my younger brother Richard, a Hollywood resident in pursuit of an acting career, committed suicide, my wife contracted and was treated for breast cancer—successfully, as it turned out—and I was traveling, performing, and lecturing in Europe (with a prolonged stay in what was then Yugoslavia), working as a journalist and, as always, writing poetry. Moreover, I was writing *Seduction By Light,* a novel I wasn't certain I would ever finish.

By spring of 1986, I had been invited (as a last-minute replacement for an applicant who had canceled) to spend three months at an artists' retreat: the Pamela Djerassi Foundation, a ranch tucked away in the bucolic hills of lush Woodside, California. That was where I happened to complete that novel, which is dramatically set in and around Hollywood. The story is narrated by Mamie Franklin, a singer and sometime-actress turned Beverly Hills maid for a prominent film producer and his foreign-born wife. Mamie, a middle-aged charmer, who knows she isn't long for this world, is, as she puts it, "setting her falling-down house in order." Not the least of Mamie's concerns is Benjamin Franklin, her only child, who has just graduated from the UCLA film school and who has yet to learn that his real father is a bigtime film and TV producer, a former employer and lover of Mamie's.

A novel about spiritual adventure, which I have found to be the most difficult of experiences to fictionalize appealingly, *Seduction By Light* is suffused with such phenomena as synchronicity, clairvoyance, ghosts, astral navigation, and one hell of an earthquake that practically devastates Los Angeles almost a decade before the 1994 disaster hit. During my stay at Djerassi—between March and May of 1986—the sound of Mamie's voice not only took over my head, it took full charge of the story; I tagged along behind her as best I could, some days pecking out between 15 and 20 pages on my beloved IBM Selectric II. Prior to that serendipitous residency, I had composed, over a period of five or so years, around 200 pages of the novel. In fewer than seven weeks at Djarassi, more than 250 pages flowed through me.

Once I left the retreat and returned to my studio, it took another 100 or so pages for the story to complete itself toward the close of that summer. Never will I forget the evening I realized the time had come to type *THE END.* Exhausted and choked with emotion (I had lived with Mamie Franklin and all the other characters for all those years, even while writing and publishing three other books), I went out and bought a six-pack of ale, checked into a motel by myself, spread the pages all over the floor of the room, then spent the night popping open can after can of beer as I stepped and crawled around the room, snatching up pages at random and reading them—silently, aloud—until I had laughed and cried myself to sleep.

The autumn of 1986 found me visiting Santa Monica, one of the settings I had more or less re-created for *Seduction By Light.* This was where Mamie lived. I remember sitting on the Santa Monica Pier, looking around me, imagining that I hadn't done badly in my depiction of that rebellious, enigmatic community which, because of its many municipal programs, was being called the People's Republic of Santa Monica. Driving back into Los Angeles along the Pacific Ocean, I picked up the lovely hitchhiker from Scotland I wrote about in the entry above.

Later, back at home up near San Francisco, I found the book she mentioned, *White Banner* (which I had never heard of before) although I had seen the movie made in the 1950s from one of Douglas's other novels, *Magnificent Obsession;* similarities between my maid character and his blew me away. Like everything else that has blossomed in time from seeds first planted in journals and diaries I've kept, the imponderable coincidence of having met Fiona Campbell—a voracious reader who had also made *The Guinness Book of World Records* by walking across the United States in 151 days—continues to blow me further and further away. The ever-melting wonder of it all!

Keeping Your Own Writer's Journal

WRITERS USE their journals to create and store inventory: the thoughts, phrases, images, and associations that come to mind or that they overhear. After reading the forty writers in this book, you may be inspired to experiment with keeping your own journal. If you haven't kept a journal before, your first steps will include procuring the writing implements and/or notebooks and then keeping them handy.

Think about where you write and when you are likely to have time to write. If this is away from home, be sure the notebook you choose is one you like carrying with you. Train yourself to keep your notebook with you. If you are most likely to write at home, keep it in a place at home where you like to sit. If your favorite way to keep a journal is using a computer, accommodate yourself by creating the necessary files. Name the files in ways that will amuse you and make you feel good about opening them. For years my word processing application has opened with the message "Sheila Bender, I'm a writer." It has kept me going on many occasions by helping me stick to this professional definition of myself. If you use different computers at home and at work, you might want to carry a floppy disk and make a copy of all files on it. Put an attractive label on the disk so you'll feel happy to see it.

It may seem intimidating to develop the journal-keeping habit. You may be thinking defeatist thoughts, such as "I can't do this regularly forever. I don't know how many times a week I'll really remember," and so on. At first, commit to keeping your journal for a month. Tell yourself that for this month you can make an entry every day or every other day or at least on weekends or on Mondays and Fridays. Whatever you decide, make sure you write at least that often. Start with an entry that describes why you created the system you did and why you bought the notebooks and pens or pencils or the disks and labels and why you committed the particular amount of time that you did. At the end of the month, make your last entry one in which you evaluate how your created system worked for you. Decide in that entry whether you want to stick with your original system for another month, make some alterations in it, or move on to a different system. After you write that last entry for the month, reread your very first entry. How do your end-of-the-month thoughts about journal-keeping compare to those you wrote down at the beginning of your month? You might want to write about the comparison. Next, make a commitment to the same or to a new journal-keeping system for one more month. Write this commitment down in your journal and then keep your entries going for another month. Do this month by month until keeping a journal is a habit.

Whether you are new at keeping a journal or have done so for a while, you can try out various ways of writing in your journal by taking ideas from the writers in this book.

Idea 1: Travel Journal

When you travel, write about your surroundings. Describe the rooms, buildings, streets, landscapes, people, and activities in which you are involved. (See the entries of Alcalá, Casteñada, Cole, Divakaruni, Hellenga, Manrique, Mori, Reich, Weimer, and Young). Jot down dialogues and conversation (see the entries of Casteñada, Hampl and Hemley). Describe yourself in your new surroundings being sure to show how you react to the people around you. (See the entries of Divakaruni, Hellenga, and Lopate.)

Idea 2: Journal Your Journaling

For consecutive days keep a journal of yourself keeping a journal, as David Mas Masumoto has done, or choose another activity besides journal-keeping and keep a journal for several consecutive days about that activity. Some examples are: training a puppy, having a visitor, planting a garden, and searching for the perfect gift for someone. Or take the same walk on journal entry days and write about the walk each time you take it. Whatever you do, capture your thoughts and behavior as you do whatever activity you are keeping a journal about.

Idea 3: Word Meditations

You might like to do a meditative writing exercise on a word as Lisa Shea does. Find a word by looking in books, newspapers, magazines, letters, signs, or billboards. If you can't decide on a word to use, locate five words in your vicinity (i.e., on your bulletin board, in a newspaper headline, on a shopping bag, on a warning label, on a card in your wallet). Write each of the five words on a scrap of paper and put the scraps in a bowl or hat. Choose one scrap and begin to write about that word. Write for ten to twenty minutes without stopping or editing yourself.

Idea 4: Tidbits, Odds and Ends

On some days you might just want to enter an apt phrase or description or an ironic question that comes to mind. Feel free. You might want to assign numbers to those kinds of tidbits when they show up, as Ron Carlson does. Or you might just leave them as short paragraphs entered under dates, as Denise Levertov and Israel Horovitz do, or leave them as paragraphs without dates as Jim Harrison and William Matthews do.

Idea 5: Journal Your Writing Process

If you are engaged in writing anything—story, poem, essay, play, or paper for school or for work—make some entries about your writing process, as do Bierds, Lesley, Matthews, Torgovnick, Tyau, and Winn. Like Bierds, be sure to say what your feelings are as you begin, revise, and finish what you are working on. What questions do you ask yourself, and what are you reading to help yourself write? What are you contemplating have happen in your writing? Or write as Matthews does, about what you think you are working against.

Idea 6: Poems

Let yourself do some entries in the form of poems, as Robert Alexander, Naomi Shihab Nye, and Elizabeth Woody do. The poems don't have to be great. They can just be litanies. See what happens if you give playfulness a chance by making line breaks and even by engaging silly rhymes.

Idea 7: Letters

Try writing letters, as Pam Houston, Fenton Johnson, and Shawn Wong do. Whether you mail them or not, and whether you choose to write them to an inanimate object, a place, a pet, a living person, a dead person, someone who knows you or never did or never will, the letter form will allow you to focus your thoughts and keep your thoughts flowing. You might want to make a list in your journal of potential people, places, animals, or things you might like to write a letter to. Try writing a letter from that person, animal, place, or thing back to you.

Idea 8: People Who Influenced You in Childhood

Diana Abu-Jaber and others write about people who were important to them as children. Make a list of all the people you can remember from your childhood and make entries from time to time in the form of ten- to twenty-minute freewrites (where you keep writing without editing or stopping yourself) about one person on this list.

Idea 9: Unloading Worries

Sometimes unloading professional worries and goals into the journal clears space for the writing self. Ilan Stavans writes down the books, colleagues, editors, and professional objectives that are on his mind.

Maybe allowing one day a week or a month for this kind of entry will be helpful to you.

Idea 10: Revision for the Fun of It

Stanley Plumly makes a journal of his revisions. Choose something you have already written in your journal. Begin to revise it, imagining you are an editor who has asked you for a specific kind of piece—memory piece, poem, essay on bus riding. Don't worry about the piece being perfect—just a sample of what can happen when you look at your writing again.

Idea 11: Fellow Enthusiasts

Write about meeting people who share your interests or hobbies, as Maxine Kumin does.

Idea 12: Weather Center

Become sensitive to the weather like Reginald Gibbons. Try describing the weather in your journal entries. Get your eye on the landscape, sky, people, animals, buildings, vehicles. Be specific with images and words that appeal to the senses. Write it so that when you reread that entry, you can taste, hear, smell, and feel as well as see the various weathers.

Idea 13: From Where You Are

Write entries that describe where you are as you write. Even if you write from the same place every day, you can describe it as it seems to you at the moment. And things change—what is on the desk, out the window, under your feet.

Idea 14: **Prompts**

Challenge yourself to write using a prompt. For example, "The last thing I ate before I sat down to write this entry was _____ and the next thing I might eat is _____. This is because . . .

When I look up from my page, the first thing I see is _____. I like/don't like this because . . .

Here are five things I should not have put in the trash and this is why . . . Here are five things I ought to put in the trash and here is why . . .

If I could describe the place where I am writing to a set designer for a movie, here is what I would say . . .

When I go to the White House for dinner, I always wear my _____ and take along my _____. That way . . .

When the nightly news director put words under the shot of me to identify me to the people, the words were _____. This is what had happened . . .

Write a list of five to ten prompts of your own that you can use from time to time. Or ask a friend to invent some for you to use.

Idea 15: **Use the Alphabet**

Make the alphabet your friend. Challenge yourself to put down your thoughts entry by entry with titles that start with each letter of the alphabet for twenty-six continuous entries. Or challenge yourself to start each entry itself for twenty-six days with words that begin with the alphabet's letters in order. Or write twenty-six meditations, one each on each letter of the alphabet.

Idea 16: **Reading Lists**

Read book reviews and make up reading lists in your journal.

Idea 17: **Library Searches**

Go to library on-line catalogs and investigate a subject and writer. Search for some of the books. Write about your search.

Idea 18: **Responses to Writers' Groups and Writers**

Write about your creative writing class, your writers' group, your reaction to a writer you are reading.

Idea 19: **Radio Prompt**

Turn on the radio for twenty seconds. Write about what you heard.

Idea 20: **Your Characters' Entries**

If you are a fiction writer, invent journal entries your characters might write. Whatever you like to write, invent journal entries your friends or relatives might write.

Idea 21: **Your Journal-Writing Employee**

Invent a persona for your journal—a character who is employed as a journal writer for you, whose job it is to make entries on a schedule you propose, someone whose creativity in dreaming up new ways to approach the genre will be rewarded. Write the job description in your journal. Write the interview with the job applicant. Assign this persona a wardrobe, a history, a reason why he or she wants this job. Write your new employee's entries. Let him or her react to the world and the people around him or her.

And of course use the journal to write whatever it is you want to write! There is no wrong way to keep a journal. It is for your eyes only or for the eyes of exactly who you want to see it.

However you do it, you will probably come to an understanding as the poet does in Lydia Davis's novel, *The End of the Story* (Farrar, Straus & Giroux, 1995). She considers a title for her collection of material and thinks:

> The best possibility may be MATERIAL—TO BE USED, which does not go as far as to say that it is ready but only that in some form it will be used, though it does not have to be used, even if it is good enough to use.

Look at journal material this way and it becomes a writer's best friend, offering timely, wholehearted, unconditional support.

Appendix 1

About the Contributors

Diana Abu-Jaber was born in Syracuse, New York, into a Palestinian/Jordanian/Irish, Muslim/Catholic family.

Her first novel, *Arabian Jazz*, won the Oregon Book Award in 1995. She was granted a National Endowment for the Arts award for work on her second novel, *Memories of Birth*. Excerpts of this unpublished novel appear in *Left Bank* (Volume 5) and in *Story Magazine* (Spring 1994).

Ms. Abu-Jaber is currently an assistant professor at the University of Oregon where she teaches writing and literature.

She cites the following authors:

Etel Adnan, *Sitt Marie Rose* (Post Apollo Press, 1990), translated by Georgina Kleege.

Louise Erdrich, *Love Medicine* (Holt, Rinehart, Winston, 1984)

Maxine Hong Kingston, *Woman Warrior: Memoirs of a Girlhood Among Ghosts* (Knopf, 1976).

Philip Roth, *Portnoy's Complaint* (Random House, 1969).

Kathleen Alcalá's first collection of short stories, *Mrs. Vargas and the Dead Naturalist,* was published by Calyx Books in 1992 after having won the King County Publication Prize in Washington State. Her newest novel, *Spirits of the Ordinary: A Tale of Casas Grandes,* has been published recently by Chronicle Books, San Francisco. She received the 1995 Washington State Artist Trust Literature Fellowship.

Ms. Alcalá is cofounder and now on the board of directors of *The Raven Chronicles,* a magazine of multicultural art, literature, and the spoken word, and assistant editor of *The Seattle Review.*

Robert Alexander is the author of eighteen plays including *Servant of the People* (a play about the rise and fall of Huey Newton and the Black Panther Party), *I Ain't Yo'*

Uncle, The New Jack Revisionist Uncle Tom's Cabin, Secrets in the Sands, and *The Hour-glass.*

A graduate of Oberlin College, Mr. Alexander has been a playwright-in-residence at the Lorraine Hansberry Theater in San Francisco. Mr. Alexander's work has been produced by the Negro Ensemble Company, the Kennedy Center, The Group Theater, Inner City Cultural Center, Los Angeles Theater Center, the Hartford Stage Company, Jomandi Productions, St. Louis Black Repertory Company, Crossroads Theater Company, and San Diego Repertory Theater. He was a 1996 Patricia Roberts Harris Fellow at the University of Iowa.

Mr. Alexander performs in the Bay Area as a spoken word artist with the Black Planet Collective. He coedited the anthology *Colored Contradictions, Postmodern African American Drama* (Signet, 1996).

James Bertolino's eighth volume of poetry, *Snail River,* was published in 1995 by the Quarterly Review of Literature poetry series. Other books include *Making Space for Our Living,* (Copper Canyon Press, 1975), *Precinct Kali & The Gertrude Spicer Story* (New Rivers Press, 1978), *First Credo (Quarterly Review of Literature,* 1986), and *New & Selected Poems* (Carnegie Mellon University Press, 1995).

Mr. Bertolino grew up in Wisconsin, graduated from the University of Wisconsin and received an MFA from Cornell University. He has received many awards including the Book-of-the-Month Club Poetry Fellowship, the Discovery Award, and a National Endowment for the Arts Fellowship. He teaches now at Western Washington University in Bellingham, Washington.

Here are some citations for the writers and books he referred to as influences on his journal-keeping:

Robert Creeley, *Pieces* (Scribner's, 1969).

Edward Dorn, *Hello, La Jolla* (Wingbow Press, 1978), *Abhorrences* (Black Sparrow, 1990), *Way West: Stories, Essays, & Verse Accounts: 1963–1993* (Black Sparrow Press, 1993).

Gary Snyder, *Regarding Wave* (New Directions, 1970).

Linda Bierds has published four books of poetry: *Flights of the Harvest-Mare* (Ahsahta Press, 1985), *The Stillness, the Dancing* (Henry Holt, 1988), *Heart and Perimeter* (Henry Holt, 1991), and *The Ghost Trio* (Henry Holt, 1994), which was a Notable Book selection of the American Library Association in 1995. Her awards include two grants from the National Endowment for the Arts, two Pushcart Prizes, the Consuelo Ford Award from the Poetry Society of America, and fellowships from the Ingram Merrill Foundation, the Artist Trust Foundation of Washington, and the Guggenheim Memorial Foundation.

Ms. Bierds' poetry has appeared in numerous anthologies and magazines, including *The New Yorker, Atlantic Monthly,* and *New American Poets for the Nineties* (Godine, 1991). She is an associate professor of English at the University of Washington.

Ron Carlson is the author of five books of fiction: the story collections *Plan B for the Middle Class* (W. W. Norton, 1992), which was selected one of the best books of 1992 by *The New York Times,* and *The News of the World* (W. W. Norton, 1987), which was also selected by *The New York Times* as one of the best books of 1987. His two novels are *Truants* (W. W. Norton, 1981), and *Betrayed by F. Scott Fitzgerald* (W. W. Norton, 1984). W. W. Norton will publish *The Hotel Eden* in 1997.

Mr. Carlson's fiction has appeared in anthologies such as *Best American Short Stories, 1987; Best of the West, Volumes 1 and 5; Sudden Fiction* from G. M. Smith Publishers in Salt Lake City; and *The Norton Anthology of Short Fiction,* 5th edition. His evening of monologues, *Bigfoot Stole My Wife,* has been widely produced. Mr. Carlson's stories have appeared in *Harper's, The New Yorker, GQ, Playboy,* and *Story* among other magazines.

He is currently a professor of English at Arizona State University in Tempe, Arizona, where he cohosts "Books and Company" on KAET Public Television.

Mr. Carlson cited Dawn Powell as an influence on his journal-keeping. Excerpts from Powell's journal appeared in *The New Yorker,* 6/26–7/3, 1995.

Omar S. Castañeda has published three novels, *Cunuman* (Pineapple Press, 1987), *Among the Volcanoes* (E. P. Dutton, 1991), and *Imagining Isabel* (Dutton/Lodestar, 1994). His collection of short fiction, *Remembering to Say Mouth or Face,* was published in 1993 by Fiction Collective Two and University of Colorado Press and won the

1993 Nilon Award for excellence in minority fiction. He has written a play, *Dance of the Conquest,* for third graders (Kane Publishing, 1993), and a picture book, *Abuela's Weave* (Lee and Lee Books, 1993). Mr. Castañeda coedited *New Visions: Fiction by Florida Writers* (Arbiter Press, 1989). His essay on Guatemalan macho oratory appears in *Muy Macho: Latino Men on Self-Identity and the Macho Myth* (Doubleday, 1996). Mr. Castañeda's short fiction and essays appear in the anthologies *Under the Pomegranate Tree: Latino Erotica* (Bantam, 1996) and *On the Wings of Peace* (Houghton Mifflin, 1995). A new collection of short stories, *Naranjo the Muse,* is forthcoming from Arte Publico Press.

Mr. Castañeda lives in Bellingham, Washington. He referred to *Writing From the Center* (Indiana University Press, 1995) by Scott R. Sanders as having influenced his journal-keeping.

Henri Cole has published three collections of poetry: *The Marble Queen* (Atheneum, 1986), *The Zoo Wheel of Knowledge* (Knopf, 1989), and *The Look of Things* (Knopf, 1995).

He is currently Briggs-Copeland Lecturer in Poetry at Harvard University.

Mr. Cole refers to the following work as influences on his journal-keeping.

Bruce Chatwin, *The Songlines* (Viking, 1987).

Colette, *The Vagabond* (Penguin, 1995). Translated by Enid McLeod.

Wallace Stevens, *Souvenirs and Prophecies* (Knopf, 1977).

Indian-born **Chitra Banerjee Divakaruni** has published three collections of poetry, *Dark Like the River* (Writer's Workshop, India, 1987), *The Reason for Nasturtiums* (Berkeley Poets and Press, 1990), and *Black Candle* (Calyx Books, 1991). She has edited a multicultural anthology, *Multitude: Cross Cultural Readings for Writers* (McGraw-Hill, 1993). Her collection of short fiction *Arranged Marriage* was published by Anchor/Doubleday in 1995.

Ms. Divakaruni teaches creative writing at Foothill College in San Francisco where she is also one of the founders and president of MAITRI, a South Asian women's service in the San Francisco area run by South Asian women volunteers serving victims of domestic violence and other abusive situations.

Janice Eidus is the author of the novels *Faithful Rebecca* (Fiction Collective, 1987) and *Urban Bliss* (Fromm International, 1994) as well as the short story collections *The Celibacy Club* (City Lights, 1996) and *Vito Loves Geraldine* (City Lights, 1990). Her nonfiction has appeared in *Publishers Weekly* and *Poets and Writers Magazine*.

She lives and teaches in Manhattan and reviews for *The New York Times Book Review, American Book Review,* and the *Review of Contemporary Fiction.·*

Reginald Gibbons has published four books of poems, the most recent of which is *Maybe It Was So* (University of Chicago, 1991), which won the Carl Sandburg Award. His novel *Sweetbitter* (Viking Penguin, 1996) won both the Anisfield-Wolf Book Award and the Jesse Jones Award of the Texas Institute of Letters. His other work includes volumes of translation, literary criticism, and edited collections, including an anthology of modern essays by poets about poetry, *The Poet's Work* (University of Chicago, 1989).

Since 1981 he has been the editor of *TriQuarterly* magazine at Northwestern University, where he teaches literature and creative writing. He also teaches in the MFA Program for Writers at Warren Wilson College.

Here are some citations for the writers and books Mr. Gibbons referred to as having influenced his journal-keeping:

Anton Chekhov, *Letters of Anton Chekhov* (Harper and Row, 1973). Translated by Michele Helm and Simon Korlinsky. *Letters of Anton Chekhov to His Family and Friends* (Chatto and Windus, 1920). Translated by Constance Garnett. *The Life and Letters of Anton Chekhov* (Cassell and Company, 1925). Translated by Koteliansky and Tomlinson. *Notebook of Anton Chekhov* (Ecco Press, 1987). Translated by Koteliansky and Leonard Wolf.

Witold Gombrowicz, *Diary Volume One 1953–1956, Volume Two 1957–1961,* and *Volume Three 1961–1966* (Northwestern University Press, 1988, 1989, 1993).

Thomas Mann, *Thomas Mann: Diaries 1918–1939* (Harry N. Abrams, 1982).

George Seferis, *A Poet's Journal, Days of 1945–1951* (The Belknap Press of Harvard University Press, 1974). *The Poet's Work, 29 Masters of 20th Century Poetry on the Origins and Practice of Their Art* (Houghton Mifflin, 1979).

Henry David Thoreau, *The Heart of Thoreau's Journals* by Odell Shepard (Dover Publications, 1961). *Henry David Thoreau, An American Landscape, Selected Writings from His Journals* by Robert L. Rathwell (Marlowe and Co., 1991).

Patricia Hampl's books include *A Romantic Education,* a memoir about her Czech heritage (Houghton Mifflin, 1981 and 1992 with a postrevolution afterword); *Virgin Time* (Farrar, Straus, and Giroux, 1992; paperback, Ballantine Books, 1993), a memoir about her Catholic upbringing and an inquiry into contemplative life; and *Spillville* (Milkweed Editions, 1987), a meditation on Antonin Dvorak's summer in Iowa. She has also published two collections of poetry, *Woman Before an Aquarium* (University of Pittsburgh Press, 1978) and *Resort and Other Poems* (Houghton Mifflin, 1983). She edited *The Houghton Mifflin Anthology of Short Fiction* (1989) as well as *Burning Bright,* an anthology of sacred poetry of the West from Judaism, Christianity, Islam (Ballantine, 1995). She has also written the screenplay for a feature film of *Spillville* for Robin Burke Productions in New York.

Ms. Hampl is the McKnight Distinguished Professor at the University of Minnesota in Minneapolis.

She referred to *The Art of Fiction* (Oxford University Press, 1948) by Henry James as having influenced her journal-keeping.

Jim Harrison's fiction includes the novels *A Good Day to Die* (Simon and Schuster, 1973), *Farmer* (Viking, 1976), *Warlock* (Dell, 1982), *Sundog* (Dutton, 1984), *Dalva* (Dutton, 1988), *Wolf* (Dell, 1989), *The Woman Lit by Fireflies* (Houghton Mifflin, 1990), *Julip* (Houghton Mifflin, 1994), and *Legends of the Fall* (Delta, 1994). He has published eight volumes of poetry, including *Plain Song* (W.W. Norton, 1965), *Locations* (W.W. Norton, 1968), *Selected and New Poems* (Delacorte, 1982), and *The Theory & Practice of Rivers* (Winn Books, 1985). His nonfiction collection is entitled *Just Before Dark* (Houghton Mifflin, 1991).

Mr. Harrison is a screenwriter for Warner Bros. and other film companies.

Here are citations for the books and authors he referred to as influences on his journal-keeping.

E. M. Cioran, *Anathemas and Admirations* (Arcade, 1991). *History and Utopia* (Seaver Books, 1987). *On the Heights of Despair* (University of Chicago Press, 1992). *The New Gods* (Quadrangle Books, 1974). *The Temptation to Exist* (Quadrangle Books, 1968).

Fyodor Dostoyevsky, *A Writer's Diary: Fyodor Dostoyevsky,* Vol. 1, 1873–1876, Vol. 2, 1821–1881 (Northwestern University Press, 1992).

Loren Eiseley, *All the Strange Hours: An Excavation of a Life* (Scribner's, 1975).

Gustave Flaubert, *The Letters of Gustave Flaubert* Vol. 1 1830–1857, Vol. 2 1857–1880 (Belknap/Harvard University Press, 1982).

Tom McGuane. Jim Harrison had a personal correspondence with this prolific novelist.

Henry David Thoreau. See biographical notes for Reginald Gibbons.

Robert Hellenga is author of the novel *The Sixteen Pleasures* (Soho, 1994, Delta, 1995), for which a screenplay is being prepared by a major motion picture company. His short fiction appears in many magazines and literary journals including the *Iowa Review, Crazyhorse, The Chicago Review, TriQuarterly, The Chicago Tribune Magazine,* and *The California Quarterly.*

Mr. Hellenga is a professor of English at Knox College, Galesburg, Illinois.

Following are citations for the books and authors he referred to as having an influence on his journal-keeping.

Dorothea Brande, *Becoming a Writer* (J.P. Tarcher, 1981).

Mrs. Dostoevsky (Dostoevkaia, Anna Grigor'evna Snitkina), *The Diary of Dostoyevsky's Wife* (Macmillan, 1928) edited by Rene Fulop-Miller and Dr. Frank Eckstein. Translated by Madge Pemberton. *Dostoevsky Portrayed by His Wife, the Diary and Reminiscences of MME. Dostoevsky* (E. P. Dutton, 1926). Translated from the Russian and edited by S. S. Koteliansky.

Mrs. Tolstoy, *The Diary of Tolstoy's Wife, 1860–1891* (Payson and Clarke, 1929). Translated by Alexander Werth.

Robin Hemley is the author of the novel *The Last Studebaker* (Graywolf, 1992) and the story collections *All You Can Eat* (Grove/Atlantic Monthly Press, 1988) and *The Big Ear* (John F. Blair, 1995). His book of practical criticism, *Turning Life into Fiction,* was published in 1994 by Story Press. Mr. Hemley's work has also been published in the Pushcart Prize Anthologies (Volumes 15 and 19), and in the *Best American Humor of 1994* (Touchstone). He is the recipient of the 1996 Nelson Algren Award.

Mr. Hemley teaches creative writing at Western Washington University in Bellingham, Washington, and is editor of *The Bellingham Review.*

Brenda Hillman has published two chapbooks of poetry, *Autumn Sojourn* and *Coffee, 3 A.M.* (Em Press, 1995, 1982). Her volumes of poetry include *Bright Existence* (1993), *Death Tractates* (1992), *Fortress* (1989), and *White Dress* (1985) (all published by Wesleyan University Press). She has also edited *The Poetry of Emily Dickinson* for Shambhala Publications (1995).

Ms. Hillman's work appears in the *Pushcart Prize Anthology* (1990 and 1992), the *Best American Poetry,* Collier Books 1990 and *A Book of Women Poets From Antiquity to the Present,* Schoken, 1980 among other anthologies.

Ms. Hillman has taught as a visiting faculty member at the University of Iowa, the University of California, Irvine, the University of San Francisco, and Warren Wilson College. She is an associate professor at St. Mary's College.

Here are citations for the books and authors Ms. Hillman referred to as influences on her journal-keeping:

John Cheever, *The Journals of John Cheever* (Knopf, 1991).

Anton Chekhov. See citations in the biographical notes for Reginald Gibbons.

Gerard Manley Hopkins, *Journals and Papers* (Oxford University Press, 1959). *Selections from the Note-books of Gerard Manley Hopkins* (New Directions, 1945).

Sylvia Plath, *The Journals of Sylvia Plath* (Dial Press, 1982).

George Seferis. See citations in the biographical notes for Reginald Gibbons.

Paul Valéry, *The Collected Works of Paul Valéry, Vol. 1* (Bollingen Foundation, 1956). Edited by Jackson Matthews. *The Collected Works of Paul Valéry,* Vol. 1, Bollingen Series XLV 1, Princeton University Press (Princeton, N.J., 1971). *The Collected Works of Paul Valéry,* Vol. 2, Bollingen Series XLV 2, Princeton University Press (Princeton, N.J., 1969). *Self-Portraits, The Gide/Valéry Letters 1890–1942* (University of Chicago Press, 1955). Edited by Robert Mallet.

Israel Horovitz is the author of nearly fifty plays, many of which have been translated and performed in as many as twenty languages worldwide. Among Horovitz's best-known plays are *The Indian Wants the Bronx, Line, It's Called the Sugar Plum, Rats, The Primary English Class, Morning, Today, I Am a Fountain Pen, North Shore Fish, Park Your Car in Harvard Yard, The Widow's Blind Date,* and *Unexpected Tenderness.*

Mr. Horovitz's filmed screenplays include *The Strawberry Statement, Believe in Me, Author! Author!* and *A Man in Love.* He has recently adapted his plays *North Shore Fish* and *The Widow's Blind Date* for the screen and has written new screenplays for Warner Bros.'s upcoming films *James Dean* and a new version of *A Star Is Born.*

He lives and works in France, where eighteen of his plays recently have been translated and performed. No other American playwright has been produced more frequently.

Mr. Horovitz is founder and artistic director of The Gloucester (Massachusetts) Stage Company and of the New York Playwrights Lab.

Here are citations for books and authors Mr. Horovitz referred to as having influenced his journal-keeping.

Samuel Beckett, *Happy Days: Samuel Beckett's Production Notebook* (Grove Press, 1986). Edited by James Knowlson.

Albert Camus, *American Journals* (Marlowe and Co., 1995). *Notebooks 1935–1942* (Knopf, 1963). Translated by Philip Thody. *Notebooks 1942–1951* (Knopf, 1965). Translated by Justin O'Brian.

Eugene Ionesco, *Fragments of a Journal* (Grove, 1968). *Notes and Counter-Notes* (John Calder, 1964).

Pam Houston is the author of the short story collection *Cowboys Are My Weakness* (W.W. Norton, 1992), which won the 1993 Western States Book Award. It has been translated into seven languages. She edited a collection of fiction, nonfiction, and poetry called *Women on Hunting* (Ecco Press, 1995).

Ms. Houston is contributing editor to *Elle* and *Ski* magazines. She teaches in the MFA program at St. Mary's College in Moraga, California, as well as at writers' conferences and festivals across the United States and England.

Fenton Johnson is the author of two novels, *Crossing the River* (Birch Lane Press, 1989/Dell, 1991) and *Scissors, Paper, Rock* (Pocket, 1993/Washington Square, 1993). *Geography of the Heart: A Memoir* was published by Scribner in 1996.

Mr. Johnson's essays have been anthologized in *Wrestling with the Angel: Faith and Religion in the Lives of Gay Men* (Putnam, 1995) and *How We Live Now: An Anthology of Contemporary Multicultural Literature* (Beacon, 1993).

Mr. Johnson is a contributor to the *New York Times* Magazine and writes scripts for public television documentaries. He is on the faculty of the Creative Writing Program at San Francisco State University and the Napa Valley Writer's Workshop.

Here are citations for the journals he mentions in his commentary:

May Sarton, *The House by the Sea, A Journal* (Norton, 1977).

Samuel Pepys, *Pepys Diary* (The Macmillan Co., 1963). *The Shorter Pepys* (University of California Press, 1985).

Maxine Kumin has authored several novels and books of poetry including *Our Ground Time Here Will Be Brief* (Viking/Penguin, 1982), *The Long Approach* (Viking/

Penguin, 1986); *Nurture* (Viking/Penguin, 1989); *Looking for Luck* (Norton, 1992), and *Connecting the Dots* (Norton, 1996).

Her collection of short stories is entitled *Why Can't We Live Together Like Civilized Human Beings?* (Viking, 1982). Her collections of essays are entitled *To Make a Prairie: Essays on Poets, Poetry and Country Living* (University of Michigan Press, 1980); *In Deep: Country Essays* (Beacon Press, 1988); and *Women, Animals, and Vegetables: Essays and Stories* (Norton, 1994).

In addition, Ms. Kumin has published a number of children's books.

Ms. Kumin has most recently been a visiting professor at the University of Miami (Florida). She has been elected to join the board of chancellors of the Academy of American Poets.

Following are citations for authors whose work influenced her journal-keeping:

James Agee, *The Collected Short Prose of James Agee* (Norman S. Bers, 1978). Editor, Robert Fitzgerald. *Letters of James Agee to Father Flye* (George Braziller, 1962).

Louise Bogan, *What the Woman Lived: Selected Letters* (Harcourt Brace, 1973). *Journey Around My Room, The Autobiography of Louise Bogan, A Mosaic* (Penguin Books, 1981). Editor, Ruth Limmer.

John Cheever, *The Letters of John Cheever* (Simon and Schuster, 1988).

Anne Sexton, *Anne Sexton: A Self-Portrait in Letters* (Houghton Mifflin, 1991).

Woolf, Virginia, *Diary of Virginia Woolf, Vol. 1–5, 1915–1941* (Harcourt Brace Jovanovich, 1977–1984). Edited by Ann Olivier Bell. *A Moment's Liberty, the Shorter Diary of Virginia Woolf* (Harcourt Brace Jovanovich, 1984). *Moments of Being, Unpublished Autobiographical Writings* (Harcourt Brace Jovanovich, 1976). Edited by Jeanne Schulkind. *A Passionate Apprentice, The Early Journals 1897–1909* (Harcourt Brace, 1990). *A Writer's Diary: Being Extracts From the Diary of Virginia Woolf.* (Harcourt and Brace, 1954). Edited by Leonard Woolf.

Craig Lesley has published three novels: *Winterkill* (Houghton Mifflin, 1984), *River Song* (Houghton Mifflin, 1989), and *The Sky Fisherman* (Houghton Mifflin, 1995). He edited *Talking Leaves: Native American Short Fiction and Dreamers* (Dell, 1991) and coedited *Dreamers and Desperadoes: Contemporary Short Fiction of the American West* (Dell, 1993) with Katheryn Stavrakis. His short fiction appears in *Writers' Forum, The Massachusetts Review, Mississippi Valley Review, The Seattle Review,* and *Northwest Review.* He is currently a professor of English at Clackamas Community College in Oregon City, Oregon.

He referred to William Ratigan's *Great Lakes, Shipwrecks and Survivals* (William B. Eerdmans, 1960) as having influenced his journal-keeping.

British-born **Denise Levertov** has lived in the United States since 1948. She received the 61st Fellowship of the Academy of American Poets for distinguished poetic achievement. She has published many books of poems as well as essays, translations, and memoirs. Her newest book of poems is *Sands of the Well,* New Directions Press, 1996. Also from New Directions are the recent poetry collections *Evening Train, A Door in the Hive,* and *Breathing Water,* as well as *Poems 1968–1972.* Ms. Levertov's latest book of essays is *Tesserae (Memories and Suppositions)*, New Directions 1995, which also published *New and Selected Essays* in 1992. A bibliography of Ms. Levertov's extensive work was published in 1988 by Garland Publishers. Critical studies of her work have been published in the last years by Hofstra University, the University of South Carolina, and the University of Michigan.

After a distinguished teaching career at Vassar College, Massachusetts Institute of Technology, Tufts University, Brandeis University, and Stanford University among others, Ms. Levertov is now emerita professor at large, Cornell University.

Here are some citations for the books and authors Ms. Levertov referred to as influences on her journal-keeping.

Samuel Taylor Coleridge, *Anima Poetae* (U-M-I Out of Print Books on Demand, 1990). Kathleen Coburn edited.

John Keats, *Letters of John Keats 1814–1821,* 2 volumes (Harvard University Press, 1958). Edited by Hyder E. Rollins.

Rainer Maria Rilke, *Letters on Cézanne.* (Fromm International Publishing Corp., 1985). Edited by Clara Rilke. *Letters to a Young Poet* (Swedgewick, Jackson, 1945).

Translated by Reginald Snell. *Selected Letters of Rainer Maria Rilke, 1902–1926* (Macmillan, 1946). R.F.C. Hull translated.

Dorothy Wordsworth, *Home at Grasmere, Extracts from the Journal of Dorothy Wordsworth (written between 1800 and 1803) and from the poems of William Wordsworth)* (Penguin Books, 1986), Colette Clark, editor.

Phillip Lopate is the author of three essay collections: *Bachelorhood* (Little, Brown, 1981), *Against Joie de Vivre* (Poseidon/Simon and Schuster, 1989), and *Portrait of My Body* (Doubleday, 1995). His novels include *The Rug Merchant* (Viking, 1987) and *Confessions of Summer* (Doubleday, 1979). He has published two poetry collections, *The Eyes Don't Always Want to Stay Open* (Sun Press, 1972), and *The Daily Round* (Sun Press, 1976). *Being with Children* (Doubleday-Anchor, 1994) is a memoir of his teaching experiences. He edited *Journal of Living Experiment* for Teachers and Writers (1979) and the definitive *The Art of the Personal Essay* for Doubleday-Anchor (1994).

He currently holds the Adams Chair at Hofstra University where he is professor of English. Here are citations for the writers and books Mr. Lopate referred to as influences on his journal-keeping.

Fyodor Dostoyevsky

André Gide, *Journals of André Gide, Volumes 1–3.* (Knopf, 1947–1949), translated by Justin O'Brien.

Friedrich Nietzsche, *Nietzsche: A Self-Portrait from His Letters* (Harvard University Press, 1971). Peter Fuss and Henry Shapiro edited. *The Portable Nietzsche* (Viking Press, 1977). Selected and translated with introduction, prefaces, and notes by Walter Kaufmann.

Jaime Manrique is a Colombian-born writer. His first volume of poetry, *Los adoradores de la luna,* received Colombia's National Poetry Award. He is the author in Spanish of *El cadaver de papa* (a novella and short stories) and *Notas de Cine* (a collection of film criticism). In English, he is the author of a volume of poetry, *Scarecrow* (Groundwater Press, 1990) and the novels *Colombian Gold* (Clarkson N.

Potter, 1983), *Latin Moon in Manhattan* (St. Martin's Press, 1992), and *Twilight at the Equator,* forthcoming Spring 1997 from Farber & Farber.

His poetry collection, *My Night with Federico García Lorca* for Groundwater Press appeared in 1996.

Mr. Manrique is currently living in New York City.

Here are citations for the author Mr. Manrique referred to as an influence on his journal-keeping.

Katherine Mansfield, *The Collected Letters of Katherine Mansfield, Vol. 1 1903–1917* (Oxford University Press, 1984). Vincent O'Sullivan and Margaret Scott created the book. *Journals of Katherine Mansfield* (Knopf, 1941). Selections edited by her husband, J. Middleton Murry, of journals kept by the New Zealand short fiction writer and novelist from 1910 to 1922. *The Letters and Journals of Katherine Mansfield.* (Allen Lane, 1977). Editor C. K. Stead has selected from material Murry didn't publish. *The Scrapbook of Katherine Mansfield* (Knopf, 1940). John Middleton Murry edited.

David Mas Masumoto has published *Silent Strength,* a book of short stories (New Currents International, 1984), *Country Voices,* a book of oral histories of the Japanese community around Fresno, California (Inaka Countryside Publications, 1987), and *Epitaph for a Peach,* a memoir of farming with his family (HarperSanFrancisco, 1995), which won the 1995 International Association of Culinary Professionals Award for best literary food writing. He has written numerous articles for *USA Today* and the *Los Angeles Times.*

Mr. Masumoto farms organically with his family on eighty acres of peach trees and grapevines outside of Fresno, California.

He refers to Joan Didion's essay "On Keeping a Notebook" from *Slouching Toward Bethlehem* (Farrar, Straus & Giroux, 1968), in which the novelist and essayist says, "It is a good idea, then, to keep in touch, and I suppose that keeping in touch is what notebooks are all about."

William Matthews's thirteen books of poems and essays include *Curiosities* (University of Michigan, 1989), *Selected Poems & Translations,* 1969–1991 (Houghton Mifflin,

1992); *The Mortal City: 100 Epigrams from Martial* (Ohio Review Books, 1995); and *Time and Money* (Houghton Mifflin, 1995), which won the National Book Critics Circle Award for Poetry, given to the best body of poetry published in 1995.

Mr. Matthews is a past president of the Poetry Society of America.

He currently teaches at City College in New York.

Mr. Matthews has referred to *Straw for the Fire: From the Notebooks of Theodore Roethke 1943–63* (Anchor Books, 1974).

Kyoko Mori's books include the novel *Shizuko's Daughter* (Henry Holt, 1994), which won the Wisconsin Council of Writer's Best Novel Award, and *One Bird* (Henry Holt, 1995); a memoir, *The Dream of Water* (Henry Holt, 1994); a book of poems, *Fallout* (Tia Chucha Press, 1994); and a new collection of essays forthcoming in 1997.

Ms. Mori's short fiction appears in *The Sun Dog, The Maryland Review, The Apalachee Quarterly, The Cream City Review, The Kenyon Review,* and *Cross-Currents* among other magazines. Her poems have appeared in *The American Scholar, The Missouri Review, The Beloit Poetry Journal,* and *The Northwest Review,* among others.

Ms. Mori is an associate professor of English and Creative Writing at Saint Norbert College in De Pere, Wisconsin.

Here are citations for the books and authors Ms. Mori referred to as influences on her journal-keeping.

John Cheever. See citations in biographical notes for Brenda Hillman and Maxine Kumin.

Anaïs Nin. There are many editions of the French-born American novelist's literary diaries. *The Early Diaries of Anaïs Nin, Vols. 1–4, 1920–1931* (Harcourt Brace and Co., 1978–1985). Volume 3 is sometimes called "The Diary of a Young Wife." *The Diary of Anaïs Nin, Vols. 1–7, 1931–1974* (Harcourt Brace, 1966). *The Diary of Henry and June: The Unexpurgated Diary of Anaïs Nin* (Harcourt Brace, 1989). *Fire: From "A Journal of Love": The Unexpurgated Diary of Anaïs Nin 1934–1937* (Harcourt Brace, 1995). *Incest: From a Journal of Love, The Unexpurgated Diary of Anaïs Nin, 1932–34.* (Harcourt Brace, 1992).

Virginia Woolf. See citations in biographical notes for Maxine Kumin.

Naomi Shihab Nye's books of poems include *Red Suitcase* (BOA Editions, 1994) and *Words Under the Words: Selected Poems* (Far Corner Books, 1995). Her picture book *Sitti's Secrets* (Four Winds Press, 1994); *Benito's Dream Bottle* was published in 1995 by Simon and Schuster. Ms. Nye edited *This Same Sky,* an anthology of international poetry, for Four Winds Press/Macmillan (1992) and *The Tree Is Older Than You Are,* a bilingual collection from Mexico, for Simon and Schuster (1995). She is featured on two PBS poetry specials: "The Language of Life with Bill Moyers" and "The United States of Poetry."

She has traveled abroad on three Arts America speaking tours and lives, writes, and edits in San Antonio, Texas. She refers to the following works/authors as having influenced her journal-writing.

David Ignatow, *The Notebooks of David Ignatow* (Black Sparrow Press, 1973).

May Sarton. The following diaries of the poet were published by Norton: *The House by the Sea: A Journal* (1977), *Journal of a Solitude* (1977).

Stanley Plumly's most recent collection of poems is *The Marriage in the Trees* (Ecco Press, 1996). His first collection, *In the Outer Dark* (LSU Press, 1970), won the Delmore Schwartz Memorial Award. In 1974 Ecco Press published *Out-of-the-Body Travel* in the American Poetry series. *Summer Celestial* was published in 1985 by Ecco Press, and *Boy on the Step* in 1989. Earlier works include *Giraffee* (LSU Press, 1974) and *How the Plains Indians Got Horses* (Best Cellar Press, 1973).

For the past ten years, Mr. Plumly has been a professor of English at the University of Maryland.

Here are citations for the authors and works he referred to as influences:

Samuel Taylor Coleridge, *Biographia Literaria or Biographical Sketches of My Literary Life and Opinions* (Cambridge University Press, 1920). Also see citation in biographical note for Denise Levertov.

John Keats. (See citation in biographical notes for Denise Levertov).

David Reich is editor of *The World,* the national magazine of Unitarian Universalism. His articles about the political power of the fundamentalist Christian right and his interviews with political figures appear regularly in that magazine.

In the 1970s and 1980s Mr. Reich's fiction and articles appeared in *Transatlantic Review, The Smith, North American Review, Beyond Baroque,* and other literary magazines.

Mr. Reich previously taught writing at Framingham State College and Northeastern University.

He referred to the following works by Jack Kerouac reprinted in *The Portable Kerouac* (Viking Press, 1995), edited by Ann Charters, as having influenced his writing: "Belief & Technique for Modern Prose," "Essentials of Spontaneous Prose."

Lisa Shea's first novel *Hula,* was published by Norton in 1994. Her essays, book and music reviews, and feature articles have appeared in *The New York Times Book Review, Interview, Mirabella,* the *Forward, Allure, The Women's Review of Books, Elle,* and *People,* among other publications.

Ms. Shea is the recipient of a Whiting Award and has taught fiction at Breadloaf and the Mt. Holyoke Writer's Conference, and at the Bennington College July program.

She lives in Brooklyn, New York.

Here are citations for books and authors Ms. Shea referred to as having influenced her journal-writing:

Samuel Beckett, *Samuel Beckett* (Simon and Schuster, 1990) by Deidre Bair.

Brontës, *The Brontës: Charlotte Brontë and Her Family* (Fawcett, 1990) by Rebecca Fraser.

Jim Carroll, *The Basketball Diaries* (Penguin, 1987).

F. Scott Fitzgerald, *The Crack-Up* (New Directions, 1956). Edited by Edmund Wilson.

Anne Frank, *The Diary of a Young Girl: The Definitive Edition* (Doubleday, 1995).

James Joyce, *Letters of James Joyce* (Viking Press, 1957). Stuart Gilbert, editor. *Scribbledehobble: The Ur-Workbook for Finnegans Wake* (Northwestern University Press, 1961). Edited and introduced by Thomas E. Connolly.

Flannery O'Connor, *The Habit of Being, Letters of Flannery O'Connor* (Vintage Books, 1979). Sally Fitzgerald edited. *Mystery and Manners: Occasional Prose of Flannery O'Connor* (Farrar, Straus & Giroux, 1961). Edited by Sally and Robert Fitzgerald.

Simone Weil, *First and Last Notebooks* (Oxford University Press, London, 1970). Translated by Richard Rees. *Notebooks, Vol. 1 and Vol. 2* (Routledge and Kagan Paul, 1956). Translated by Arthur Wills. *Simone Weil: An Anthology* (Virago Press, 1986). Edited by Sian Miles. *The Simone Weil Reader* (David McKay Company, 1977). Edited by George A. Panichas.

Kim R. Stafford's publications include *Rendezvous: Stories, Songs, & Opinions of the Idaho Country,* a collection of folklore (Idaho State University Press, 1982); *Having Everything Right: Essays of Place* (Confluence Press, 1986, rpt. Sasquatch Books, 1997); and *Entering the Grove,* a book of essays in celebration of trees with photographer Gary Braasch (Peregrine Smith, 1990).

Mr. Stafford teaches at Lewis and Clark College in Portland where he directs the Northwest Writing Institute, which assists writers and writing teachers through the Oregon Writing Project, Workshops in Writing and Thinking, and the Imaginative Writing Seminars series.

He refers to Dorothy Wordsworth as having influenced his journal-writing. Here are two citations: *Journals of Dorothy Wordsworth: the Alfoxden Journal 1798,* and *The Grasmere Journals 1800–1803* (Oxford University Press, 1973).

Ilan Stavans is the author/editor of several books, including *Sentimental Songs/La poesia cursi by Felipe Alfau,* a bilingual edition (Dalkey Archive Press, 1992); *Imagining Columbus: The Literary Voyage* (Twayne-Macmillan, 1993); *Growing Up Latino* (Houghton Mifflin, 1993) (coedited with Harold Augenbraum); *Tropical Synagogues: Short Stories by Jewish—Latin American Writers* (Holmes and Meier, 1994); *The Hispanic Condition, Reflections on Culture and Identity in America* (HarperCollins, 1995); *Bandido:*

Oscar 'Zeta' Acosta & the Chicano Experience (HarperCollins, 1995); *The One-Handed Pianist and Other Stories* (University of New Mexico Press, 1996); *Art & Anger: Essays on Politics and the Imagination* (University of New Mexico Press, 1996); *The Urban Muse: Stories on the American City* (forthcoming from Delacorte); and *New World: New Latino Writers* (Delacorte, 1997).

Mr. Stavans's literary criticism, essays, and short fiction appear in many U.S. and Latin American publications including *The New York Times, The Washington Post, The Boston Globe, The Nation, Salmagundi, TriQuarterly, Tikkun, Hungry Mind, Utne Reader, El Observador, Excélsior,* and *El Nacional* among others.

Mr. Stavans teaches at Amherst College in Amherst, Massachusetts.

Here are some citations for the books and authors Mr. Stavans mentions in his commentary.

Hannah Arendt, *Between Friends: The Correspondence of Hannah Arendt and Mary McCarthy* (Harcourt Brace, 1995). *Eichmann in Jerusalem, A Report on the Banality of Evil* (Penguin, 1977).

Isaac Babel, *1920 Diary* (Yale University Press, 1995).

Jorge Luis Borges, "Autobiographical Essay," in *The Aleph and Other Stories, 1933–1969* (E.P. Dutton, 1970).

Graham Greene, *A World of My Own* (Viking, 1995).

Mary McCarthy, *Memories of a Catholic Girlhood* (Harcourt Brace, 1957). *How I Grew* (Harcourt Brace, 1987). *Ideas and the Novel* (Harcourt Brace, 1980).

V. S. Naipaul, *The Loss of El Dorado* (Penguin, 1973).

Pablo Neruda, *Memoirs* (Penguin, 1987).

Isaac Bashevis Singer, *In My Father's Court: A Memoir* (Farrar, Straus and Giroux, 1962).

Marianna de Marco Torgovnick is the author of many books and articles including *Gone Primitive: Savage Intellects, Modern Lives* (University of Chicago Press, 1990) and

The Quest for Ecstasy: Primitivism at the Millennium (forthcoming from Knopf, 1997). Her book of personal essays and literary criticism, *Crossing Ocean Parkway: Readings by an Italian American Daughter* (University of Chicago, 1994), won an American Book Award. She edited *Eloquent Obsessions: Writing Cultural Criticism* (Duke University Press, 1994). Ms. Torgovnick teaches English at Duke University.

Kathleen Tyau's first novel, *A Little Too Much Is Enough,* was published by Farrar, Straus and Giroux (1995). Her writing appears in *The Stories That Shape Us* (Norton, 1995) and in magazines and journals such as *American Short Fiction, Story, Glimmer Train, Left Bank,* and *ZYZZYVA.*

She has received writing fellowships from Fishtrap Inc. in 1992, from Oregon's Literary Arts, and from the Oregon Arts Commission.

She lives outside of Portland, Oregon, where she teaches writing workshops.

Ms. Tyau has gathered ideas for her journal writings from lectures by other writers including Teresa Jordan, Andrea Carlisle, and Sallie Tisdale.

Joan Weimer is the author of the memoir *Back Talk: Teaching Lost Selves to Speak* (Random House, 1994, and University of Chicago Press, 1996). She is coeditor of *Literature of America* (McDougall Littell, 1975) and editor of *Women Artists, Women Exiles,* a collection of stories by Constance Fenimore Woolson (Rutgers University Press, 1988). She is currently working on a spiritual memoir.

Ms. Weimer is a professor of English at Drew University where she teaches American literature and advanced nonfiction writing.

Following are citations for books and authors Ms. Weimer referred to as influences on her journal-keeping.

Ralph Waldo Emerson, *Emerson in His Journals* (Belknap Press, 1982).
   The Heart of Emerson's Journals (Houghton Mifflin, 1939).

Henry James, *The Ambassadors* (Houghton Mifflin, 1960). Edited by Leon Edel. Also see citations in biographical notes for Patricia Hampl and Marianna de Marco Torgovnick.

Henry David Thoreau, *Walden* (Princeton University Press, 1989). Edited by J. Lyndon Chanley. *Walden and Resistance to Civil Government,* Norton Critical Edition, 2nd edition (Norton, 1992). William Rossi edited. Also see citations in the biographical notes for Reginald Gibbons.

Virginia Woolf, *To the Lighthouse* (Knopf, 1992).

Steven Winn is the co-author of a book on a serial killer, *Ted Bundy: The Killer Next Door* (Bantam, 1980). His stories have appeared in *Alaska Quarterly Review, Carolina Quarterly, Indiana Review, Prism International,* and other magazines. His articles have appeared in *ARTnews, Connoisseur, National Lampoon, Parenting, Sports Illustrated,* and the Arts and Leisure section of the *New York Times.* He has published essays in the *Baltimore Sun, Buffalo News, Cleveland Plain Dealer, Milwaukee Journal,* and the *Seattle Times* among other newspapers.

He has been a journalist since 1975, when he joined the start-up staff of *The Weekly* in Seattle. He is currently the theater critic of the *San Francisco Chronicle.*

Shawn Wong has published two novels, *American Knees* (Simon & Schuster, 1995) and *Homebase* (Reed and Cannon, 1979 and Plume/NAL, 1990). He has edited and coedited several anthologies, including: *Aiiieeeee! An Anthology of Asian American Writers* (Howard University Press, 1974 and Mentor, 1991); *The Big Aiiieeeee! An Anthology of Chinese America and Japanese America in Literature* (Meridian/NAL, 1991); *Asian American Literature* (HarperCollins, 1995); and *Before Columbus Foundation Fiction/Poetry Anthology: Selections from the American Book Awards, 1980–1990,* two volumes of contemporary American multicultural poetry and fiction (W.W. Norton, 1992).

Mr. Wong publishes his poetry, fiction, essays, and reviews in numerous periodicals and anthologies and has written screenplays.

Mr. Wong is a professor of English and the director of the Creative Writing Program at the University of Washington, Seattle.

Elizabeth Woody's first collection of poetry, *Hand Into Stone,* was published by Contact II Press (1988). Her second collection, *Luminaries of the Humble,* was published by University of Arizona Press (1994); and her third, *Seven Hands, Seven Hearts,*

Prose and Poetry, by The Eighth Mountain Press (1994). Her collaborations with artist Joe Feddersen have been shown at Tula Foundation Gallery, Atlanta, Georgia, and toured in an ATLATL-sponsored Submuloc Show/Columbus Wohs exhibition. Her work is featured in a 1994 portfolio of prints published by *Reflex* magazine in Seattle and included in collections at the Portland Art Museum and the Cheney Cowles Museum. An essay by Ms. Woody is included in the anthology *Everything Matters,* edited by Brian Swann and Arnold Krupat for Random House (Winter, 1997).

Elizabeth Woody, of Navajo, Warm Springs/Wasco/Yakima descent, is a professor at the Institute of American Indian Arts.

Al Young's newest books are *Drowning in the Sea of Love (Musical Memoirs),* which won the PEN/USA Award for best non-fiction of the year, The Ecco Press, 1995; *African American Literature: A Brief Introduction and Anthology,* HarperCollins Mosaic Series, 1996; and *Conjugal Visits (And Other Poems in Verse and Prose),* Creative Arts Book Co., 1996. The University of California Press will reissue his 1975 novel *Who Is Angelina?* in paperback as a California Classic.

With Ishmael Reed, Mr. Young was cofounder of the legendary pioneering multicultural journal, *Yardbird Reader.* Widely anthologized, his prose and poetry have been translated in more than a dozen languages, including Italian, French, Spanish, Polish, Serbo-Croatian, Norwegian, Japanese, Chinese, and Tamil.

Al Young has lectured and performed his work (often to music) worldwide. He has taught at Stanford, University of California Berkeley and Santa Cruz, Rice University, Bowling Green State University, and the University of Michigan. Mr. Young was born in Mississippi, grew up in Detroit, and has resided most of his life in the San Francisco Bay Area.

Here are citations for the works and authors Mr. Young referred to as influences on his journal-keeping:

Albert Camus. See citations in the biographical notes for Israel Horovitz.

André Gide. See citations in the biographical notes for Phillip Lopate.

Tristine Rainer. See citation in Appendix II.

William Saroyan, *The Twin Adventures* (Harcourt Brace, 1950).

Appendix II

Helpful Books on Keeping Journals

ADAMS, KATHLEEN. *Journal to the Self, Twenty-two Paths to Personal Growth* (Warner Books, 1990). The author uses dreams, images, unsent letters, lists, and stream-of-consciousness writing for healing grief and getting to know one's self.

————. *Mightier Than the Sword: The Journal as a Path to Men's Self-Discovery* (Warner Books, 1994). Dedicated to helping men overcome stereotypic role models who taught them to constrict their emotions, this book provides, in the author's words, "practical, immediately useful ways to use a journal for personal growth, problem-solving, stress management, creative expression and a whole host of other applications."

BALDWIN, CHRISTINA M. *Life's Companion, Journal Writing as Spiritual Quest* (Bantam Books, 1990). This useful book has short quotes from the journals of writers along with journaling exercise ideas on the left-hand pages; on the right-hand pages, the author offers a narrative on keeping journals and the spiritual quest.

————. *One to One: A New and Updated Edition of the Classic Self-Understanding Through Journal Writing* (Evans and Company, 1991). As the back cover explains: "In this completely new revised edition of a classic, Christina Baldwin approaches journal writing as a free-flowing form of self-expression that can add dimension to anyone's life. She discusses what a journal is and the many reasons for keeping a journal."

CAPACCHIONE, LUCIA. *The Creative Journal* (Newcastle Publishing, 1989). A guide to discovering and releasing your inner potential through writing and drawing.

CHAPMAN, M. A. *Journaling for Joy, Writing Your Way to Personal Growth and Freedom* (Newcastle Publishing, 1991). Write on through to the other side!

EDITORS OF STORY PRESS. *Idea Catcher, An Inspiring Journal for Writers.* (Story Press, 1995). Blank pages with writing prompts at the top of each one.

FINLAYSON, JUDITH. *Season of Renewal: A Diary for Women Moving Beyond the Loss of a Love* (Crown, 1993). A blank book for journal-keepers with pithy quotes as prompts for writing.

HOLZER, BURGHILD. *A Walk Between Heaven and Earth, A Personal Journal on Writing and the Creative Process* (Bell Tower, 1994). A very fine instrument for helping writers keep and use a journal. Kept in journal form itself, this book demonstrates the creative process and how staying open to the present moment and recording whatever one finds there is important to writing.

MALLON, THOMAS. *A Book of One's Own: People and Their Diaries* (Hungry Mind Press, 1995). Quoting from authors who have kept daily chronicles, travel journals, made entries of apology, confession, and spiritual expression of the heart, this author analyzes the significance of diary genres and encourages readers to keep their own.

METZGER, DEENA. *Writing for Your Life: A Guide and Companion to the Inner Worlds* (HarperSanFrancisco, 1992). Metzger says both the creative and spiritual paths "demand a commitment to truth and a willingness to be trusting, disciplined, and aware." Her book is filled with thoughts and examples on how to do this.

MOSLE, SARA. "Writing Down Secrets." *The New Yorker* magazine, September 18, 1995. A third-grade teacher working in a predominantly Dominican and African American community, Mosle uses her students' journals to start dialogues with each of them and realizes the similarities all children share no matter what their background and geography.

MURRAY, JOHN A. *Nature Writing Handbook* (Sierra Club, 1995). The first chapter is entitled "The Journal." It discusses those of nature writers and offers ideas for keeping your own. At the book's end, publication is discussed.

PROGOFF, IRA. *At a Journal Workshop, Writing to Access the Power of the Unconscious and Evoke Creative Ability* (J. P. Tarcher, 1992). These ideas from a master of journaling help you get to know the inner core of your life on ever deeper levels.

RAINER, TRISTINE. *The New Diary: How to Use a Journal for Self Guidance and Expanded Creativity* (J. P. Tarcher, 1978). This book includes lucid, valuable discussions of diary-keeping including erotism and the diary, the diary as time machine, and using the diary to transform personal problems. It includes a comprehensive bibliography of interest to journal-keepers.

ROSENWALD, LAWRENCE. *Emerson and the Art of the Diary* (Oxford University Press, 1988). This critical theoretical study of Emerson's journals contains a thoughtful and instructive chapter, "From Commonplace Book to Journal," valuable for anyone interested in the history of the diary as well as in how Emerson used his.

Appendix III

Writer's Anthologies

ARTESEROS, SALLY, ED. *American Voices: Best Short Fiction by Contemporary Authors with Comments by the Authors* (Washington Square Press, 1992). This work includes fiction by Joyce Carol Oates, Frank Conroy, Tobius Wolff, John Updike, Raymond Carver, Harriet Doerr, Charles Baxter, Jane Smiley, and Sandra Cisneros among others. Each story appears with commentary about how the author wrote it.

BRETT, SIMON. *The Faber Book of Diaries* (Faber and Faber, 1987). This is an anthology composed of excerpts from four centuries of British diaries. Evelyn Waugh, Virginia Woolf, Lord Byron, Mary Shelley, Noel Coward, Elizabeth Barrett, Thomas Moore, Gerard Manley Hopkins, and George Eliot are represented in the 1,400 entries taken from over 100 diaries. The acknowledgment page at the book's end is a rich source on published diaries.

DILLARD, ANNIE. *The Writing Life* (Harper & Row, 1989). These thoughts on writing and glimpses into her writing life by the Pulitzer Prize–winning novelist are like journal entries grouped into seven chapters.

EPEL, NAOMI. *Writers Dreaming. William Styron, Anne Rice, Stephen King and 23 Other Writers Talk About Their Dreams and the Creative Process* (Carol Southern Books, 1993). In about seven pages each, the writers included in this book comment candidly on their dreams and the use they make of them in their writing.

FRIEDMAN, BONNIE. *Writing Past Dark: Envy, Fear, Distraction and Other Dilemmas in the Writer's Life* (HarperCollins, 1993). Eight delightful, touching, and soul-building personal essays about writing.

HALPERN, DANIEL, ED. *Our Private Lives, Journals, Notebooks and Diaries* (Vintage Books, 1990). Originally published by Ecco Press's *Anteaus* as *Journals, Notebooks, and Diaries,* in 1988, this volume contains solicited journal entries from thirty-nine writers. Tess Gallagher, Annie Dillard, then-governor Bill Clinton, Gail Godwin, Donald Hall, Ursula K. Le Guin, Edna O'Brien, Oliver Sacks, William Matthews, Joyce Carol Oates, Charles Simic, and V. S. Naipaul are among them. Some of the entries are raw, some prettied up, and some begun when heretofore the writers hadn't kept journals.

————. *Who's Writing This? Notions on the Authorial I with Self-Portraits* (Ecco Press, 1995). Fifty-six writers discuss the difference between the person writing and the fictional persona created of that writer by the public. Jane Smiley, James Michener, Cynthia Ozick, Alice Hoffman, and John Updike are among the writers represented.

HEFFRON, JACK. *The Best Writing on Writing* (Story Press, 1994). This book contains essays and lectures on writing from twenty-seven writers in 1993, collected from various periodicals and literary magazines. Writers include Donald Hall, Kim Stafford, William Kittredge, Adrienne Rich, and Edward Albee.

————. *The Best Writing on Writing, Vol. 2* (Story Press, 1995). Kathleen Norris, William Goldman, Joyce Carol Oates, Margaret Atwood, and Dorothy Allison among twenty-three writers' essays and lectures from 1994.

JUNKER, HOWARD. *The Writer's Notebook* (HarperCollinsWest, 1995). West Coast poets and writers including Native American writer Sherman Alexie, African American writer Charles Johnson, Chinese American writer Maxine Hong Kingston, environmentalist poet Gary Snyder, and doctor writer Ethan Canin are represented, sketches, scribbles, and all.

LIFSHIN, LYN, ED. *Ariadne's Thread: A Collection of Contemporary Women's Journals* (Harper & Row, 1982). Arranged around themes of work, self, love and friendship, family, being somewhere else, society, and nature, the journal contains entries of fifty-two women, including Anne Sexton, Marge Piercy, Carol Bly, Miriam Sagan, Rita Mae Brown, Patricia Hampl, Janice Eidus, Maxine Kumin, and Denise Levertov.

————. *Lips Unsealed* (Capra Press, 1990). More confidences of contemporary women writers.

MALLON, THOMAS. *A Book of One's Own: People and Their Diaries* (Hungry Mind Press, 1995). Quoting from authors who have kept daily chronicles, travel journals, made entries of apology, confession, and spiritual expression of the heart, this author analyzes the significance of diary genres, leaving readers hungry to read more.

MOFFAT, MARY JANE, and Charlotte Painter. *Revelations: Diaries of Women* (Random House, 1974). Divided into sections called "Love," "Work," and "Power," excerpts from the diaries of well-known and lesser-known women from many historical periods and places reveal the transforming effect of honest writing. Anaïs Nin, Anna Dostoevsky, Sophie Tolstoy, and Alice James appear among thirty-two others.

The New Yorker, June 26 and July 3, double summer issue, 1995. James Atlas, Nicholson Baker, Leonard Michaels, Dawn Powell and Richard Ford offer journal excerpts.

PLIMPTON, GEORGE, ED. *Poets At Work: The Paris Review Interviews.* (Viking, N.Y., 1989). Selected interviews with famous writers that have appeared in *The Paris Review* since 1953.

————. *Women Writers at Work: The Paris Review Interviews.* (Penguin Books, N.Y., 1989).

————. *The Writer's Chapbook: A Compendium of fact, opinion, wit, and advice from the 20th century's preeminent writers.* (Viking, N.Y., 1989).

————. *Writers at Work, The Paris Review Interviews,* 2nd, 3rd, 4th, 6th, 7th Series. (The Viking Press, N.Y., 1963, 1972, 1976, 1984, 1986).

————. *Writers at Work, The Paris Review Interviews,* 5th Series, 8th Series. (Penguin Books, N.Y., 1981, 1988).

RUBIN, MICHAEL. *Men Without Masks: Writings from the Journals of Modern Men* (Addison-Wesley, 1980). Excerpts from the journals of Pope John XXIII, Richard E. Byrd, James Dickey, Howard Nemerov, Franz Kafka, Frederick S. Perls, and Thomas Merton among thirty entries arranged on the theme of being sons, fathers, husbands, lovers, seekers, and workers.

SCHLISSEL, LILLIAN. *Women's Diaries of the Western Journey* (Schocken Books, 1982). Experience the trip from the East Coast to Oregon or California between 1840 and 1870 in the diary writings of over 100 women.

STERNBURG, JANET. *The Writer on Her Work,* Volumes 1 and 2 (Norton, 1980 and 1991). Susan Griffin, Janet Burroway, and Michele Murray offer journal entries in volume one. Volume 2 includes thoughts from Patricia Hampl, Harriet Doerr, Maxine Kumin, and Ursula Le Guin among others.

TALL, DEBORAH, ED. with Stephen Kuusisto and David Weiss. *Taking Note: From Poets' Notebooks* (Norton, 1995). Thirty-two poets, including Stephen Dunn, Carolyn Forche, Rita Dove, Marvin Bell, Heather McHugh, Garrett Hongo, William Matthews, William Stafford, and Mary Oliver, share excerpts from their journals.

Appendix IV

Published Journals of Literary and Historical Figures

ALCOTT, BRONSON. *The Journals of Bronson Alcott* (Little, Brown, 1938).

ALCOTT, LOUISA MAY. *Louisa May Alcott: Her Life, Letters and Journals* (Chelsea House, 1980). Edited by Ednah D. Cheney.

ARKSEY, LAURA, AND PRIES, NANCY, EDS. *American Diaries: An Annotated Bibliography of Published American Diaries and Journals, Vol. 1 1492–1844, Vol. 2 1845–1980* (Gale Research, 1983–1987).

AUDEN, W. H. *A Certain World: A Commonplace Book* (Viking Press, 1970).

BENJAMIN, WALTER. *Moscow Diary* (Harvard University Press, 1986).

BENNETT, ARNOLD. *The Journal of Arnold Bennett* (Viking Press, 1933).

BISHOP, ELIZABETH. *One Art: Letters* (Noonday/Farrar, Straus & Giroux, 1994).

BLAISE, CLARK, AND MUKHERJEE, BHARATI. *Days and Nights in Calcutta* (Hungry Mind Press, 1995).

BOSWELL, JAMES. *The Heart of Boswell, Highlights from the Journals of James Boswell* (McGraw-Hill, 1981). Edited by Mark Harris.

———. *The Journals of James Boswell 1762–1795* (Yale University Press, 1994).

———. *The London Journal 1762–1763* (McGraw-Hill, 1950).

———. *Journal of a Tour to Hebrides with Samuel Johnson* (McGraw-Hill, 1961).

BOWLES, PAUL. *Days: Tangiers Journal 1987–1989* (Ecco Press, 1991).

BRECHT, BERTOLT. *Diaries 1920–1922* (St. Martin's Press, 1979). Edited by Herta Ramthun.

———. *Journals 1934–1955* (Routledge, 1993).

BROUGHTON, JAMES. *The Androgyne Journal* (Broken Moon Press, 1991).

BROWNING, ELIZABETH BARRETT. *Diary of Elizabeth Barrett Browning, 1831–32* (Ohio University Press, 1969).

BURROUGHS, JOHN. *The Heart of Burroughs's Journals* (Houghton Mifflin, 1928).

BURROUGHS, WILLIAM S. *My Education: A Book of Dreams* (Viking, 1995).

BUTLER, SAMUEL. *The Note-Books of Samuel Butler* (Jonathan Cape, 1952).

BYRON, GEORGE GORDON BARON. *Byron's Letters and Journals. Vol. 1–5. 1798–1817* (Belknap Press, Harvard University Press, 1972–1976).

CARR, EMILY. *Hundreds and Thousands: The Journals of Emily Carr* (Clark, Irwin & Company Limited, 1966).

CHANDLER, RAYMOND. *The Notebooks of Raymond Chandler and English Summer: A Gothic Romance by Raymond Chandler* (Ecco Press, 1976).

CHESNUTT, CHARLES W. *The Journals of Charles W. Chesnutt* (Duke University Press, 1993).

CLAIRMONT, CLAIRE. *Journals of Claire Clairmont* (Harvard University Press, 1968).

CLEMENS, SAMUEL. *Mark Twain's Notebooks and Journals, Vols. 1, 2, and 3 (1835–1891)* (University of California Press, 1975).

COOPER, JAMES FENIMORE. *Gleanings in Europe: The Writings of James Fenimore Cooper* (State University of New York Press, 1980–1986).

DREISER, THEODORE. *Theodore Dreiser, American Diaries, 1902–1926* (University of Pennsylvania Press, 1982).

———. *Notes on Life* (University of Alabama Press, 1974).

ELLIS, EDWARD ROBB. *A Diary of the Century: Tales from America's Greatest Diarist* (Kodansha International, 1995).

FISHER, M. F. K. *Stay Me, Oh Comfort Me: Journals and Stories, 1933–1941* (Pantheon Books, 1973).

FLANNER, JANET. *Paris Journal Vol. I, 1944–1965 and Vol. II 1965–1971* (Atheneum, 1971).

———. *Paris Was Yesterday 1925–1939* (Harcourt Brace, 1972).

FORSTER, E. M. *Commonplace Book* (Stanford University Press, 1987).

FRISCH, MAX. *Sketchbook 1966–1971* (Harcourt Brace Jovanovich, 1971).

GARROS, VERONIQUE; NATALIA KORENEUSKAYA; and THOMAS LAHUSEN. *Intimacy and Terror: Soviet Diaries of the 1930's.* Translated by Carol Flath.

GINSBERG, ALLEN. *Journals, Early Fifties, Early Sixties* (Grove Press, 1977).

GORKY, MAXIM. *Fragments from My Diary* (Robert M. McBride & Co., 1924).

GRUMBACH, DORIS. *Coming Into the End Zone, A Memoir* (Norton, 1991).

———. *Fifty Days of Solitude* (Beacon Press, 1994).

GUEVARA, CHÉ. *The Motorcycle Diaries: A Journey Around South America* (Verso, New York, 1995). Translated by Ann Wright.

HAMPL, PATRICIA. *Virgin Time* (Farrar, Straus, and Giroux, 1992).

HAVLICE, PATRICIA. *And So to Bed: A Bibliography of Diaries Published in English* (Scarecrow, 1987).

IRVING, WASHINGTON. *The Western Journals of Washington Irving* (University of Oklahoma Press, 1944). Edited by John Francis McDermott.

ISHIKAWA, TAKUBOKU. *Romanji Diary and Sad Toys* (Charles E. Tuttle, 1985).

JAMES, ALICE. *The Diary of Alice James* (Dodd, Mead & Co., 1964).

KAFKA, FRANZ. *The Diaries of Franz Kafka,* Vols. 1 and 2 (Schocken Books, 1948–1949). Volume 1 covers the years 1910 to 1913. Volume 2 is composed of entries from 1914 to 1923. Edited by Max Brod.

KAZIN, ALFRED. *A Lifetime Burning in Every Moment,* from the Journals of Alfred Kazin (HarperCollins, 1996). Selected and edited by author.

KIERKEGAARD, SØREN. *Journals and Papers, Vols. 1–6* (Indiana University Press, 1967–1978). Howard V. Hong and Edna H. Hong edited and translated.

———. *The Last Years: The Kierkegaard Journals 1853–1855* (Harper & Row, 1965). Edited and translated by Ronald Gregor Smith.

KUMIN, MAXINE. "Journal—Late Winter—Spring 1978," in *Deep Country: Essays* (Viking, 1987).

LE MARQUE, TINA. *Warrior Woman: A Journal of My Life as an Artist* (Artists and Writers Press, 1992).

LINNEA, ANN. *Deep Water Passage: A Spiritual Journal at Midlife* (Little, Brown, 1995).

MATTHIESON, PETER. *Nine Headed Dragon River: Zen Journals 1969–1982* (Shambhala, 1986).

MENCKEN, H. L. *The Diary of H. L. Mencken* (Knopf, 1989).

MERTON, THOMAS. *Run to the Mountain, the Journals of Thomas Merton, Vol. I 1939–1941* (HarperCollins, 1995).

MICHELET, JULES. *Mother Death, The Journal of Jules Michelet 1815–1850* (University of Massachusetts Press, 1984).

MONTGOMERY, L. M. *The Selected Journals of L. M. Montgomery, Vol. 1 1889–1910.* (Oxford University Press, 1985). Edited by Mary Rubio and Elizabeth Waterson.

MORGAN, KAY E. "Blood Talk: Day Pages of a Psychotherapist." *The North Atlantic Review,* May/June, 1995.

MORLEY, HELENA. *The Journal of Helena Morley* (Noonday Press, 1995).

NEMEROV, HOWARD. *Journal of the Fictive Life* (Rutgers University Press, 1965).

ORTON, JOE. *The Orton Diaries* (Harper & Row, 1986). Edited by John Lahr.

PATCHEN, KENNETH. *The Journal of Albion Moonlight* (New Directions Press, 1961).

PAYN, GRAHAM, AND MORELY, SHERIDAN, EDS. *The Noel Coward Diaries* (Little, Brown, 1982).

PRICE, EUGENIA. *Diary of a Novel* (Lippincott & Crowell, 1980).

RICH, ADRIENNE. *What Is Found There: Notebooks on Poetry and Politics* (Norton, 1993).

ROREM, NED. *Setting the Tone: Essays and Diary* (Coward-McCann, 1983).

SARTRE, JEAN-PAUL. *The War Diaries, November 1939–March 1940* (Pantheon Books, 1984).

SCHERER, MIGUEL. *Still Loved by the Sun* (Plume, 1993).

SHELLEY, MARY WOLLSTONECRAFT. *The Journals of Mary Shelley 1814–1844* (Johns Hopkins Press, 1987). Edited by Paula R. Feldman and Diana Scott-Kilvert.

————. Selected Letters of Mary Wollstonecraft Shelley (The Johns Hopkins University Press, 1995). Edited by Betty T. Bennett.

SHELLEY, PERCY BYSSHE, AND MARY W. *History of a Six Weeks Tour* (Cassell Publishing, 1991).

————. *Rambles in Germany and Italy in Eighteen Forty, Eighteen Forty-two, and Eighteen Forty-three* (Folcroft Library Editions, 1981).

SHORE, EMILY. *Journal of Emily Shore* (University of Virginia Press, 1991).

STRONG, GEORGE TEMPLETON. *The Diary of George Templeton Strong* (University of Washington Press, 1952).

TRUITT, ANNE. *Daybook, The Journal of an Artist* (Penguin Books, 1984).

————. *Prospect: The Journal of an Artist* (Simon & Schuster, 1996).

WARHOL, ANDY. *The Andy Warhol Diaries.* (Warner, 1989).

WAUGH, EVELYN. *The Diaries of Evelyn Waugh* (Little, Brown, 1976). Edited by Michael Davie.

WELLS, IDA B. *The Memphis Diary of Ida B. Wells: An Intimate Portrait of the Activist as a Young Woman* (Beacon Press, 1995). Edited by Miriam Decosta-Willis.

WHITLEY, OPAL. *The Singing Creek Where the Willows Grow* (Penguin, 1994).

WHITMAN, WALT. Notebooks spanning the years from 1847, when Whitman was twenty-eight, to 1863, at the height of the Civil War. Unpublished notebooks, Library of Congress.

WILDER, THORNTON. *The Journals of Thornton Wilder, 1939–61* (Yale University Press, 1985). Edited by Donald Gallup.

WISE, THOMAS T. and SYMINGTON, J. A. *The Brontës: Their Lives, Friendships and Correspondence* 4 vols. (Oxford: Basil Blackwell, 1932).

WISTER, SALLY. *Sally Wister's Journal: A True Narrative Being a Young Girl's Account of Her Experiences During the Revolutionary War* (Applewood Books, 1995).